T0375125

*An Insider's Guide to University
Administration*

An Insider's Guide to University Administration

Daniel Grassian

Johns Hopkins University Press • *Baltimore*

© 2020 Johns Hopkins University Press
All rights reserved. Published 2020
Printed in the United States of America on acid-free paper
9 8 7 6 5 4 3 2 1

Johns Hopkins University Press
2715 North Charles Street
Baltimore, Maryland 21218-4363
www.press.jhu.edu

Library of Congress Cataloging-in-Publication Data

Names: Grassian, Daniel, 1974– author.
Title: An insider's guide to university administration / Daniel Grassian.
Description: Baltimore : Johns Hopkins University Press, 2020. |
    Series: Higher ed leadership essentials | Includes bibliographical references
    and index.
Identifiers: LCCN 2019025618 | ISBN 9781421437071 (paperback) |
    ISBN 9781421437088 (ebook)
Subjects: LCSH: Universities and colleges—United States—Administration. |
    College administrators—Vocational guidance.
Classification: LCC LB2341 .G668 2020 | DDC 378.1/01—dc23
LC record available at https://lccn.loc.gov/2019025618

A catalog record for this book is available from the British Library.

*Special discounts are available for bulk purchases of this book. For more information,
please contact Special Sales at specialsales@press.jhu.edu.*

Johns Hopkins University Press uses environmentally friendly book materials,
including recycled text paper that is composed of at least 30 percent post-
consumer waste, whenever possible.

Contents

*An Insider's Guide to University
Administration*

Don't Panic!

Education is the most powerful weapon which you can use to change
the world.
—Nelson Mandela

An administrator in a bureaucratic world is a man who can feel big by
merging his non-entity in an abstraction. A real person in touch with
real things inspires terror in him.
—Marshall McLuhan

I t is 6:30 on a Friday evening. You didn't expect to be in the office late on a Friday. You made plans with your spouse for dinner. There was a cocktail with your name on it at a happy hour
that you had intended to go to before dinner, as a reward for a
long week full of challenges, drama, escalation, de-escalation, re-
escalation, and then what you thought were final resolutions.
However, that turned out to be only an illusory calm before the
storm. And now the storm has hit on multiple fronts. On one
side, students at your college are demanding that a campus event
featuring a controversial speaker be shut down. Words like "racism," "sexism," and "discrimination" have been uttered, and while
no one's name has been attached to these words yet, it might not

be far off. Yours may be close to the top of the list along with the college president, who recently texted senior staff (including you) and asked them to work on these issues ASAP.

Meanwhile, other students are demanding that the same speaker be heard. Words like "free speech," "no silencing," and "discrimination" are being uttered aloud. Once again, while no one's name has been mentioned, yours, the president's, and other senior staff's may be cited soon. You also just received news that a couple of hours ago there was a reported sexual assault on campus. This morning your supervisor has told you in your weekly one-on-one meeting that she lacks confidence in one of your staff and not so subtly tells you that you should let this person go or you will be responsible for her performance. Yesterday, you found out that a faculty member recently denied tenure has not only enlisted his department and faculty allies, but he has also hired legal counsel for what will almost certainly be a contentious appeal. You think about a meeting you had yesterday in which one of your peers, who has been vying for attention and compliments from his supervisor (who is also your supervisor), demeaned you in front of your colleagues, and you didn't have the tenacity to push back. You wonder if this has something to do with your supervisor's most current subtle suggestion that you consider letting go of one of your staff. Are you being tested? Even if you are, should this be something you care about, and how important is it compared to all of the other important issues that are going on now?

You tell your spouse to eat without you; this will be a long night and a long weekend. As you settle down at your desk to come up with some preliminary thoughts and an action plan, the lyrics to the Talking Heads song "Once in a Lifetime" come into your head: "And you may ask yourself, 'Well, how did I get here?' . . . And you may say to yourself, 'My God! What have I done?'" How did you get here? What have you done? What will you do? Is it too late to get out, and where would you even go? Do you have a moral compass that can direct you in anything approaching a "right" direction, or is there some kind of personal or institutional calculus you can utilize that can successfully weigh the costs and benefits of various decisions you could make? You try to put these questions aside as you know you have no time to dive into this administrative rabbit hole now. You have a job to do. You roll up your sleeves and get to work on this long Friday night.

So you think you may want to take a plunge into administration at a college or university? If so, take a minute and consider how you would react to the previous scenario, as it is real. And some, if not all of it (and more), can happen to you as an administrator, all at once or over a period of time. The work of a college or university administrator can be energizing, exhilarating, and rewarding, especially since the stakes can be very high (multimillion-dollar investments, initiatives put in place to eliminate the equity gap for undergraduates, hiring, promotion, and giving tenure to a number of people, etc.) and the effects can be so significant and current (this is quite a contrast for traditional faculty-scholars or staff). It can, however, also be extremely stressful and enervating work. At times, it will be both, sometimes even in the same day.

If you are currently a faculty member, you have probably heard the analogy equating joining the administration to joining the "dark side," along with the general and specific disdain directed against certain administrators deemed to be cruel, power hungry, vindictive, or just incompetent. Of course, *you* are no Anakin Skywalker; *you* are no Dean Vader in the making. You are morally centered and professionally accomplished, and you have a number of noble ideas you would like to implement as an administrator—from increasing graduation and retention rates to making higher education more accessible for students from historically underserved groups. You won't be like the lackluster or even abhorrent administrators you have served under, seen, or heard about; you are more than competent, morally centered, and unconcerned with power and politics. After all, you are you, and you are a good person. You've got this.

But wait, are you so sure about that? Most college and university administrators never know until they are in their respective positions for a period of time whether being an administrator is right for them, and it is not uncommon for new administrators, especially if they come directly from the faculty, to have no training and to learn mostly through careful analysis as well as trial and error. It is the primary intention of this book to help those currently in faculty positions determine whether a career in college or university administration (mainly but not exclusively in academic affairs) is right for them (in particular, director, chair, dean, to provost and other mid-tier up to senior-level administrative positions) while providing critical engagement with some of the most pertinent and important current administrative issues: fund-raising, budgeting, marketing, leadership, diversity, and management. It can also provide other prospective and current staff and administrators (regardless of whether they hail from the faculty ranks, especially those who may currently be in a more entry-level administrative position, such as a chair or director) an in-depth critical analysis of areas pertinent to college and university administration. In addition, the book offers readers external to higher education a more holistic understanding of what those in college and university administration may do and the important practical, political, and ethical issues with which they engage that may affect so many millions of people directly or indirectly.

Why do we need another book about college and university administration, one might wonder? It is, of course, true that a number of monographs have been published about administration, including end-of-career reflections from presidents (e.g., William M. Chace's *One Hundred Semesters* and William G. Bowen's *Lessons Learned: Reflections of a University President*), stinging critiques of the supposedly bloated administration from embittered faculty (e.g., Benjamin Ginsberg's *The Fall of the Faculty*), and guidebooks for administrative success (e.g., Jeffrey L. Buller's *The Essential Academic Dean or Provost* and C. K. Gunsalus's *The College Administrator's Survival Guide*). Monographs about college and university administration tend to come in three varieties: a lesson-filled end-of-career memoir, a detailed critique or endorsement of some aspect or aspects of higher education, or a prescriptive administrative self-help book with guiding lessons.

Bridging critical analysis with practical, real-world experience and theory, the present volume is a combination of these three varieties. Whereas other books on administration may simplify the roles and the issues involved, this one does not aim to distill the complexities into oversimplified guidelines. For instance, in *The Essential Academic Dean or Provost*, Buller describes his "goal" as "to provide readers with clear, concise recommendations that can be absorbed in ten minutes or less."[1] I would argue that any administrative "recommendation" that can be "absorbed" in such a short period of time is likely to be oversimplified and not ultimately helpful. While I understand that, as Buller writes, administrators can be "busy" and "time is of the essence," the job of most college and university administrators is complicated and nuanced.[2] At the same time, this is not a "how-to" book that charts out step-by-step what an administrator may do to conduct, for instance, program reviews, assessment, and a reaccreditation site visit. Not only can those tasks be more easily taught and learned (unlike how to lead and how to build relationships with colleagues), but they are not ultimately key to an administrator's success and longevity in her or his position. Rather, I aim here to reveal the complexities of administration; the nuances involved in decision-making, which can depend on the kind of institution one serves at as well as the existing institutional culture; and the distinctions between faculty life and administrative life.

The kind of institution where one serves at—public or private, religiously affiliated or secular, primarily teaching- or research-oriented, elite or open enrollment and so on—is extremely important and relevant yet not often discussed by those who write about college or university administration, who themselves often have been at only one or two colleges or universities their entire career or at one kind of institution (e.g., public, research-oriented, private, or elite). This is unfortunate as it is critical for an administrator to consider the kind of institution she or he serves at, as well as the existing culture there when considering options and making informed decisions. What may work at a Yale or UC Berkeley, for instance, may not work at a Boise State University or a Hillsborough Community College.

This distinction cannot be emphasized enough. Consequently, anyone writing about college and university administration (unless one is addressing a specific, narrow audience such as those at elite, private research institutions) should not promote anything approaching a one-size-fits-all model. For better or worse, I have served as a faculty member and administrator at eight different colleges and universities, from a small, private, semi–religiously affiliated institution to a medium-to-large institution that is part of the largest university system in the country, from a community college to a research-oriented PhD-granting institution. I have served at an institution that had only been in existence three years before my arrival and another that is more than two hundred years old. I have served in rural and urban areas in the Southeast, Northeast, Southwest, and the Great Plains that range from minimal diversity to the most diverse area of the country.

In considering all of the different institutions I have served at and the difficult decisions my colleagues and I have had to make, I would have chosen differently depending on the institution and the existing culture there. Consequently, if you are looking for a book that will provide you with easy answers, this book is not for you. While this book does take specific positions and makes arguments, these are sometimes nuanced positions and arguments, which should be dependent on the kind of institution one serves at, the culture there, the position one is in or strives to be in, and one's own personality and style. I hope that this nuance is not mistaken for equivocation, as these are not one and the same.

There are multiple methods to teach effectively, pending a person's individual style and the class itself, and the same is true for college and university administration, which should not be boiled down to "essential principles."[3] While it may be tempting, especially for the many mid-tier and senior administrators (e.g., department chairs, deans, provosts, vice presidents, associate vice presidents) who enter these positions from the faculty or from another industry with no direct experience in higher education, to gravitate toward bite-size, simplified, easy-to-digest-and-recall guidelines, such an approach is more likely to make a (new) administrator's position and life more challenging than engaging, with the often nuanced complexities of college and university administration. These complexities generally defy categorization and distillation into simplified guidelines and can be and often are contingent on the kind of institution where one currently serves, as well as the present climate and existing leadership there. While there are workshops designed to help adjust faculty and staff[4] into (more) administrative roles, these, at most, multiday sessions, if they are attended,[5] cannot suffice to prepare a college or university administrator for the radically different professional life that awaits her or him, especially if her or his entire previous experience at a college or university was as a faculty member or if her or his main professional experience was working in a non-higher-education-related business, industry, or organization.

For faculty or those coming to higher education from other businesses, industries, or organizations, moving into an administrative role at a college or university can be jarring and challenging. Unless they are lucky enough to have a mentor (or mentors) who can provide advice or guidance,[6] such individuals generally have little to no training or preparation for the job to come other than their own perceptions of administration from their previously held faculty or business perspective (which may be biased and limited), their own personal experiences when a student, or other secondary means (readings, anecdotal information, etc.). Careers in college and university administration can be extremely rewarding and meaningful, in some ways even more so than faculty and staff careers, since as an administrator, one can often perceive direct effects and successes more directly or tangibly, and these successes can be more widely significant than what may be accomplished as a singular faculty or staff member. At the same time, administrative positions and careers can be horrific, incredibly stressful, and riddled with numerous kinds of professional pitfalls.

I recognize and understand that the same may be stated for faculty (and employees in other organizations) as well, albeit for different reasons. Unlike other writers such as Buller, who somewhat facetiously compares the job of a dean and provost to "wading into the academic equivalent of a septic tank,"[7] I would argue that the issues a college or university administrator may encounter, while potentially having more widespread effect, are not necessarily worse than issues with which faculty and staff may deal. They are just different in scope and magnitude. As faculty who have had to deal with extremely disruptive, hostile, or challenging students can understand, managing difficult students can be as challenging (or even more challenging) in its own way than managing problematic staff and faculty or trying to raise low retention rates. Further, any lower-level staff member can more easily feel vulnerable, replaceable, and even preyed upon because of their relative lack of power. It is true that the decisions an administrator makes (e.g., to tenure, to dismiss, to hire, to financially support or not) may be more legally or ethically fraught; however, she or he often has policies and procedures to guide these decisions, colleagues who are involved in the decision-making process, and even, at times, the assistance of legal counsel. In that sense, at least at some institutions, administrators can have more institutional and external support and recourse than faculty and staff, who rarely have (direct) access to legal counsel. In addition, just as the successes in administration may be more visible and public, so can the failures.

Part of an administrator's experience will depend on the institution, the culture, the personnel, and the position, some of which she or he may not be able to change much if at all. However, the more prepared one is, the better one's experience should be, and the more engaged one is with the complexities of administration, the more one can develop the wisdom to distinguish the things that can be changed for the better from the things that may have to be accepted as they are. Are you ready? Not sure yet? That's OK, and my hope is that if you are uncertain, this book will help you decide if administration is the right career path for you. If college or university administration is already your chosen career path, my hope is that this book will reenergize your interest in the area, if not help you to advance your career, should that be your desire. If college and university administration is more or less foreign to you, my hope is that this volume will live up to its title by providing you with insight into the professional lives of those who make extremely important decisions that shape the lives of millions.

Chapter 1

College and University Administration 101

Those that can, do. Those that can't do, teach. Those that can't teach become administrators.
—Adapted from George Bernard Shaw

My sincerest apologies that you have to work on a holiday that honors your work.
—Anonymous to an administrator working on Labor Day

A Personal Anecdote

My hands were sweaty, and I readjusted my tie for what was probably the third or fourth time as I sat in an overstuffed chair outside the president's office. To stay focused and motivated, I mentally replayed Eminem's song "Lose Yourself," which I had repeatedly listened to that morning to get properly amped up. This was my moment. I'd own it and never let it go, or so I hoped. I knew this interview could be fraught, but I wanted this job badly because at the time I was at an institution where I did not fit and which was in existential peril. What made this a unique interview for me was that I knew the president personally, even though we hadn't seen each other in six years. She was single-handedly responsible for my decision to go into administration ten years before and the closest thing I ever had to an administrative mentor. Now the president of a small but growing public university, she had hired me as an assistant professor of English at an even smaller public college twelve years previously, which at the time consisted of one building (a refurbished vitamin factory) surrounded by five hundred acres of desert. This equally new campus, a renovated mental hospital, was a step up!

The position I was interviewing for oversaw faculty affairs. Among other responsibilities, the position managed faculty development and faculty contracts, and the person would be expected to investigate and adjudicate faculty grievances, conflicts, and collective bargaining negotiations. I enjoyed resolving conflicts, mentoring faculty members, and advocating for them, so the position had appeal for me. At the same time, I recognized that it would be a challenging job, the worst of which would presumably involve dealing with Dwight Schrute-like faculty, griping at every perceived slight under the sun; embittered/underpaid lecturers; part-time faculty angling for something better; and socially awkward or mentally unstable egomaniacs. I knew the types because I had worked with them (or tried to work with them) during my collective time as a faculty member and administrator. While the majority of faculty are outstanding, devoted, and often brilliant, faculty (even excellent faculty) can possess an oxymoronic combination of arrogance and insecurity. Anyone who would be in this position, which is roughly equivalent to being a director of human resources for faculty, would inevitably have to deal with some incredibly challenging, demanding, or certifiably mentally ill faculty. But I was confident that I could handle it. After all, I had ten years of college and university administrative experience under my belt at this point, which included the following situations and challenges (sometimes addressed successfully and sometimes not):

1. Being the subject of four individual faculty grievances during my first year as department chair due to my rigorous performance reviews and an inherited lack of rigor by the previous chair. (All of the grievances, though, were eventually dismissed.)

2. Serving at an extremely frugal institution with a large endowment yet still having to lobby for and eventually get across-the-board faculty salary raises along with salary equity redistributions.

3. Being on the promotion and tenure committee of a dean who supervised me and who hadn't met the scholarship criteria for promotion and tenure, then voting to deny tenure to said dean, who ended up not only receiving tenure but was informed about my solitary denial vote. (This was one factor that led to my desire, soon realized, to "Get the hell out of Dodge.")

4. Beginning a key administrative position soon after the president and board of directors had suspended tenure, and subsequently working extremely hard (and eventually being successful) in restoring tenure by convincing the president and board of its importance while acknowledging their (sometimes) valid objections and proposing ways to address these objections.

5. Overseeing a school with many difficult and vindictive faculty who were all older than I (and, in some cases, who had been at the institution longer than I had been alive) and who were mostly tenured full professors, while I was untenured and to be evaluated by them for tenure, promotion, and reappointment. Improving the culture of the school so that by the end of my three-year period there, faculty who hadn't talked to one another (let alone collaborated) for years were now doing so,

and the school had halted its downward enrollment
spiral.

6. Being described as sexist and racist for entirely opposing reasons (either predisposed to favor female faculty
and staff or predisposed to favor male faculty and staff;
either predisposed to favor White faculty and staff or
predisposed to favor traditionally underserved faculty
and staff) yet eventually being recognized with a
campus-wide diversity award.

7. Overseeing certifiably mentally ill faculty and staff
(e.g., suffering from schizophrenia, depression, bipolar
disorder, and substance abuse, among other conditions).

8. Lobbying for untenured faculty and staff who were
unfairly targeted or evaluated by other administrators
and sometimes (but not always) saving their positions
or successfully advocating for their tenure or promotion but consistently winning the respect of those for
whom I advocated.

9. Having served as ad hoc security at a campus without
public safety in a situation that required me to remove
verbally and physically threatening students (which,
miraculously, I did successfully).

10. Having been critiqued by a president of a university
for not being sufficiently "open" to terminating staff
in order to meet budget cuts, which could have been
made in other, less intrusive ways. (I mostly lost this
battle.)

11. Having been personally threatened by a faculty member
who vowed to "get back" at me and "sue" me when I did
not give him a class he wanted to teach. The latter, I
subsequently discovered, was just an empty threat that
he often hurled at people, hence leading to his departmental nickname, "I Will Sue You Guy." However, he
did try (unsuccessfully) to remove me by voting against
my tenure and continuance as school director.

12. Overseeing an impulsive and passive-aggressive faculty member who "acted" out his disdain for me by attempting a cartwheel outside a classroom where I was teaching. The cartwheel was interrupted by the presence of a trash can, which the faculty member did not calculate into his attempt, leaving him sprawled in the hallway, unharmed, although wounded in pride. In this case, the trash can did my administrative work for me.

So, I wasn't really intimidated by the job description. I was, however, intimidated by the president, who I was about to see for the first time in six years. In many ways, I had learned more from her than I had from anyone else—how to create and maintain a mutually reinforcing and positive institutional culture, how to build strong coalitions, how to hire effectively, how to identify and address problems before they fester or explode, how to motivate faculty and staff, how to delegate difficult responsibilities to others while still keeping your hands (relatively) clean, how to encourage problematic faculty and staff to leave in an indirect manner, and, perhaps most importantly, how to know when to fight your battles and how to mask your intentions, intelligence, and abilities at times in order to ultimately get what you want (or most of what you want) with as much faculty and staff buy-in and collective ownership as possible. This was an opposite approach to how I, as a faculty member, tended to operate: by projecting my voice, interpretations, and arguments while overtly pushing back against others. It was a hard adjustment for me, and one that I could never have made without her guidance.

Yet, I had made a significant mistake while working for her, one that I later regretted, even though it seemed like the right thing to do at the time. In hindsight, it perfectly illustrates the different orientations and perspectives faculty or staff and college or university administrators often have. In this situation, I did not renew a full-time administrator, who happened to be a very close friend of the now president (then dean), to teach a specific class (as a part-time faculty member, on top of her full-time administrative position). Instead, I chose to give this class to another part-time instructor (not a full-time administrator or staff and not a friend of the dean) who appeared to be more effective as a teacher and more experienced in the field, and who had received stronger student evaluations. It seemed simple enough at the time and, in its own way, rather like assigning grades, which, I believed, must be done as much as possible in an unbiased manner, according to merit and quality, irrespective of what students might think or how they might react. Knowing that the dean's friend really wanted to continue teaching and seeing, if not the potential for improvement, her commitment to teaching, I thought that I had paved the road for her to teach in another department.

However, the chair of that department, who also didn't think highly of her teaching but who was also my administrative rival (and on better terms with the dean), delayed his staffing (either on purpose or not). Not wanting to engage with the dean's friend, who I knew could be challenging, and not feeling that I was bound to do so, since I did not do that for other part-time faculty when I did not offer them classes and since she would likely teach for another department, I did not mention anything to her, so she found out that she wasn't teaching for me by looking at the posted class schedule. Due to the procrastination or purposeful delay on the part of the other chair, the dean's friend wasn't listed to teach any classes at all. This made her extremely upset, evident by a blistering email she sent to me. At the time, I felt her grievances were mostly unfounded, and that I was just doing my job to the best of my abilities.[1] For certain, the dean would have to support me in this, I thought.

It did not turn out to be as simple as that, though. While the dean did not directly rebuke me, she made it clear that she was not pleased with my choices and decision. From her perspective, given that the friend was a full-time administrator, she (the friend) should be treated differently than if she was just a part-time faculty member since we all had to work together, regardless of what might occur (which was true). From my perspective at the time, all part-time faculty should be treated equitably, regardless of whether she or he was also a full-time staff or administrator, or, in this case, a close friend of the dean. Who/what was right? If you believe that I was mainly in the right, then you may not be in good stead for a long and successful college or university administrative career, because your idealism or commitment to what you believe to be equity can ultimately alienate you from others and damage your professional relationships. This may not matter so much for faculty (especially tenured faculty) or nonmanaging staff, but it matters a great deal to administrators who must consider the personal and professional ramifications of their actions and decisions. Not realizing this at the time, I pushed back against the dean, and we got in a heated argument. The conversation ended on a tense note. While, with time, this specific disagreement faded away, there was a noticeable and lasting change and frostiness in my professional relationship with the dean thereafter, and within a year, I ended up taking another position elsewhere, although I was careful to leave on good terms with her and others (as much as I could).

But now, six years had gone by. The dean became a provost and now was a president. I had moved from department chair to director to dean and vice president for academic affairs. She had served as a strong reference for me in the past, and we subsequently exchanged several friendly and positive emails. Surely, enough water had gone under the bridge—or had it? I knew going into my meeting with her that I would have a pretty clear sense of my chances of getting the position based on her behavior, questions, and responses. It seemed to start promisingly enough. We gave each other a short, professional hug. She asked how things were going in my current position. However, once she told me that this would be a very difficult job, and she wasn't sure why I would want it, my hopes dimmed. I did my best to explain why I would be a good fit for the position, how it would be, in many ways, rewarding for me to resolve faculty issues as I had been doing for the past decade as well as play a leading role in hiring and mentoring new and ongoing faculty. Despite this, I pretty much knew I was doomed for failure when she told me that the decision would be that of the incoming provost, and that she would have nothing to do with it. Even though I praised her repeatedly during the interview, she did not say a single positive word about me or my application, even though she spent several minutes praising others with whom we had previously worked. That told me all I needed to know. This, after all, was the same person who consistently (albeit surreptitiously) intervened in faculty, administrator, and staff search committees, and stacked the search committee ranks with people she knew, trusted, or believed would be loyal to her and especially productive. Any difficult decisions, ones that could potentially carry any negative ramifications, she left to her subordinates (while guiding them), thereby keeping her hands clean. I knew this personally because there was a time in which she trusted me enough to do this for her more than anyone else.

When our meeting concluded, she extended her hand, which I shook. I now pretty much knew I would not get the job, and I also knew that I would, in all likelihood, never see her again. Whatever I had achieved, whatever things I might or would eventually say during the remainder of the entire-day interview would probably not matter, as they would not take away from the fact that (in her mind) I had not been sufficiently loyal, that I had challenged her when I should have been submissive, that I had been idealistic when I should have been pragmatic. In short, I had not learned the political realities and nuances of power, loyalty, control, management, and leadership in college and university administration. And it's true: I hadn't developed a sufficient understanding of them then, but over time, and through some painful lessons, trial and error, and hard work, I learned a great deal, which I hope to impart to readers here.

So Why on Earth Would Anyone Want to Be a College or University Administrator?

It has been frequently suggested that a sizeable number of millennials or post-millennials want to become famous or wealthy, that many want to become entertainers, software designers, or successful entrepreneurs, or at least pursue professions that allow some kind of individual distinction. Certainly, there has been and will continue to be a number of young people who want to pursue careers in healthcare, law, criminal justice, business, and so on. Of these, a small fraction of determined individuals may decide that they want to become college professors, and an even smaller fraction may make a determination that they want to work at a college or university as a staff member or administrator. When does this revelation (if it is a revelation) tend to occur? It is hard to imagine many high school or college students making a determination that they want to be a college or university administrator (let alone a staff member). Chances are good that in most cases, high school or college students wouldn't even know what a dean, a provost, a vice president for student affairs, a vice president for business and administration, a vice provost for enrollment management, and so forth does beyond some kind of vague college or university work or management. If these positions appear to be of interest to high school or college students, it is probably due to the perceived power, prestige, or compensation the title of the position seems to bestow or imply (which is also applicable to organizations not affiliated with higher education).

Indeed, faculty beginning their careers may not know what it is that various college or university administrators do, let alone how they got in their positions in the first place. The same may be true of staff, but they may immediately become part of the hierarchy upon hire, and subsequently, they will presumably get to know (directly or indirectly) others (e.g., undergraduate advisors, a director of admission, a director of graduate studies) with whom they and their units work. Whereas there is generally a straight trajectory for faculty from graduate school in their respective field to teaching in the same or a similar field, there are generally four paths that lead to a career as a college or university administrator:[2] (1) a successful path through the faculty ranks as a professor that leads concurrently or subsequently to an administrative role or roles, (2) graduate or professional training or experience in an area related to college or university administration,[3] (3) comparable or successful work in another private or public industry (e.g., a chief financial officer of a nonprofit who becomes a CFO of a university), or (4) for staff, successive promotion to a mid- or senior-level administrative position (e.g., from an institutional research consultant to a vice provost for institutional effectiveness and research or from an admissions counselor to a dean of students). It is not uncommon for the second and fourth paths to be interrelated. That is, in order to move to a senior administrative level, a staff member may feel, for good reason, that he or she will be more competitive with a PhD or EdD. Indeed, it is not uncommon to find administrators at colleges and universities working on their PhD or EdD, mainly in order to maximize their chances of moving up the hierarchy.

It has been asserted, mainly by faculty, that the first of the four paths just mentioned was generally the main, if not the only, path to administrative positions in the past. For staff, the fourth path was the most common path toward promotion to administrative positions. However, in recent years, the second and third paths appear to have become much more common and, some argue, have helped produce administrative bloat along with the perceived corporatization of the contemporary college and university, which, they contend, has allowed even more career administrators and private industry "interlopers" to flourish.[4] It is not my intention in this book to involve myself in this ongoing and presumably never-to-be-settled argument, and my focus is admittedly more on the first group (faculty who become administrators) than on the other groups, because not only was that my own career progression, but those who move into college or university administration from faculty (especially those who move into administrative positions that aren't strictly academic in nature) may have a rather significant learning curve once beginning their new positions, unlike staff who may "naturally" ascend their unit's hierarchy with time and, possibly, additional education (e.g., an advanced degree or doctorate).

This is not to suggest that "career staff or administrators" or those who come from the other groups would not have (potentially steep) learning curves. In the case of administrators who have graduate degrees in administration or something related to administration, while they may bring with them significant (theoretical) administrative experience or knowledge, they may not have had much, or any, firsthand experience as faculty. This, coupled with a general faculty-held belief that professional degrees (e.g., an EdD in higher education leadership) are analogous to a PhD-lite, may mean that such administrators are not respected as much by the faculty. Ironically, administrators or staff who do not pursue such advanced degrees may be respected more by faculty-administrators, although this group will probably not see them as equals, and they will probably find it more challenging to ascend the professional ladder. In the case of administrators who come to colleges and universities with little to no higher education experience, while they may bring with them a wealth of important organizational, position-specific, and administrative expertise, colleges and universities may be a different environment than their previous environment, and they may have a significant adjustment period.

Among other things, faculty considering a career in administration should be aware that many of their new colleagues will be staff who do not have a faculty background, and in some cases do not have advanced degrees, let alone a substantial educational background. This can give rise to various spoken and unspoken tensions and unnecessary or unfortunate conflicts. Conversely, administrators who do not begin as faculty or who did not work their way through the faculty ranks might sense arrogance and entitlement in their administrative faculty colleagues (and perhaps rightly so), and those same administrative faculty colleagues may underestimate the abilities and intelligence of nonfaculty staff. Faculty-administrators who are able to bridge this gap will be more likely to succeed, although this, in itself, is certainly not enough to do so. There are, indeed, many potentially significant, even career-ending, pitfalls in college and university administration, probably more than there are for faculty (although possibly not for nontenured/tenure-track faculty or staff), especially if the institution has an ineffectual or vindictive human resources division.

With all of this in mind, a valid question is: Why would anyone want to pursue a career in higher education management or administration? Generally, the reasons include the following: (1) higher salary, (2) increased power, (3) preferred work environment (e.g., for those who were previously employed in a less meaningful or relatively cutthroat position or industry), (4) greater future employment opportunities, (5) perceived ability to effect change more widely and tangibly, (6) perception that those in administrative positions are ineffective and that one can be more effective, and (7) growing disenchantment or burnout from teaching and scholarship.[5]

I suspect that most college or university administrators, if asked why they chose their specific career path (especially if they come from the faculty), would be inclined to give either some variation of the fifth reason just mentioned or possibly some variation of the third and sixth. Administrators may be less likely to state the other reasons because they suggest greater self-interest, although in the end, these reasons are no less important. In particular, it is hard for anyone to admit that what draws them and keeps them in a position may be money or power. It is even more challenging to admit this in the mostly nonprofit world of academia, where the primary focus is or should be on education, students, ideas, and knowledge. Indeed, in *The College Administrator's Survival Guide*, experienced administrator C. K. Gunsalus reports that she has never had a former faculty member at her institution "tell me he or she does it [administration] for the money."[6]

This may be so; however, not only did Gunsalus spend the majority of her career at the flagship University of Illinois campus, where faculty salaries tend to be considerably higher (especially when adjusted for cost of living) than most colleges and universities (thereby making the salary of an administrator somewhat less compelling than it might be elsewhere), but it is not surprising that administrators may be reluctant to mention that one of the factors that drew them to their current position is the level of compensation, as doing so might be embarrassing to admit (even to one's self). While Gunsalus claims that the "money is not adequate compensation for the burdens of the job—if taken on conscientiously," I would argue that it is more complicated and dependent upon the position and the institution. In some ways, the faculty life can carry significant, if not greater, burdens than the administrative life, and one should not privilege the "burdens" of the administration, as doing so is not only unfair to faculty and staff, who shoulder their own respective burdens by being on the proverbial front lines, but can also be symptomatic of a large sense of administrative entitlement for shouldering these supposedly more weighty or oppressive "burdens."

In the end, whether or not it is directly stated, money and power do play a role in what can and does draw a number of people to, in particular, senior-level college and university administrative positions (e.g., dean, vice presidents, presidents), especially if the individual does not have a faculty position as a safety net should her or his administrative position not continue. If, for instance, a tenured faculty member received approximately the same salary (or even less) as she or he would as an administrator, how many would move into or continue with administration? Not very many, I believe. Yet, there are a number of administrators who move (back) to the faculty of their own volition despite the almost inevitable accompanying decrease in income. Whereas in *The Essential Dean or Provost*, Jeffrey L. Buller argues that one should not pursue college or university administration for the additional compensation, and that those who do will be unhappy or ultimately unsuccessful, I believe that there is nothing intrinsically wrong with pursuing a career in college or university administration *in part* because of the additional compensation, as doing so is not mutually exclusive with enjoying the position (most of the time) and accomplishing one's goals (as long as those goals are appropriate, reasonable, and realizable).

Administrators may assert that they work much harder (all year and longer daily and weekly hours) than faculty and staff, for instance, and sometimes this can be true. Generally, administrators are expected to be in the office during normal office hours, Monday through Friday (and many mid- and senior-level administrators often work on weekends and into the evenings on weekdays, especially during campus crises), whereas faculty generally set their own schedules (except the time they teach and other required on-campus time for office hours, service work, etc.). Staff, of course, work similar hours to administrators, but they are generally not expected to work outside their normal business hours, as are administrators. Further, non-exempt or hourly staff are not allowed to work beyond their normal business hours without mutual agreement and the granting of overtime. While it may be true that faculty (especially tenured full professors) are able to get by or get away with working considerably less than administrators or even staff, all categories have their extremes—from the perpetually underperforming to overperforming workaholics. Further, as with most positions, after a person earns a certain salary range for a period of time, she or he can get accustomed to it and even feel that she or he needs a considerably higher income than she or he really does.[7] Further, not many people are willing to take salary cuts, and so once someone moves high enough up the college or university administrative ladder, it can become harder to want to descend (and those who do tend to either do so because of personal reasons, because they are pushed into it, or because they are getting close to or are at retirement age). That being stated, if money ends up being the exclusive or nearly exclusive reason for why a person works in an administrative position, it will become increasingly harder to feel motivated or feel that one does meaningful work. The likelihood, then, is one way or the other (e.g., termination, quitting, or leaving for another job), the position or the person will not last much longer.

Sometimes there is nothing wrong with this, though. Just as the faculty and staff life is not for everyone, the same can be said for the college or university administrative life. As mentioned previously, faculty who move into administrative positions are often, somewhat tongue-in-cheek, accused of joining the "dark side" by the existing faculty. While this academic cliché is often delivered in jest, as with most sarcastic statements, it possesses an element of truth. One of the primary reasons faculty tend to view administrators as part of a "dark side" is because there is a perception that those involved in (senior-level) administrative positions can lose their moral compass (if they had one to begin with!) when moving into positions of power and removing themselves from what faculty may rightly perceive as the primary function of the college or university: educating students and enriching their lives. Further, administrative roles generally carry (more) managerial responsibility and corresponding power. For both faculty and staff, the more power an administrator has, the greater the chance for corruption or abuse of that power. Consequently (and for other reasons), a sizeable number of faculty (and staff) regard administrators with some level of distrust, if not outright contempt.[8] For James C. Garland, former president of Miami University in Ohio and author of *Saving Alma Mater*, this is more of a phenomenon specific to "disgruntled faculty," who, he argues, tend to depict administrators as "authoritarian, autocratic, haughty, and arrogant."[9] Further, he suggests that such faculty believe administrators to "act unilaterally," that they have "contempt for shared governance" while being "high-handed, disrespectful, undemocratic, and poor communicators."[10]

While I do not dispute Garland's claims, I would argue that there is more widespread, anti-administrative sentiment among faculty (although presumably not as extreme as the views he expresses here), regardless of if they are disgruntled or not. First, faculty tend to be, by and large, antiauthoritarian. Trained by nature to question supposed authority and to perpetually question, faculty can be skeptical of those in positions of power (and often, rightly so). Also, as entrepreneurs of sorts, faculty tend to be more libertarian or conservative (not politically) when it comes to administrative governance. Indeed, to many faculty, the best administrators (as well as programs, departments, and schools or colleges) tend to be those who govern or administer the least, especially when it comes to them and their respective units. When it comes to more mundane, difficult, or fraught issues (e.g., student disciplinary actions, honor code violations, legal issues, technology, facilities, bureaucratic paperwork), faculty tend to be more than happy to have staff and administrators involved or to just take care of these issues for them. Administrators may indeed endear themselves to faculty and staff if they are able to effect tangible benefits in their lives (e.g., through increasing salaries, adding departmental funds, procuring grants, and offering significant professional development opportunities), yet this does not happen frequently. For their own part, administrators (and staff) may feel that faculty display a certain arrogance and condescension (although, in fairness, administrators may convey this same attitude toward faculty), especially if those administrators (and staff) do not possess the same scholarly qualifications that they do (e.g., a doctorate, a wide and esteemed body of scholarship, years of effective teaching, having successfully navigated the faculty promotion and tenure process). Intellectual egos can be tremendously important to faculty, and college and university administrators and staff who do not bear that in mind may end up having a short and unhappy tenure.

It is true that the college or university administrative life may seem and often will be unappealing to many, if not a large majority of, faculty. It can also be unappealing to staff but generally for different reasons than for faculty, for whom being more directly supervised by someone, having more rigid working hours, and gaining often managerial-related, stressful, and weighty responsibilities can be a challenging adjustment. As William M. Chace, former president of Wesleyan University and Emory University explains in his memoir, *100 Semesters*: "Very few professors think they will become administrators. And few do. Seen from afar, a career in administration looks dull or suggests that one's career as a scholar has dried up."[11] For others, though, the appeal of (senior-level) administrative work, whether the draw may be more for the money, power, or the altruistic desire to serve the institution (or a combination of these factors), can sometimes be more meaningful than the faculty life, especially if one feels that one's scholarship (e.g., after one has been tenured and promoted to full professor) lacks meaning and significance or if a faculty member feels burned out by the perpetual demands of teaching and scholarship. For staff, the perks of money, power, prestige, and a feeling of professional accomplishment may be equal draws. To be certain, while it can be exciting and rewarding, the administrative life can also be and sometimes is dull (although staff positions can be even duller), no matter what level one may be at, from a clerical or administrative assistant level to the presidential level. The dull part of the position may include completing bureaucratic paperwork, responding to a mountain of emails (sometimes nonessential emails), and attending tiresome and ineffectual meetings with staff, faculty, trustees, and community members. At the same time, faculty can experience a similar dullness in assessing and evaluating student work, especially at basic levels (e.g., introductory courses for nonmajors and developmental courses). It is truly in the eye of the beholder as to which work or career lifestyle is ultimately more satisfying or appealing.

The Landscape of College and University Administration

One aspect of college and university administration that may not be appealing to faculty and is one of the biggest differences between faculty and administrators has to do with a change in lifestyle.[12] As stated previously, there is an expectation that most administrators will keep at least normal business hours, and there is often the expectation and reality of longer hours, which can, and often does, extend into the evenings, early mornings, and weekends. At the same time, pending the position and the institution, it can be somewhat easier to draw boundaries between professional and personal time as an administrator, since there can always be more one can do as a faculty member.

Gunsalus argues that administrators should keep "boundaries between personal and professional lives."[13] However, this can depend on the position, the institution, and the culture. In one of my previous positions, administrators regularly befriended faculty and staff and other administrators, attending social events and activities as well as visiting each other's homes. To some degree, this can help engender a community, and the dean at the time was socially savvy enough to use it to her benefit as a leader, for there is much more that faculty and staff may consider doing for someone they consider a real friend. At the same time, there were negative aftereffects of this approach, in that some believed members of the administration to have favorites, with the nonfavorites being treated inequitably. While in this case, the pros ended up outweighing the cons, at other institutions, this might not have been the case. Work-related "social" events such as staff lunches, holiday parties, and off-campus retreats are generally safer, although the proverbial payoff isn't as potentially large as it can be when administrators, faculty, and staff genuinely become off-campus friends. At the same time, the "payoff" can turn extremely negative and ugly if one is accused of favoritism or even discrimination by others, which is why, as a general rule, I advise those in (senior-level) administrative positions to be cautious and sparing in engaging with one's staff in non-university-related social events outside campus.

Further, depending on the administrative position, there may be a considerable amount of mundane, bureaucratic work that needs to be completed.[14] Beyond that, for faculty (not staff), there will be an immediate change, in that, by and large, administrators tend to have a more directly involved supervisor, and administrators (especially at the senior level) often supervise an array of faculty, staff, and administrators themselves. Many, if not most, administrators (especially if they come directly from the faculty) will bring with them little to no managerial experience (especially for faculty, with nonfaculty staff and administrators) beyond the classroom, which is dissimilar to being a faculty and staff supervisor. Becoming an effective manager is something that many new administrators will often need to learn on the job, hopefully through the guidance of a mentor or mentors but almost certainly, at least to some degree, through trial and error.

Part of trial and error involves personnel adjustments and calculations. While there certainly are interfaculty and interstaff conflicts, it is, of course, not uncommon for faculty and staff to befriend one another. However, once one moves into a higher-level administrative position (e.g., a department chair, a dean, or a provost, an admissions director, a dean of students), that can and will change the dynamics one has with other faculty, staff, and administrators who are no longer peers. As Chace aptly writes in *100 Semesters*: "The most painful lesson coming to me when in the dean's office was that while my circle of acquaintances had greatly expanded, my number of friends had not. Even the slender power seemed to act as a disincentive to friendship. Once people believed I could 'do something' for them or fail to do so, easy amicability withered."[15] As an administrator, one's circle of peers tends to be other administrators (or others outside of the college or university).

At healthy institutions, there can be and usually are genuine friendships that form between administrators (and, at times, between administrators, faculty, and other staff), although the higher one goes up the administrative ladder, the more one's circle of peers shrinks, as well as the pool for potential equal professional or personal friendships within the institution. Further, at unhealthy institutions, where faculty and staff might more easily band together against the perceived problematic administration, administrators themselves can often fight with one another for resources or the attention of top-level administrators (e.g., the president or provost). Indeed, it can sometimes be quite isolating and lonely to be a senior-level administrator. This, though, may not be as unhealthy as it seems. While the opportunities for real professional or personal friendships can decrease the higher one goes up the proverbial administrative ladder, and these opportunities may be virtually nonexistent at especially dysfunctional colleges and universities, if one is engaging with external community members (e.g., board members, working professionals, or potential donors), there may be more extensive opportunities for external friendships beyond the college or university. Additionally, while the quantity of professional or personal friendships may decrease, the quality may increase, given the narrowed pool of peers and the increased intensity of administrative work.

Still, while it may be asserted and argued that one should trust no one completely in the workplace or in administration, for one's own mental health as well as for political reasons (e.g., to protect one's own position), it is important for an administrator to have at least one (pending the size, complexity, and existing culture of the institution, likely more than one) trusted and reliable colleague. I use the word "colleague" on purpose because, ideally, this individual is a peer or close to a peer. Some administrators who feel isolated or who want immediate validation use their support staff (e.g., their administrative assistant) to unburden themselves and to gain sympathy. However, not only is this an unfair burden to put on another person who holds considerably less power and is essentially a captive audience, one can never know whether one's support staff appears or is sympathetic because they feel it is in their interest or professional role to do so, or because they truly are sympathetic and supportive.

While some might advocate trusting no one, especially since it is true that anything one says to another can potentially be revealed to others, there is no either/or dynamic to trust in college and university administration (let alone for people in one's personal life). Rather, there is a range from complete distrust to complete trust, and while one may be wise to never completely trust anyone in the workplace, mostly trusting (or at least making that person feel that she or he is trusted or enjoys a privileged position) at least one fellow administrator (or at least making that person feel that he or she is trusted) is very important. Sometimes this kind of trust can be built through compliments on presentations, actions, or behaviors. Trust can also be built by revealing common opinions or attitudes about other initiatives, ideas, or even other faculty, staff, and administrators. For instance, if a colleague shares a story of feeling disrespected by a certain staff member and one has a similar experience to share, that experience can be revealed to the other person in the spirit of trust-building and reciprocity. That being stated, generally less is more when discussing other staff or administrators negatively, with the possible exception of staff and administrators who have already left an institution. Regardless, as much as possible, one should not express a much greater sense of disdain about a person than what a colleague has expressed, nor should one ever put such language or content in writing. Strong bonds may be difficult to form if an administrator focuses too much on sharing negative experiences. Another technique is to collaborate on positive, culture-building initiatives. For instance, a department chair might build respect and trust by collaborating with another department chair on developing an initiative to recognize and reward outstanding part-time faculty.

Trust and respect, though, are only part of the politically tinged administrative landscape. This landscape can be dotted with various stated and unstated alliances, which themselves can be proverbial minefields. As is the case for most organizations, and as is the case for most administrators regardless of where they work, it is inevitable that alliances form in administration, but even these alliances can be mutable. Although it may be distasteful to do so, one can (and in many cases should) form pseudo-alliances or pseudo-friendships with other administrators (who one may not fully respect or appreciate). In fact, this may be a necessity when working in certain positions or at institutions that have a challenging or even hostile culture, or when there are powerful administrators who are so ingrained that they or their behavior is mostly beyond control. On a smaller level, political alliances can and do certainly occur in departments and units among faculty and staff, but they are generally more issue related and sporadic, especially with faculty, whereas they tend to be more pronounced in administration since administrators and staff work with each other on a regular and sometimes daily basis for extended periods of time (whereas faculty may rarely see, let alone engage with, one another except at departmental, school, or university meetings or committees). Further, the higher the stakes, as they tend to be with multimillion-dollar budgets, salaries, personnel decisions, and so forth, the more significant and pronounced the dissent can be and the more likely that administrators will be either blamed or given the challenging task of resolving or mitigating the dissent.

Challenging Administrative Types, Personas, and Styles

Given this, it is crucial for any college or university administrator to become politically savvy and to hone her or his interpersonal skills. While it is always dangerous to generalize, there are certain potentially challenging kinds of managers or types of managerial styles and approaches that one may encounter as an administrator (as direct reports, colleagues, or a supervisor). The wisdom lies in successfully engaging with these individuals, styles, and approaches, which sometimes means some delicate navigation. I am purposely leaving out especially competent and effective kinds of administrators (e.g., The Reliable, The Worker Bee, The Honorable) as, like excellent students in a class, there is little one needs to do with them beyond creating an environment in which they can thrive. These are the kind of people administrators should want to hire and retain, if possible. These are also the kind of peers with whom administrators should want as colleagues, and they also tend to be ideal supervisors.

However, while some environments may be better than others, no college or university administrator works on an idyllic or utopic campus, where everyone at the institution is truly outstanding and mutually supportive. If problems arise, it will probably have something to do with one of the types or styles detailed in the following sections. Although it may be rare for a single individual to neatly fit into only one of the categories, and most will probably fit into more than one, I do believe that current college and university administrators should recognize supervisors, peers, and direct reports according to the following, admittedly generalized, catalog of the kinds of challenging administrative types and styles. The more an administrator prepares to engage with them, the better off she or he will be.

The Autocrat and the Bully

The autocratic college or university administrator is often a micromanager who tends to like to control the work, information, and even behavior of others. Such individuals are often either in a position of power (e.g., a president or provost) or have been at the same institution for years, if not decades, thereby allowing them to accrue power. She or he is often, but not always, a bully who uses her or his power to control, intimidate, or coerce others.[16] Autocratic administrators usually are, at heart, insecure about their own abilities or about themselves and may seek to control others in order to validate their own egos and ensure that their own image or position is protected. In other circumstances, autocratic administrators are arrogant, and they may feel that they ultimately know better or are more capable or intelligent than others. Sometimes, the two blend into what is often a dangerous combination of arrogance and insecurity. As autocrats tend to have thin skin and be hypersensitive to criticism, it is important to be careful, especially if one ends up reporting to an autocratic administrator, to sparingly (if at all) challenge her or him and to know when to hold one's tongue. It is usually better to come across as nonassuming as well as nonthreatening and to flatter, even at times when the flattery is not warranted. One may then be able to proverbially fly under the radar and get a good deal accomplished after the trust (or if not the trust, then at least not the ire) of the autocrat or bully has been earned.

There may be times, though, in which an autocratic administrator may either ask or push her or his direct report(s) into doing something questionable (often because she or he does not want to do it her- or himself or, perhaps, as a test of one's mettle when one is beginning a position).[17] If one is asked to do something unethical, potentially fraught with danger, or unreasonable, then one may need to make a decision as to whether or not to comply. If the decision is not to comply with an autocratic administrator, it is generally best to do so privately in a gentle, demure manner and, ideally, by presenting a different, better path. Generally, the worst thing to do is to emphatically make dissent public (especially if one serves at an institution with a weak human resources office or little to no real employee protections), as that can make the problems worse.

There are circumstances, though, in which making dissent or critique public is something one should either do or seriously consider doing, despite the fact that there may be, and often are, consequences to one's actions. If, for instance, an autocratic administrator makes public or confirmable racist or sexist comments, asks a direct report to do something that is illegal, or if she or he engages in sexual harassment, then it is better to report the action(s) to the appropriate human resource (or analogous) administrator and possibly the administrator's supervisor rather than keep it to oneself. Yes, there can be consequences for these actions, and yes, the autocratic administrator will probably deny any wrongdoing on her or his part, but if there is no record of her or his actions, it may be harder for one to act in the long run, or the behavior will likely continue unchecked.

While the place to report, of course, should be a human resources (or analogous) office, at some colleges and universities (generally smaller private colleges or universities), this office may be overseen directly or indirectly by the autocratic administrator her- or himself (especially if she or he is the college or university president) and some who work there might be confederates for her or him. Having been in this position myself, I can relate that in this circumstance, as difficult as it may be, it may be better to not report anything unless the action(s) are grievous (e.g., overt sexual harassment, racism, or fraud) and unless one has clear evidence. Rather, as difficult as it may be, it may be better to try to move on somewhere else. If the autocratic administrator is a colleague (not a supervisor) or if one is at a public institution with a strong and independent human resources division, there may be more options on the table. However, one should still be just as careful around peers as one's supervisor, as autocrats can have a network of sycophantic confederates who report back to her or him. If the autocrat gets wind of what she or he perceives to be anything disrespectful, insulting, or challenging, she or he may lash out in ways that can be injurious, if not devastating, to one's career.

The Listener

College and university administrators who are listeners may be so by nature (e.g., introverts) or by design, like a cautious poker player holding his or her cards close to his or her vest. While often seeming to be the least politically engaged or savvy of administrators, listeners can actually be the opposite. By cultivating trust among others and not seeming overly assertive or politically savvy (when they sometimes are one or the other in reality), administrative listeners can often gain many allies and alienate few. At tumultuous institutions, listeners may appear to be the most secure in their respective positions, as not only do they often not stand out, but they may seem meek, unassuming, sympathetic, and supportive. Listeners often have an open door policy, respond to emails or calls very quickly, and give personal cues that may elicit sympathy, to which they often respond. While they may not always be the most productive workers (in part due to their receptivity or extreme responsiveness via email, text, or phone), they often work longer hours in and outside the office, thus, at least, projecting excellent work habits.

Although it may seem tempting to trust listeners, such trust should be tempered, at least at the outset, until one has a better sense of whether the listener also has a tendency to be a gossip or whether her or his listening is a front. Sometimes, when starting a new position, the best way to gauge this is by mentioning something relatively innocuous (e.g., a hobby or some basic information about one's family or previous life) just to this person in order to see if it comes back in other ways. If it does, the likelihood is that the listener is not to be trusted. If it does not come back, one can try testing her or him with somewhat more sensitive information to see what happens. It may seem safe and secure to take on the role of the listener, but doing so can have its drawbacks—namely, such administrators may be seen as disengaged, shy, or not (sufficiently) ambitious. These qualities may solidify or protect an administrator in her or his current position, but they may not be helpful if she or he wishes to move into a more senior administrative role.[18]

The Diplomat

It has been asserted that one of the most important skills an administrator needs is diplomacy—namely, the ability to mediate conflicts or opposing interests and successfully engage with a diverse group of people while, as much as possible, not offending, insulting, or irritating anyone. It is a tall order for anyone in college and university administration, where disputes are common and, to quote a common cliché, the reason the "politics" can be "so vicious is because the stakes are so small." Of course, they do not seem like small stakes to college and university faculty, staff, and administrators, many of whom (especially in the former category) build their reputation or brand on staking their claim to a small area of research or scholarship. Consequently, those who are skilled diplomats are often the most esteemed and valued of all academic administrators.[19] However, this does not necessarily mean that they are the most productive or useful, nor does it mean that they will be the most helpful. Those who are diplomatic tend to be extremely careful not to ruffle anyone's feathers, and in doing so, they may be apt either to be indecisive or to slough important or potentially fraught decisions onto others, like listeners who may also be diplomats. Being a diplomat may be one of the safest roles for administrators to take, but like being a listener, it may not take an administrator very far in her or his career advancement because real leadership is inevitably fraught with risk and danger. This is not to state that it is mutually exclusive with being diplomatic, but, as the adage goes, "Those who stand for nothing fall for anything."

Diplomats may indeed have strong personal or professional beliefs, but those can be sidelined or obscured by her or his desire to ensure that, as much as possible, the greatest number of people are placated. This approach can lead to indecisiveness or long periods of time before decisions are eventually made, and those decisions may be half-baked or vague. It can also lead to misunderstandings between people who might take the diplomat's good-natured empathy to mean that she or he agrees with them when she or he does not. As with listeners, diplomats rarely become significant senior administrators because they usually do not tend to project strength, vision, courage, and independence.

The Ambitious Administrative Politician

As with politicians, it is hard to rise in college or university administration if one does not have accomplishments to display, a clear and inclusive agenda, and an ability to inspire trust and confidence. Ambitious administrative politicians are generally able to do all this for a specific reason or reasons: to build community or buy-in for their ideas or visions, to climb the administrative ladder, or to build themselves up in their current position so that they are as close to invulnerable as possible. It is best to presume that administrative politicians will not put anyone else before them, even if it seems at times that they will or do. Chances are this is a calculated attempt on their part to win the trust of others, which they would like to have to the point that one would jump on a proverbial grenade for them. Colleagues are important and valuable insomuch as they can help the ambitious administrative politician move up the professional ladder or protect themselves.

As in the political realm, there are a number of distinct kinds of ambitious administrative politicians. Some are more overt in their ambitions and desire to be liked or even loved. They are usually among the most outspoken in meetings, the ones who tend to take control, and the most apt to spend additional time socializing with colleagues, community members, or anyone else who might either forward their position(s) or increase their power. Administrative politicians are also generally excellent public speakers and charismatic. They can also be apt to dichotomize their colleagues into allies or adversaries, which can often mean that they have a wider range for success or failure. The most successful ones may often rise (sometimes meteorically) into positions of great power, including most definitely the college or university presidency. They can also dramatically fail, ostracize or irritate their colleagues, and be summarily terminated, especially if their administrative social climbing appears to get in the way of their work, and that work is either not consistently done or not done well, or others feel resentful for, in their view, having to do the lion's share of his or her work. Still, all things considered, it is definitely advisable to avoid becoming a perceived adversary of an ambitious administrative politician, as not only can it be difficult to know how high she or he may rise administratively, but she or he could retaliate in ways one may never know until it is too late.

The Slacker

On the opposite side of the administrative spectrum is what we might loosely call "the slacker." All colleges and universities (or, for that matter, any organization or business) have employees who are not particularly hard or effective workers. There may be various reasons for this. The individual may suffer from low morale, the work may be dull and uninspiring, or she or he may just generally be lazy or not particularly competent. Sometimes, when starting a new administrative position, one discovers slackers in positions that were mismanaged (or not managed). There may also be administrative bloat, allowing some individuals to continue in positions that are mostly not necessary. Colleges and universities that have strong unions or labor protection for their employees, while providing important labor relations and equity services, can also sometimes inadvertently protect slackers, especially if they have been in their position(s) for a long period of time and have never really been evaluated (or have never or rarely ever received any written criticism).

There are different approaches and considerations in dealing with (or not dealing with) administrative slackers, pending whether the slacker is a direct report or colleague. It may be tempting to want to dismiss slackers who are direct reports as soon as possible, but it is important to be cautious and prudent before doing this. It is also important to perform a cost-benefit analysis and consider the consequences of potentially rash actions that one may later regret. It may be impressive to one's supervisor or send a clear message to direct reports or to the campus community if one rebukes or demotes/terminates a slacker, but it can also send ripples of fear or even disdain throughout one's department, if not the entire school, college, or university, if the slacker is personable and well liked.[20] If the slacker is generally not well liked by others and others have complained about her or his work habits, an administrator will be in much better stead to respond more forcefully (e.g., critiquing or demoting/terminating).

If, though, the slacker is popular among her or his colleagues and has been at the institution for quite a while (e.g., a number of years), not only may it be harder from a human resources perspective to do much, but the consequences of doing something significant (e.g., demoting or terminating) may be greater. Further, if one of the issues is low salary and there doesn't appear to be a viable path going forward to increase the salary of the position should it be vacated, it may very well not be worth it to aggressively pursue the slacker as long as she or he is basically functional. In these circumstances, it is generally better to try to work with the slacker to get her or him to improve their performance. When the slacker is a colleague, the main question is whether to complain to her or his supervisor (which may also be one's own supervisor).

There is ultimately no right answer or approach to this situation. It can depend on the institution, the extent of the slacking involved, the extent to which it may affect an administrator or others, and the perceived reaction of the supervisor. When I was in a previous position, an administrative colleague once told me that she made it seem like she was really busy when she actually was not. (To this day, I am unsure why she told me this. Perhaps she thought I would be impressed—I wasn't—but more likely, she just said what was on her mind at the time.) While I didn't immediately tell her supervisor (who was also my supervisor), when it later appeared that her weak work habits were affecting my units and me, I did tell my supervisor, who ended up not doing anything because he tended to avoid conflict and, ironically, didn't want this to affect this person's work habits (anymore), as many were considering leaving the institution, as its future was uncertain. While telling my supervisor about her was risky, it was a risk I consciously took because I had heard other colleagues complain about her. As it turned out, doing this solidified my relationship with my supervisor, as he confessed that he had had doubts about her, which this confirmed. As this incident illustrates, it is important to weigh the slacker's relative popularity and potential impact on others before doing this, along with how significant the slacking is in terms of affecting one's own position. If this is not something affecting one's day-to-day work life much and others appear to think highly of the slacker, it is often better to not complain or make it an issue.

The Incompetent

There may be an overlap between slackers and incompetent staff or administrators at colleges or universities, but this is not always the case.[21] Those who are unable, unwilling, or more or less incapable of doing their job may actually not appear to be slackers at all; in fact, if they are still in their positions, chances are that they are either diplomats, flatterers, or autocrats. Sometimes, these individuals are promoted internally because they are popular with others or because they appear to be the safe political choice. Undoubtedly, an institution would be better off without incompetent staff, so it would seem that immediate or prompt demotion or termination would be the most obvious course of action. However, it may not be as easy to do just that. As with slackers, those who are incompetent may be protected by unions, labor laws, or especially protective human resources units, especially if they have been at the institution or in their positions a long time. Further, if they are well liked or politically savvy, there may be significant consequences if they are demoted or terminated (or if one moves toward doing so with a strongly worded performance evaluation or official letter to be placed in their file). However, unlike slackers, who may have the ability to be effective in their position, incompetent staff are usually either unable or unwilling to change. They are most definitely not an asset to an administrator or to her or his institution, although, if an administrator is new to the position or to the college or university, it may take some time to distinguish between slackers and the more generally incompetent.

One has to tread carefully, though (and with the assistance of the human resources or analogous office), especially if an administrator has inherited incompetent faculty, staff, or other administrators who have been with the institution for a long time and never received (or rarely received) any negative performance evaluations. One will need to document the nonperforming individual's missteps and failings in a way that is clear and constructive, and (as much as possible) cannot be viewed as retaliation or as personal in nature. If the incompetent faculty, staff, or administrator gets upset or makes false claims, it is also important not to respond emotionally or personally. Rather, keep it objective, cool, calm, and professional. It may take time before an administrator can move toward demotion or termination. In some cases, the individual will see the writing on the wall, try to retaliate, or bait an administrator into a response that she or he can later use against her or him. If one is fortunate, the incompetent staff, faculty, or other administrator may leave or retire before one is able or needs to do anything. The more others see and document the faculty, staff, or other administrator's incompetence, the better and easier it will be to move forward. If an administrator does receive oral complaints about the individual, she or he should ask the grievant if she or he is willing to put the grievance in writing, as this is something that can be used in in the future. One should also consult with one's supervisor and the human resources office (unless they are among the incompetent) so that the incompetent person is on notice. Those who are incompetent in a work situation can actually be extremely clever or even ingenious in acting unethically by accusing others of discrimination, harassment, or something similar as an advance tactic, before one even gets a chance to proceed in their demotion or termination.

The Flatterer

It has been said that flattery can get a person far or even anywhere. While that may be an exaggeration, successful flatterers can certainly help create a safe and secure place for themselves at a college or university, just as anywhere else. Their flattery, though, tends to be motivated by two interrelated reasons: self-protection and to gain allies. If a person is commended for a job done especially well in a way that seems authentic and heartfelt, it will probably make her or him feel more sympathetic toward the person who made the comment or evaluation, which is, of course, the flatterer's main purpose. However, flattery and compliments are not one and the same. Flattery tends to be hyperbolic. For instance, one can compliment a colleague by letting him or her know that one was impressed by the way he or she answered difficult questions about a proposed tuition increase. Alternatively, one can flatter the same colleague by telling him or her that one was floored by their response, that the program review or assessment they submitted was brilliant, the best one has ever seen, and so forth.

With the right kind of person (e.g., an autocrat, a politician, or a bully), flattery can be especially effective because it is exactly the kind of extraordinary impact they want to have, but with others, flattery can seem fake and unauthentic. This does not mean that flatters can't be helpful, even if one isn't convinced by their flattery. If, for instance, the flatterer puts his or her flattery in writing, one will have it for perpetuity, no matter how hyperbolic the praise may be. It could prove useful later. At the same time, flatterers can also be gossips, and they tend not to be monogamous in their flattery (or, at least, their flattery tends to be proportional to the level of the corresponding administrator—the higher the power of the position, generally, the greater the flattery). Flatterers, though, tend to respond to flattery themselves. As long as one does not put anything in writing that one might regret later, flattering the flatterers is worth considering, as it may provide one with occasional useful allies.[22]

The Miserable, the Unstable, and the Eccentric

In all organizations, businesses, and, yes, institutes of higher learning, there are individuals (in the case of colleges and universities, faculty, staff, and administrators) who are off-kilter, nasty, mean, unwell, or just absolutely miserable. In some (and perhaps many) cases, their attitude or even personality has something to do with the work environment or their lack of satisfaction in their position. There are certainly some college and university faculty, staff, and administrators who feel that they work in an unsatisfying, hostile, exploitative, or even racist or sexist environment. That environment can make for miserable staff, and misery at a college or university (especially at a small college or university) can spread like a virulent cancer. If an administrator finds her- or himself in this environment and something can be done to help improve morale, she or he should do it. If, however, she or he finds that there isn't much that can be done about it, the worst thing to do is succumb to the misery, which often leads to apathy, nihilism, and, eventually, even morally bankrupt behavior.

Faculty, staff, and administrators at colleges and universities can be among the most intelligent, engaged, and good-hearted professionals one will ever have the good fortune to work with. However, as with other organizations, there can also be a contingent of faculty, staff, and administrators who have deep-seated psychological illnesses or conditions, or who are socially awkward, eccentric, or just downright mean and nasty. The life of the mind, as much as it can be a beautiful thing, can also lead a person down the road of solipsism and eccentricity, if not, in extreme cases, (further) mental illness. Moreover, in certain organizations, some administrators can rise to their respective position by just being overly aggressive, narcissistic, and vindictive. Putting down others, or demoting or terminating others without compulsion is not something that often comes easy to many administrators (especially those who come from the faculty ranks). At healthy organizations, there are protections (e.g., unions, the human resources office) to protect faculty and staff from such behavior, but at less healthy or less functional organizations, there may be little to nothing in the way of protection from an especially vicious or vindictive administrator.

When an administrator has the chutzpah to respond with extreme force and action (e.g., stringent policies, cutbacks, demotions, and terminations without pressing need to do so), it can create a ripple effect of fear among other administrators. It is important, especially if one is working for someone like this, to be cautious before challenging her or him regarding her or his actions or by overly asserting one's perspective. At the same time, she or he might be looking to see if one has the ability to make what she or he considers tough decisions (actions that she or he would do). In this case, it is probably either demoting or terminating another staff member or administrator who is perceived to be nonperforming. An especially vicious, monarchical, or Machiavellian administrator may even judge one's actual or potential worth as an administrator on one's ability to critique, demote, or terminate others with impunity. In that, while this is an admittedly (somewhat) hyperbolic statement, it can be sort of like a proverbial gang initiation act in which an new administrator is asked to commit a drive-by shooting of a rival gang member to prove her or his relative toughness and loyalty.

As awful as that may sound (and it is indeed awful, as I can personally attest to, having been asked by my supervisor mere weeks into a new position to terminate someone that my supervisor believed, with scant evidence, was not performing and who he ultimately did not like), it can sometimes be even more challenging to work with psychologically unstable or mentally ill staff. Whether these faculty, administrators, and staff have delusions of grandeur (e.g., their work has or will revolutionize their respective discipline or disciplines, that they were single-handedly responsible for saving the institution from a multimillion-dollar lawsuit), subscribe to paranoid conspiracy theories, talk to themselves or the walls, think that a pen a colleague gave them has a hidden microphone in it,[23] or think that someone has been breaking into their office to steal their ideas or writings,[24] it is better, as much as possible, to steer clear of them. This may be relatively easy to do if they are not colleagues, supervisors, or direct reports. However, if they are, an administrator has to learn strategies to deal with them until either they resume to some relative level of normalcy or they act out enough that (finally) a human resources or analogous office is able and willing to act. This may involve bringing human resources into related matters and documenting actions, but it also means not overreacting or calling anyone sick (or anything analogous). If they are indeed sick, it is important, within reason, to treat them with compassion, understanding, and respect, even if what they state or ask for appears unreasonable. If one can find a way to address their concerns without expending much time, energy, or institutional money, it may be worth doing so, as demoting and terminating such faculty, staff, and administrators can be a long and even untenable process.

The Popular

Every organization has faculty, staff, and even administrators who are well liked by their colleagues, who are socially adept, or who are just charismatic. Colleges and universities are certainly no different. Popular administrators may be this way naturally because they have a magnetic personality, because they inspire enthusiasm or optimism, because they are funny or eloquent, or because they are incredibly warm and friendly. Others may become popular (and sometimes attempt to become so) through ulterior motives (see the flatterer), by being dependable/reliable, by being trustworthy/respectful toward others, or by way of their seemingly very long work hours and easy accessibility. Popular administrators, though, are not necessarily untouchable, as their likeability can lead to jealousy among other less popular or effective staff. Especially if they have been in their position(s) or at their institution a long time, the likelihood is that they are not going anywhere. If an administrator comes into a new position or a new college or university, it is important to recognize that these faculty, staff, and administrators are the ones who she or he should generally want to impress the most and disappoint the least, as they often carry a significant amount of power and influence at the institution.

Popular administrators who are not especially effective or who are not effective at all can be especially challenging. It is hard for anyone to want to critique, let alone demote or terminate, a faculty or staff member or administrator (if it is even possible) who is extremely well liked. Not only can it be challenging for an administrator if she or he has to manage faculty, staff, or administrators like this, but there can be repercussions if such faculty, staff, or administrators are critiqued, demoted, or terminated (again, if this is even possible). This does not mean one should not do so, and certainly, there is great danger in succumbing to one's own desire to be liked. There may be even more danger in treating faculty, staff, or administrators inequitably because of their relative popularity (which can be a form of implicit bias, whether one realizes it or not).

Especially at smaller institutions where administrators may be friends with one another (or with staff or faculty), or where alliances have formed and solidified over the years, perfectly justifiable actions aimed at a noneffective but popular faculty, staff, or administrator can lead others to either want to retaliate or to view an administrator with concern and distrust. They might ask, How could that nasty administrator do that to Jane or Jim? She or he is such a nice person, has done so much, and is so devoted to the institution. On the plus side, popular faculty, staff, and administrators generally want to be liked by others, and if one is their supervisor, it is generally best to work with the person (or people) to try to improve their performance by conveying how enjoyable it is to work with them and how much one wants to them to succeed in their position. Not always, but often, an administrator will find that with support, clear directions, and clear expectations, these faculty, staff, and other administrators can and often do improve in their overall performance. If they do not, it is important to recognize that one's primary responsibility is to the institution. This may mean considering demoting or terminating a popular faculty member, staff member, or an administrator (although, in some cases, an administrator will not be able to do this at all, and, in other cases, she or he will probably need to wait until there is sufficient documentation and they have the assistance and support of the human resources office or equivalent).

Who Is an Ideal College or University Administrator, Then?

The aforementioned is, again, an admittedly overgeneralized accounting of (potentially) challenging faculty, staff, and administrators one may manage, work with, or work under as an administrator. Ultimately, an effective administrator defies classification by adopting many styles and approaches depending on the situation, the institution, the position, and the individual(s). It helps if she or he is a skilled negotiator, inclusively engaging those below (faculty and administrative staff) and above (senior-level administrators) with finesse. In addition, she or he can be politically savvy with these groups as well as with her or his administrative peers. Being politically savvy does not mean being deceitful or Machiavellian, though. Honest praise, if not flattery, can be especially effective as a political tool. If, for instance, a faculty member, a staff member, or an administrator makes a strong point at a meeting or makes an effective presentation, a politically savvy administrator may verbally praise that person.[25] Further, in order to gain the trust of others, an administrator can also make her- or himself generally available (within reason) to those who wish to talk and learn how to become an effective listener. However, one should do so within reason. It can be counterproductive at certain institutions and in certain positions to have an open door policy, as that could lead to inefficiencies, demands, and overaccessibility. This can be an excellent way to build coalitions, teams, and community, which is something an effective administrator will do.

Being an engaged listener involves not only empathy or sympathy but also trying to find common ground, even when (especially when) other faculty and staff may make relatively unconvincing points or when they make claims with which one may disagree. For instance, if another staff member, faculty member, or administrator suggests prioritizing an event or new hire with which one does not equally value, it is important to respond by emphasizing the aspects of the event or new hire that are worthy (e.g., "I think it would be great to have a fall carnival and a new professor of German language and literature."). At the same time, one can also stress the importance of other things without directly stating that it is more important (e.g., "I'm also worried about affordability for students, and I'd like to see more funding available for student scholarships and for professional tutors to help with our retention rates, which have gone down in the past two years."). This may seem like a more passive approach, but it is one that validates the other person while emphasizing one's own position. The other person may feel more willing to change her or his mind or position this way, since there would be little to no loss of face. Developing lists of comparable value can also help or divert a discussion that may not seem like it is going one's way in a committee meeting. For instance, in a budget-cutting situation, if a colleague is aggressively pushing for a specific elimination of a program or event that one feels strongly about but the colleague appears to be gaining ground, one may propose developing collectively agreed upon guiding principles for budget cuts or suggest that written proposals are developed and submitted. Not only can doing so buy more time and opportunities to form alliances with others, but also, in the long run, it may buttress one's own position(s).

While life as a college or university administrator will inevitably be at least somewhat political, that does not mean it is or will be a professional life of constant (coldhearted) calculation, nor should it diminish the amount one may be able to accomplish, which can directly and indirectly improve the lives of so many students, staff, and faculty. It does mean, though, that if one wants to be successful (and who doesn't?), one will need to enjoy collaborating with others and be attuned to their needs and desires. The faculty life (especially in certain disciplines, such as the humanities, where it is rare for scholarship to be collaborative) can be focused on individual achievements. Similarly, the staff life can also be driven by individual achievements (whereby one does one's job, hopefully well, and largely keeps it or tries to keep it distinct from one's personal life). In contrast, the administrative life (which can easily bleed into one's personal life) tends to be focused on collective achievements (of which each individual involved and each supervisor can and often do claim credit). Being an effective college or university administrator is, of course, not simply about developing strong interpersonal and management skills (although these are very important); there is also a crucial fiduciary component, which can override virtually everything else. I explore this critical aspect of college and university administration in the next chapter.

Chapter 2

Finances, Fund-Raising, and Budgeting

The best things in life are free. But you can keep them for the birds and bees. Now give me money (that's what I want).
—Berry Gordy and Janie Bradford, "Money (That's What I Want)"

A wise man should have money in their head, but not in their heart.
—Jonathan Swift

Money is only a tool. It will take you wherever you wish, but it will not replace you as the driver.
—Ayn Rand

Don't tell me what you value. Show me your budget and I'll tell you what you value.
—Joe Biden

W hy didn't you use the economy lot?" a senior university administrator, who was also my supervisor, asked me.

"Uh, I'm sorry; I was in a bit of a rush?" I responded. It came out more like a question than a statement. I did not expect that this is what we would talk about after getting back from a very successful final reaccreditation affirmation trip to a regional accrediting body.

"And you are going to charge it to the university, I'm sure. Go ahead, then. I guess you earned it," the senior administrator told me, only partially in jest.

After all those long hours and weekends in which I served as the university's accreditation liaison officer, scrambling to get the campus in decent shape for a reaccreditation visit and review, which I needed to complete a year after I started my position, mostly by myself, I guess I *had* earned it. At the end of that year, I created a document detailing the number of policies and procedures (nearly fifty) I had created, cocreated, and led, from credit unit policies, to internship policies, to transfer policies, and so forth. Yes, I guess I had earned that $18, which was precisely the difference between parking in the economy and long-term airport lot for two days.

This is a true story of something that occurred when I was an administrator at a very small private institution that had an endowment of more than $100 million. I use it to illustrate that no matter how well-endowed an institution may be, it is ultimately individuals who make budgetary decisions, and individuals who are frugal by nature in their personal lives will almost certainly be frugal in their professional lives, regardless of what kind of fiscal cushion they may (or may not) have. Further, institutions that have frugal governing boards or who have been through not-so-distant difficult financial times may become risk-averse to finances and investments. It goes without saying that one will have problems as an administrator at a cash/endowment-strapped institution; however, this does not mean finances will necessarily be much or any easier at wealthier institutions, where the phrase "Mo' money, mo' problems" can be surprisingly apt.

One of the biggest adjustments many have when moving from a faculty or staff position to an administrative position involves the oversight and allocation of a budget, as well as, for many, the expectation that one will successfully fund-raise.

Along with these expectations may come the (often stark) realization that it is money more than anything else that drives a college or university, regardless of whether the school is nonprofit or for-profit, cash-strapped or extremely well-endowed, for, in many ways, a college or university is a business, albeit a business that offers specific products. Generally, the vast majority of faculty and staff have little to no experience overseeing a budget, let alone a financial enterprise, as part of their job portfolio, and for many faculty and staff who move into administrative roles, dealing with finances and asking for financial gifts (if this is part of their position or expectations) can be the most uncomfortable, if not the "dirtiest," part of their respective positions. It can also change the nature of one's relationships with colleagues if one has the ability or even just the perceived ability to make fiscal decisions or to increase or decrease salaries. Most administrators find that, when it comes to money, it is impossible to please everyone, and the real issues are how financial decisions are made (including the communication of decisions) and how funds are allocated to units.

As is the case with private life, much of a university, college, or department's problems can and often do revolve around finances—namely, not having enough money or knowing how to effectively and equitably spend money. There is never really a case of a university or college having too much money,[1] nor are there really any administrators who feel that they have too much money in their or budgets. Even well-endowed, elite colleges and universities have heated discussions of how to prioritize and allocate monetary funds or how to compensate administrators, faculty, and staff in a (relatively) equitable way. Still, pending the nature of the institution, finances and the manner in which fiscal decisions are made may be distinct. Whereas public institutions tend to receive funding according to state-determined allocation formulas (e.g., using the number of full-time-equivalent students to determine allocations), private institutions generally have much more autonomy (especially if they have a sizeable endowment) to make funding determinations. This can be both a blessing and a curse for administrators, in that they may have more decision-making power (although at institutions that have a strong and active board, this may not be the case), but they can then be held accountable (by the board, faculty, staff, and even students) for those decisions. Further, that power, like virtually any power, can be abused. In this case, it can lead to patronage-type relationships between those who control the money and those in need of it. In particular, at private institutions, where external gifts are often paramount, it can elevate the relative importance of donors (who often have a strong presence on the institution's board, which may have an annual requirement of rather sizeable dues) as well as those in advancement, development, or an equivalent office (e.g., an athletics office at a competitive Division I university) that can bring in sizeable gifts or funding either directly or indirectly. Given that this book focuses more on academic administration and on faculty considering moving into administrative roles, I am not focusing on areas such as athletics and facilities, which are usually within the purview of a vice president for student affairs or administration (or analogous title).

Budgets and Budget Cuts

It can be wonderful to be at an institution that is thriving and has an ongoing and growing influx of capital, but more commonly, administrators serve at financially challenged institutions. They may have to make difficult decisions in terms of allocations, funding or not funding programs, or even, in more drastic circumstances, laying off quality (as well as nonquality) faculty, staff, and other administrators. Not only can these decisions have devastating effects on the lives of those who work at an institution, but they can also devastate the decision maker's career through certain repercussions (e.g., widespread campus disdain, votes of no confidence), not to mention her or his mental or physical health. When the future is uncertain because of finances and the institution is in a financial hole, it can be extremely difficult to get out of it, let alone make any progress on major initiatives. In such circumstances, administrators need to make difficult decisions, and if those decisions are not made collectively, with constructive, wide-ranging dialogue and inclusion, it can be detrimental, if not destructive, to institutional culture and morale.

Consequently, it is important whenever considering whether to accept an administrative position at a college or university to have a (relatively) clear understanding of the institution's budget and the budget(s) one would inherit, as well as the knowledge of whether one's potential institution or offices have experienced recent deficits. If they have, one of an administrator's most important objectives (which may not be expressed or made clear until after beginning a new position) may be to turn the financial situation around. In these circumstances, her or his supervisor(s) and the institution itself may be looking for someone to make difficult decisions that they may not want to make themselves (e.g., eliminating units and personnel). As horrific as this may sound (and it truly can be horrific when a person unwittingly comes into a position and quickly realizes that she or he is expected to be a financial or personnel butcher), there is sometimes a silver lining that she or he may be able to completely rework one's offices or the organization itself. However, this cannot be done effectively without collective buy-in or some kind of financial investment. If, when considering a position, an administrator discovers that the institution or offices she or he would inherit have experienced recent and rather significant financial losses, it is important to determine (as much as possible and as soon as possible) if there will be an expectation to cut (and if so, generally how much) or whether there will be some capital to spend for investments. If the answer is or appears to be no to investments, then it is extremely likely that an administrator will either be unsuccessful in the new position or that she or he will be viewed with fear or disdain by her or his colleagues (some of whom may eventually need to be terminated or demoted).

From the aforementioned example, it may seem like I am asserting that money is the lifeblood of a college or university, and that fiscal issues are intrinsically paramount. While this can be the case at financially strapped institutions, fiscal issues are extremely important, but not necessarily paramount, at most institutions. Other things, such as academics, institutional morale, student life, ethics, and community outreach, may be equally important, although each of these areas can themselves have an important financial component. In *Crisis in Higher Education*, Geoffrey R. Docking (at the time of this writing, president of Adrian College) argues that "when the money runs out, an institution ceases to exist. It is that simple. Money is the life-giving nourishment that every college needs, and when there is no money, there is no college."[2] While it is indisputable that when the money nearly or completely evaporates, there is no college or university, in reality, it is more complicated than Docking suggests. Institutions that experience sizeable enrollment declines and do not have significant endowments may close, nearly close, or be threatened with closure, but even those that do possess significant endowments may be closed or threatened with closure if they experience ongoing or less than significant financial losses, or if they do not have enough support from private or public sources.[3] If there's a perception that a college or university is a losing investment, trustees, board members, or senior-level administrators may make a preemptive move to dismiss key staff (e.g., the chief advancement officer, the chief financial officer), close programs, or even close the institution itself to stem further losses. Public institutions that do not have widespread community support even if they experience a significant or steady increase in enrollment may also experience the same or a similar fate.

When money is tight at a college or university, just as in the "real world," it can bring out the best and worst of people and an institution as a whole. In such circumstances, some institutions may collectively agree that all faculty, staff, and administrators (or just those making above a certain threshold) will take salary cuts and furloughs rather than cut people. Others may take on additional work or responsibilities for no additional compensation. Still others may collaborate and come up with ingenious solutions to do more with less. Institutions may create thoughtful, inclusive, and ethical guiding principles for budget prioritization. While applying these guiding principles to general and exact schools, units, and departments can be challenging, doing so is generally the best approach. Additionally, being transparent with the budget at school, unit, or department meetings (which includes sharing details of the budget, not just its broad strokes) can also help promote a sense of transparency, inclusion, and community, which can mean so much if and when an institution hits rough financial times.

I am not suggesting, though, that this kind of transparency will always lead to a beneficial result. At times, budgetary transparency, especially if it is not handled well, can lead to jealousy and anger. For instance, if a certain faculty member, staff member, or administrator discovers that another peer, college, or unit is receiving more than they or their division receives, it can lead to accusations, hostility, and discord. Most administrators will or should instinctively know that they should not reveal individual salaries to others (unless there is a legitimate need to know), even if those salaries are a matter of public record. Pending the institution, revealing college- or unit-level funding can be beneficial, although not if there are clear discrepancies that cannot be addressed immediately, unless there is a clear plan or commitment to change them in the future. If faculty and staff feel that they are being provided with the most important financial data in a transparent manner, and, as much as possible, only individual salaries are being withheld, the campus community is more likely to keep up its morale and institutional devotion, even during challenging and uncertain times.

At the same time, though, there can also be a phenomenon that Docking describes as "forced selfishness" at economically challenged institutions.[4] Academic units, faculty, staff, and other university constituents can and sometimes do go into retrenchment and battle mode when there are impending or actual cuts. This is more likely to occur at institutions without a strong culture or that lack shared governance, but it can truly occur anywhere on a small or large scale. Having agreed upon guiding financial principles that help guide budget cuts as well as a strong budgetary or financial guiding committee with, as much as possible, equal representation from different schools and units can help minimize dissent and damage. However, in the end, only the very senior administrators at a college and university (or the board itself) are able to determine whether to be this inclusive. Instead, they may decide that they want to make the decisions (or control the decisions) as to how to cut the budget themselves. This, though, can create or encourage a hostile culture and in worst-case scenarios lead to votes of no confidence and subsequent removal from their respective positions. It is rare for senior administrators to persist much longer if significant portions of the campus community (e.g., the faculty senate) vote no confidence in their leaders. In such cases, where there should be solidarity, transparency, and communication, there can be fighting, recrimination, accusations, fear, and hostility.

As much as one may want to change the culture at such institutions, if that culture is sufficiently ingrained and fostered by senior administrators or the governing body or bodies, it may be incredibly difficult, if not impossible, to change it. Those at public institutions with strong unions and strong shared governance systems may be able to push back against senior administrators through votes of no confidence, through collective complaints, or by other means. However, at other institutions, especially non-elite private, for-profit, or other nonunionized institutions, it is often more challenging, if not foolhardy, to believe a person or even a group of people can change a culture, even if one or an entire group believes they are completely in the right to do so. Instead, it may be wise or even essential to play along according to the cultural rules of the institution until the crisis passes, the current senior administrators leave, or one finds a position at another institution.

College and university administrators do not always have the sole ability to determine what to cut when there are cutbacks, even if the cutting is to their own units. To some degree, this can be beneficial if it means avoiding the responsibility of making difficult decisions and the consequences that sometimes accompany these decisions. However, administrators may also be asked by their supervisor(s) to do morally questionable or particularly challenging things that could jeopardize their own careers (e.g., make certain cuts or cut certain people). For instance, I once worked at a private institution where the two most powerful and entrenched senior-level administrative leaders immediately "asked" some of their staff to cut personnel (even though the staff had already been cut multiple times in the past several years) when faced with budget cuts because they felt that those were the only real or long-lasting cuts. Instead of seeking recommendations or engendering a discussion, the administrators merely "recommended" to their staff who should be cut (literally and specifically), regardless of whether there could be (and there were) any other ways to save the same amount of money in a less intrusive manner. If the staff pushed back, these two senior administrators (who had been at the institution for decades) would become angry and say that they were "insulted" and "disrespected." If the staff continued to resist or even refused, they were either written up or critiqued in their next performance review as a not-so-subtle indication that any future resistance would be dealt with swiftly. For, after all, these senior administrators knew best, and they were safely entrenched in their positions since they had been at the institution for decades and were extremely close with the board.

In truth, these senior administrators had ulterior motives. William G. Bowen, former president of Princeton University, asserts that "Serious adversity can make it politically possible to reshape institutions in desirable ways."[5] Indeed, for some administrators, budget cuts present an opportunity to "trim fat" when there is a perception that there is fat to cut. As former mayor of Chicago and former Clinton and Obama administrator Rahm Emanuel has stated: "You never want a serious crisis to go to waste."[6] It is never as easy to terminate, reorganize, reshape, and bulk up the portfolios of staff and administrators deemed to be lazy or inefficient as it is during a budget crisis. While, theoretically at least, doing so can be helpful to an institution, the danger of the latter (a "bulking up" or merging approach) is that it assumes that nonproductive administrators and staff will become productive if they are given more work or responsibility. If the approach is to terminate and there is no funding or ability to hire anyone better, the end result may be placing more work on others and having either unfilled positions or positions that end up being filled with equally nonperforming staff. In the end, good work is generally internally, not externally, motivated. Administrators and staff who have additional work hoisted upon them can end up being even less productive or even actively adversarial, unless this comes with a mutually agreeable salary increase (although, as doing this may not be enough to ensure productivity, a conditional increase is usually best). Further, when the opportunity is taken to restructure, it is important to ask the question: According to whose desire is the institution reshaped? If it is reshaped according to one individual's or small group's whim or to a small group (e.g., a board of trustees or members of the senior staff) who holds a large amount of power and who has vested interests in supporting one unit, group of people, or area over others, this can end up being an abuse of power.

In this case, the essential question may be: What does one do in a situation in which an administrative supervisor seemingly abuses his or her power by strongly recommending, for instance, the termination of individuals who do not need to be or deserve to be terminated or when the loss of their positions will create a significant burden upon one's unit(s), much greater than what would be experienced through other cuts that would produce the same level of savings? Of course, one can just go ahead and do what one feels is best, regardless of what one's supervisor(s) may "recommend." This, though, can risk damaging or even destroying one's relationship with one's supervisor, possibly beyond the point of repair. One can try to reason with one's supervisor, present the reasons for a preferred path, and hope that it will be enough to change her or his mind. Sometimes it will be, but more often, the best path will be to compromise and accept some of the recommendations, even if one does not agree with all of them. To be sure, it may depend on the extent of what is being asked, the amount that can be "swallowed," and the perceived impact on one's unit(s). However, one must tread carefully before outright rejecting the recommendations given by a supervisor, especially if she or he (or the institution itself) has an established history of dismissing or undermining her or his subordinates. Even if this is not the case, and one is already planning an exit strategy, it is still important to maintain a professional relationship with a supervisor as much as possible (within reason), since she or he may be needed as a reference later, and prospective employers may want to speak with previous supervisors or colleagues regardless of whether they are put down as a reference.

Leaving aside disagreements and potential conflicts about what to do in the face of declining finances, once an institution has experienced significant budget cuts or extreme cost savings, it can be hard to regain a sense of financial stability, let alone personal or community stability, even if financial normalcy returns. Further, institutions that have a powerful and aggressively frugal chief executive officer or chief financial officer may place a virtual stranglehold on most financial investments and spending. Doing so, while tempting, is ultimately a mistake, for, as Docking accurately states, "You can't cut your way to prosperity," because of the level of competition colleges and universities face with one another.[7] He also argues effectively that "the only thing that keeps our colleges on the front line of progress is constant improvement and the momentum that inevitably surfaces when people know that they are part of a prosperous and thriving institution."[8] While it is true that one can minimize additional expenses and still promote an institution as thriving, if not prosperous, and one certainly should not overspend after a fiscal crisis, it is important not to be completely risk-averse. Investments can indeed be risky, but if they are not undertaken at institutions that are in a financial downward spiral, the best one can hope for is a kind of uninspiring stasis. One can emphasize the positive aspects of an institution, for instance, a small faculty-to-student ratio, internship opportunities, and so forth, but without an institutional level of optimism and excitement, the future will not look bright for a college or university, and the best and brightest may end up leaving. Further, low morale and negativity are contagious, if not cancer-like, and once they settle in at a college or university, it can affect virtually everyone and everything there, including the students.

Fund-Raising

Investments, of course, are not the only way a university or college can bring in additional funding. More than any other area, fund-raising (or "advancement" or "development," as it is more frequently called at colleges and universities) has the potential to transform the college or university, for, as with virtually all other industries and organizations, nothing can happen without money. While the corollary that money makes things happen is not necessarily or intrinsically true (at least not necessarily positive things), an insolvent or nearly insolvent college or university is more or less destined for the chopping block. Indeed, in the face of budget cuts or bleak financial situations, fund-raising can take on additional, even critical, importance.

For faculty who move into administration, fund-raising may be the activity they dread the most, since it can seem so foreign and so seemingly beneath the abstract pursuit of knowledge that drew them to a career in higher education in the first place. To some extent, the dread is warranted, especially when one sees senior-level administrators fawning over existing or potentially wealthy donors to the point of seemingly compromising their integrity or the integrity of the institution. As an example, when I was a humanities department chair, a dean once brought me to lunch with a potential donor. After the lunch, when we realized that the potential donor had strong interests in the humanities, the dean asked me to look into having her teach for us, despite the fact that the potential donor did not have any teaching experience at all, let alone an advanced degree in the humanities (although she had taken a few graduate classes in a humanities field). I also worked for a senior-level administrator who regularly took phone calls from donors at almost all times, regardless of whether you were engaged in an important conversation with him at the time. These calls would last anywhere from a couple of minutes to more than fifteen minutes, during which I waited patiently and either stared out the window or used my smartphone. The message was abundantly clear: I was, by far, less important than a wealthy donor. I did not take this personally, though, as he did it with all other university administrators, faculty, and staff who reported to him. And rightly so, it could be argued, if fund-raising is or should be preeminent. Regardless, in some circumstances and for some administrators, fund-raising can also be enjoyable and engaging in ways that many faculty and staff may not realize until they start doing it.

Some colleges and universities (either internally or externally) call fund-raising "friend-raising." I can think of no better term to describe the positive aspects of fund-raising than that. Whether or not the potential or actual donors end up becoming one's actual friends is another matter. They may become more like professional or workplace friends, but in some instances, they may actually become a part of one's personal life. In fact, successful fund-raisers can befriend donors to the point that the donors can become the closest friends of the fund-raisers themselves. This can, of course, be advantageous in that donors who are one's legitimate friends may be more apt to contribute not just financially but also in terms of their time (e.g., becoming part of a university board of directors or trustees). However, there can also be drawbacks in that such donors might expect or desire certain things. On more than one occasion, for instance, I have been pushed by senior administrators to bend the rules for families of donors or donors themselves. Further, if these donors who become personal friends are also members of the board of directors (or trustees), it can create both positive and negative dynamics and consequences. These individuals may be more apt to support an administrator in general, but in difficult times, they may be less apt to communicate their dissatisfaction because of their personal relationship with the administrator. This dissatisfaction could then be internalized and bottled up, and can eventually explode in rather destructive ways (both personally and professionally).

Despite this frightening scenario, for the most part fund-raising, although challenging in its own ways, is mostly innocuous and can be extremely rewarding. The best way to look at fund-raising is an opportunity to do two things: help an institution and make professional contacts, if not friends. It might seem preposterous to many faculty that, as William G. Bowen claims, fund-raising can sometimes be "great fun," but this is truly the best attitude to have when engaging in fund-raising.[9] If one believes in the institution and what it can do for students and the community, then, as Bowen explains, "there is real satisfaction in helping people make better use of their resources than they could ever have made on their own."[10] Further, if one is able to engage with community members generally outside of academia about higher education–related matters, one can gain an important external perspective about these issues as well as a deeper appreciation and understanding for how to communicate the values and virtues of the school, college, or university to a wider, external audience.

When fund-raising, one of the first tasks is getting to know the potential donor and his or her interests and passions. The key is to focus on an area of interest that the potential donor may have (e.g., art, social justice, teaching) and to help lead them toward related gift-giving opportunities that will benefit the institution while providing the donor or donors with a sense of fulfillment or purpose. This may be through sending invitations to significant events on campus that could be of particular interest to them and eliciting (as well as, ideally, using) their input and feedback. Generally, a donor or potential donor will be more willing to contribute if the following exists: (1) interest in the organization, activity, event, or person making the ask; (2) active participation on the part of the (potential) donor(s) in the organization, activity, or event; and (3) a sense that there will be some kind of return on investment—for instance, through student achievements, through a named center of the arts, and so forth. Displaying some of the highlights of a college or university (e.g., the opening of a student-led art gallery, final presentations of a service learning class involved in community development) to the potential donor can also be extremely important in connecting her or him to the institution as well as opening up new, previously not considered areas, where she or he could also contribute.

This, though, is not to minimize an extremely important aspect of fund-raising: In order to be a successful fund-raiser, one must be able to engage effectively with community members. In this, extroverts will have an immediate advantage. Administrators who are introverts may struggle with fund-raising, but this does not mean that they will be doomed to failure or that they will not end up not being as successful as extroverts. Introverts can even end up being more successful than extroverts. However, introverts will need to learn to project themselves socially, be able to tell engaging and witty stories, and be comfortable engaging with small and large groups. It also means that, in particular, for introverts who may not naturally do this or who may feel uncomfortable doing this, attention needs to be placed on the potential donor(s) in order to discover their interests and engage with them on those issues, to ultimately find an area where those interests can converge with a gift or donation to the institution. These discussions are generally best in person, usually over a meal or drink in some location off campus. Introverts generally fare better in one-on-one, discussion-based meetings, whereas extroverts may thrive in larger groups, and while it is ideal to be able to choose between these kinds of venues, as choice is not always available, it is important to become comfortable in both settings.

In some ways, professional relationships with (potential) donors may feel like office friendships, situationally based but not real or lasting. However, the more one can legitimately become friends with the very people being courted for gifts, generally, the better chance one has of receiving substantial gifts. This can be easier at schools with a specific mission or focus, such as religiously affiliated institutions, in which there may be an existing community (e.g., Catholic, Baptist, Jewish) of people who may be especially or intrinsically interested in what an institution is doing or the corresponding administrator may be heavily involved in that same community (e.g., members of the same congregation). Regardless, in order to pave the road for a potential gift, an administrator should be prepared to engage with the individual(s) at social occasions on a smaller, more intimate level. Receptions at one's home or the home of a university sponsor can also be especially promising venues because they may also open up personal connections, which could lead to deeper connections and eventual gifts.

There is no way around the fact that asking potential donors for gifts can be awkward at first and may not necessarily get much easier over time. The first time one makes an ask, one can feel rather like an inexperienced teenager nervously asking someone out on a first date. However, one need not and should not go it alone. Writing for *The Chronicle of Higher Education*, Kathryn Masterson argues that administrators who are expected to fund-raise should "get trained," through workshops and conferences, and should "have clear goals" that "fit into a college's vision and objectives." Such "training," if available, can certainly help. However, it cannot and should not replace collaborative efforts with an advancement or development office (or equivalent). Depending on the quality and experience of those in this office, external training may, ultimately, not be necessary. Further, some colleges and universities prefer that advancement and development (or an analogous office) either collaborate or take the lead on virtually all gifts. This could mean that an administrator has a partner or partners all along with presumably more experience in fund-raising, or it could mean having "behind the scenes" advisors who provide guidance as to the right time to make the ask and how to make the ask.

There is no universal agreement on how to make an ask, though. Masterson suggests that one should "talk about money upfront" and that newer fund-raisers should begin by asking for smaller gifts as opposed to larger ones, as smaller donations are easier to secure and can help a person "build credibility." However, others suggest taking it slow by getting to know the potential donor or donors first, possibly by asking them to serve on an advisory board and helping them learn about the college, school, program, or students before actually making the ask. The truth is that it more often depends on the situation and the potential donor or donors. Just as some personal relationships develop quickly and others develop slowly, the same is true for relationships with potential donors. Further, some potential donors will not be as or at all interested in developing professional or personal relationships. Rather, they will prefer it if one transparently and efficiently cuts to the chase with the ask. Is there a limit to which there may be too much engagement with community members? Perhaps so. I once worked at an institution where the president had lunch (off campus) virtually every day with community members for fund-raising and "friend-building." This same president was instrumental in building up a sizeable endowment at the university, and given his position, no staff member would say anything about these activities, even though it meant that he was rarely in the office before the mid-to-late afternoon (and was just there for a few hours, if at all). In fact, it wasn't until the institution and president faced a couple financially challenging years that the board began to be critical of him and his approach, which ended, tumultuously, in his eventual exit.

Superficially, it might seem that any gift is a good gift, and no gift to a college or university should be turned down except in the most extreme of circumstances (e.g., the donor is a member of the KKK, the gift comes from a donor suspected of embezzlement). In truth, it is more complicated. Sizeable gifts are usually not scrutinized by the university community itself as well as by the public, and the acceptance of gifts (and naming buildings, centers, or schools after a donor) can send a message to the public about the values (or lack thereof) of the college or university. For instance, if a college or university accepts a gift in which it is stipulated that a building, initiative, program, or something of that nature must be named after a corporation or organization with specific commercial or political connotations (e.g., the Goldwater School of Business, the Koch Library, the BP Foundation), it can produce aftereffects that can cause more trouble than benefit for the college or university. That being stated, donations from large and powerful corporate groups as well as wealthy donors with political aims often anticipate this and mask their gifts cleverly with little to no indication of the strings attached.

While in the world of college or university development it may be hard to turn down a "free lunch," it is important to consider seriously what one is about to consume before one actu-

ally does to avoid a case of proverbial indigestion, or even proverbial food poisoning. It may not be (relatively) challenging for
elite colleges and universities to turn down occasional gifts.
However, even these institutions sometimes have difficulty
turning down a "free lunch." This can be seen, for instance, in
the case of funding provided by the actively conservative Charles
Koch Foundation, whose donations, Paul Basken, writing for the
Chronicle of Higher Education, identifies, have been accepted by
some of the nation's most elite institutions (e.g., Harvard and
MIT) as well as much more fiscally strapped, non-elite institutes
such as Montana State University, which was offered a $5.7
million gift from the Koch brothers. Even though Montana State
University has experienced recent financial challenges[11] and is
located in a conservative part of a conservative state, faculty
and students there protested an "economics research center,"
which was slated to be built from Charles Koch Foundation
funding.[12]

While it may not be possible to evaluate whether this particular gift has any strings attached, there is evidence that Charles
Koch Foundation gifts to colleges and universities have come
with strings attached.[13] However, most campus community constituents would have no way of knowing this, as not only is
donor information often not made public (unless, of course, the
donation is for a named gift), even if the donor is revealed, but
the specifics of the gift are rarely ever revealed in any kind of
detail. Faculty, staff, and students may try to obtain this information themselves, but they have no intrinsic right to receive
it. Still, if they are sufficiently persistent and vocal in their demands for information or if the donor is revealed to have strong
political leanings, those that have decision-making power may
feel either pushed into not accepting the gift or releasing some
information related to the donor or gift.[14]

As much as colleges and universities sometimes can be figurative ivory towers of professors and professionals seeking a life
of the mind as well as intellectual and social improvement, they

can be more like literal ivory towers (notable by striking facilities and sometimes by resort-like amenities) that can and often are the catalyst for research and development, which drives big businesses and produces millions or even billions of dollars. As identified by *R&D Magazine*, research and development at colleges and universities "globally performs between 5% and 68% of a country's R&D, with an average of 23%—the average of 37 countries for which data is available. In the US, about 15% of the R&D is performed in academia."[15] Further, foundations, even at public institutions, are not required to disclose their agreements with other organizations, and in many cases, they do not want this information to become public because they may fear,[16] for good reason, that doing so may jeopardize the gifts themselves. Donors or those engaged in for-profit business activities (which can and do exist even at nonprofit colleges and universities) generally do not want to feel beholden to anyone, if they can avoid, in particular, the scrutinizing eyes of politically active faculty (and students).[17]

Further, foundations can be provided "backdoor" methods or "shells" for institutions to bypass university or state budgets, which operate more or less like for-profit businesses.[18] If the foundation compensates administrators for services (which it can do as a private organization), those who are compensated or may be compensated in the future can become biased in the foundation's favor. This can lead directly or indirectly to patronage-like relationships as well as campus-wide inequities if the foundation tends to support those deemed most valuable to it (e.g., development and advancement staff, athletic coaches, recruitment of athletes) and the college or university already has seemingly equitable independent budgetary allocation processes and methods. In situations like this, certain administrators, staff, faculty, units, and colleges could end up receiving compensation from multiple sources,[19] leading to what may appear to be (and what may actually be) significant campus-wide inequities.

This brings me to one of the most eye-opening revelations I have had as an administrator: Staff who have a successful track record in bringing in sizeable gifts, whether they are housed in the advancement/development office (or equivalent) or elsewhere (e.g., athletics), can gain and possess a huge amount of figurative capital by bringing in literal capital. Successful fundraisers may not be the most inspiring employees or leaders at a college or university (although they can be), but their fundraising successes can provide them with a kind of golden halo, if not provide them with a kind of (semi-)exalted status at the university or college.[20] This status can empower them to accrue more resources (staff, salary, or otherwise) and also justify a more "flexible" work schedule, which means that such individuals may rarely be in the office as they are out purportedly "fundraising." (This being stated, senior administrators and board members generally tire of these same individuals quickly if their fund-raising lessens or ceases.) Other administrators who are not in such a position may feel that this is inequitable, and they may become envious and upset. However, it is important not to act on these feelings. As much as it may be difficult for some to acknowledge, as stated earlier in this chapter, colleges and universities are businesses (some more than others), and money is critical to an institution, regardless of whether the institution is for-profit or nonprofit. Individuals who are instrumental in bringing in substantial funding can be and often are extremely valuable and powerful, often much more valuable than those who do not bring in funds.

Salaries and Spending

Given the growing demand on the part of students for campus amenities, from top-notch athletic and residential facilities to innovative and gourmet dining options, campus finances have taken on an even greater importance. As Ryan Craig argues in

College Disrupted: "Colleges and universities have been rewarded" for spending.[21] He also identifies that "US News and other rankings evaluate colleges based on how much they spend per student."[22] For Craig and many others, this is a disturbing phenomenon, one that detracts from what is often considered the primary purpose of a college or university: educating students. However, anyone who thinks that educating students can exist in a financial vacuum is woefully naive. To draw and retain students, and to draw and retain quality faculty and staff, one must be willing to spend, and in order to spend, one must, of course, have a sufficient amount of capital. Therefore, in particular, anyone considering moving into a (senior-level) college and university administrative position should examine the endowment and spending trends of the institution as well as the specific budget(s) of the school(s) or unit(s) she or he would be overseeing. Administrators who find themselves at penny-pinching institutions (or under extremely frugal senior administrators) will find their own ability to accomplish their goals to be significantly limited.

Further, as has often been stated colloquially, one gets what one pays for. This adage generally holds true in academia, just as it does for most, if not all, businesses or industries. Issues of compensation are extraordinarily important, not just in terms of attracting and retaining talented and capable faculty and staff but also in terms of institutional culture. If there is a reality or even a perception that certain faculty and staff are being compensated more (unfairly so) than others, it can lead to a malignant institutional cancer. Herein, though, lies a general and important difference between public and private institutions. Whereas salaries at public institutions tend to be a matter of public record, private institutions generally do not disclose individual salaries (at least not of their own volition), and often, the most one can discern about salaries at such institutions are general salary ranges for types of positions (e.g., dean of students, assistant professor, associate professor).

In addition, public institutions usually do not have the same latitude that private institutions have in setting salaries. To some degree, this can be helpful for public institutions, in that statewide salary parameters and guidelines may be mostly predetermined. This can allow administrators to have a convenient scapegoat either in the state educational offices or state government if salaries are lower than desired. Further, public institutions that have strong unions may take the fight directly to the state, bypassing administrators completely. Still, with the exception of the elite (e.g., UC Berkeley, University of Virginia, UCLA), public institutions generally do not have the same ability as elite private universities do to offer high salaries, which can attract extremely talented and capable faculty and administrators. Additionally, as mentioned earlier, salaries at public institutions can be a matter of public record (even though it may take some work to find them), and especially high salaries at public institutions can invite public criticism. At such institutions, with the exception of additional compensation through alternative means, which need not be disclosed (e.g., a college or university foundation), there can be no real secrets about how much each person makes. This can give faculty and staff the wherewithal to question what they may perceive (rightly or wrongly) as inequitable discrepancies between faculty and staff salaries. That being stated, even though salaries at private institutions tend to be just that, private, they can sometimes be disclosed online or leaked by other administrators, staff, or faculty.

The lack of transparency that can exist at private colleges and universities may lead to rampant speculation and misinformation. While it is possible that no one will ever know with any degree of certainty the specific salaries at such institutions, the uncertainty can breed suspicion, unfounded rumors, paranoia, and jealousy, especially if it appears that certain offices or employees have special advantages or perks that others may not. Perhaps, for instance, an academic office is asked to give up what they perceive to be an important staff position while, at the same time, a new position in the advancement or athletics office is being filled. Or, perhaps, a budget/hiring freeze is placed upon all offices, college- or university-wide, with the exception of the advancement or athletics office. Especially if it is not clear how the advancement or athletics office is truly advancing the college or university or the specific units with their additional funding, it can certainly breed disdain.

Still, even in the best of circumstances, when morale at a college or university is high and the budget and enrollment are strong, issues of salaries can never be too removed from the life of an administrator, especially one who supervises a large group of staff, faculty, and other administrators. There are two distinct paths when considering what (if anything) to do about salaries for direct reports. One path is taking an immediate comprehensive look at staff, faculty, and administrator salaries upon commencing a position, then attempting to affect change if one so determines. The other path is to wait until a faculty, staff, or administrator who is a direct report makes it an issue. The latter is usually the safest and best option. Although it may seem responsible and proactive to address existing salary inequities upon beginning a position, doing so can be akin to opening a Pandora's box, leading to all kinds of issues and collateral involving those who one may have thought (for good reason) that they were being compensated equitably, who after discovering that others are getting raises may raise "holy hell." However, this need not happen, and there are some instances in which the inequities are so blatant and are already affecting campus morale so much that it is best to address them as quickly as possible.

No matter what one does or does not do in regard to salaries after beginning a new administrative position, even if one had nothing to do with the existing salaries (which will be true for those just beginning a position), one must own them after starting a position and not be surprised if there are a number of ex-

plicit or implicit requests (or even demands) for salary increases.[23]
These requests (or demands) can run the gamut from being polite and demure to aggressive and threatening, from being well
founded to completely unfounded, and from being very realizable to completely unreasonable. If an administrator is able to
get certain salary increases, it is important to realize that, especially at smaller institutions, word may get out to others, who
might feel comparatively slighted or even discriminated against
for not receiving increases themselves. One must be ready to
defend salary increases if asked (by someone in human resources,
an equal opportunity office, etc.). At the same time, one can take
comfort in the fact that administrators can rarely unilaterally enact a change in salary. These changes generally need the approval
of (other) senior administrators (e.g., a vice president for human
resources), but without an administrator's initial impetus or
agreement, they will almost certainly not occur.

Since it is all but certain that she or he will not receive all of
the salary increase desires for her or his faculty and staff, an
administrator should be tactical in her or his approach both to
those who can grant the additional funding and to those who
ask for salary increases. In the case of the latter, no matter how
outlandish or assertive the request may be, it is important to take
it seriously and try to let the other person know that their work
is valued, and, if it is reasonable and possible, that one will genuinely look into it and get back to them. Taking a hard line and
arguing with anyone who seeks a salary increase is likely to
backfire and lead to a disgruntled employee, who can negatively
affect institutional culture. If, as an administrator, one is seen
as an actual or probable roadblock preventing faculty and staff
salary increases, it will be extremely difficult to maintain positive morale and culture. This does not mean that an administrator needs to work to increase salaries as soon as he or she begins
a new position, and, in fact, as mentioned earlier, this decision
will rarely be completely up to just one person. However, it is an
issue with which an administrator will almost certainly engage

in at some point in her or his tenure, even if it is just at the hiring stage of new direct reports (which can have ripple effects on the relative compensation levels of existing administrators, faculty, or staff, who, if they discover the new, higher salaries, may demand raises of their own).

One of the first tasks in considering administrator, faculty, and staff salaries is to get both a broad and specific understanding of how salaries have been determined and continue to be determined at the institution or within the unit. Some institutions have virtually no rhyme or reason to this process, which can be dependent on the hiring agent at the time as well as whoever may be in the finance/administration and human resources offices at the time of hire. At the other extreme, some institutions (public) that have strong and active unions may have already negotiated for specific salary increases and ranges. At those institutions, there may be little to nothing an administrator can do to change salaries (which, as alluded to earlier, can be a blessing more than a curse, overall, since this largely takes a difficult responsibility off one's plate). At the same time, even at public institutions, an administrator may notice some salary issues and discrepancies among her or his staff. For instance, since salaries for entry-level staff and faculty increase over time, those in a position for longer may ironically end up being compensated at a lower rate than those more recently hired in a similar position. If this becomes known or publicly disclosed, it can lead to demanding and potentially disgruntled staff and faculty. In worst-case scenarios, it can lead to grievances and even lawsuits.

When and if an administrator discovers what appears to be salary inequities, it is usually not as simple as just requesting adjustments. Several factors need to go into the research and deliberation process. First, getting data on comparative salaries for analogous positions at colleges and universities can certainly help one make a stronger case for equitable salary increases. At most public colleges and universities, this information can probably be located online without too much effort. For other colleges and universities, a useful starting point is the *Chronicle of Higher Education*, which regularly posts faculty salaries, and higheredjobs.com, which regularly posts administrative salary ranges. When doing this, especially if one lives in a costly urban area (e.g., the Bay Area, New York City, Los Angeles), it is important to factor in the relative cost of living. A salary of $50,000 a year, for instance, may be perfectly adequate for a rural area, whereas it would be rather low for a person living in a costly urban area. Equity with other faculty and staff, though, can also be a factor. In this case, the major roadblock may be someone or a group of people from human resources or the finance/administration office. If one is told, though, that a specific salary or a group of salaries cannot be raised because of salaries in other offices, this is not a compelling reason to give up, because it is not an administrator's responsibility that others who are not in her or his unit(s) may not be compensated as much.[24] Perhaps their supervisor(s) did not attempt to do what one is now attempting to do. At the same time, it does not mean that one will end up getting all that one wants. An administrator should also consider whether she or he wants to grant a salary increase immediately if there appears to be an inequity that she or he would like to correct. Instead, the increase can be made contingent upon an employee's performance over a period of time instead of providing it all at once without any additional accountability. If an administrator grants an immediate salary increase, the employee's work habits could suffer, and there would not be a performance evaluation to use as a comparative baseline for any compensation increases.

If one must deal with senior-level administrators (e.g., a chief financial officer or a vice president for human resources) who are themselves the major roadblocks to salary increases, it is important to be polite and respectful in making a case and to be cautious of pushing too hard. If one pushes too hard, one may end up receiving nothing and also alienate one's administrative peers who themselves might complain to one's supervisor. Also, if one pushes too hard with a supervisor or other senior-level administrator, one may alienate her or him. This is not to suggest that an administrator should be lackadaisical if the roadblocks appear to be coming from other administrative peers or staff. While it is true that an administrator may be able to push more in such circumstances, those very individuals could be acting on behalf of their supervisors, which could also lead to a conclusion in which an administrator receives nothing and alienates her or his supervisor. Still, even if one is unsuccessful in getting across-the-board, collective, or individual salary increases, or in getting as much as one hoped (or just in getting something), one can still convey transparently to faculty, staff, and other administrators that one advocated for them. If an administrator trusts certain staff, faculty, and other administrators enough, and if the message will be well received, she or he can allude to the general or even actual location of the roadblocks. However, if she or he is unsure of the response or whether it may be leaked, it is best to be cryptic. She or he may also convey that she or he will try again (perhaps in better financial conditions).

The example described in the previous paragraph, though, does not allude to what an administrator can or should do when faced with issues of compensation equity. This has been an issue at every college or university I have ever been at and is close to, if not completely, ubiquitous. Even at rare colleges and institutions that have streamlined precise and publicly accessible compensation for all faculty, according to rank or years of experience, there is bound to be differences in administrator and staff salaries, and (most or all) faculty may be unhappy with the level of compensation they currently receive. If the aforementioned measures to increase or promote salary equity and adjustments mostly or completely fail, there are some additional measures to consider. For instance, if an institution does not currently have a merit system related to annual or periodic reviews, such a system could be put in place to encourage and reward strong work. For administrators who do not want those who aren't performing well to receive automatic salary increases, or who are concerned about a future decline in work habits if salary increases are just doled out automatically, a merit-type system can be more palatable than across-the-board equity or cost of living increases. Such a system, though, will only work effectively at institutions where performance evaluations are not perfunctory, and where everyone is not reportedly doing an excellent job or, as Garrison Keillor might state, "where all the women are strong, all the men are good looking, and all the children are above average." Further, the establishment of a merit system can also lead to disgruntlement and grievances by those who do not receive merit.

Still, even if one inherits an established merit system, it will not eliminate inherited salary inequities among administrators, faculty, and staff. There is, of course, little to nothing one can or would even want to do in terms of lowering the salaries of highly compensated individuals. The most one can do is work toward (or advocate for) raising the compensation levels of those who are comparatively compensated the least. Ironically, those who strongly advocate for their own salary increases are often those in least need or not particularly deserving of salary increases. In some circumstances, one will be able to state authentically that one would love to raise salaries, but for various reasons (e.g., lowered enrollment, a fiscally conservative senior management team) it is not possible to do so now, even if the real reason is that one does not really want to grant the specific individual a salary increase. Even if this is the case, though, it is important to appear sympathetic to her or his cause, even if one ends up not granting it to avoid unnecessary conflict and dissatisfaction.

Regardless, one way to justify salary increases, if agreeable to the staff, faculty, or administrator as well as to senior administrators, is through the reclassification or restructuring of positions with greater responsibility and authority, thereby justifying an appropriate salary increase. An example of this would be transferring the academic duties of assessment and program review to a faculty member in exchange for a stipend and course releases (as opposed to hiring a specific person for assessment and program review). This measure, in fact, is usually the most palatable path at budget-strapped institutions, as doing so can theoretically save the institution money while rewarding a specific individual with greater compensation. That being stated, one must always be wary of going this route. Not only can it result in a decreased quality of work if the individual is stretched too thin, but the same individual might suffer from burnout or complacency later on. Further, if the budgetary "lean" times pass or the responsibilities of one part of the person's position increase, it may be quite challenging to reclassify that individual's position again.

Budgeting

Beyond matters of individual or collective compensation, most administrators have to determine ways to effectively and equitably allocate budgets and make funding decisions. These decisions can vary widely depending on the relative fiscal health of an institution as well as its general willingness to invest (or not). I once interviewed at a prominent research university where the hiring senior administrator stated that she was, thus far, able to secure every position and budgetary request for which she had asked. Perhaps primarily because of this reason, the staff, faculty, and administrators had very positive things to say about her during the interview process (in particular, about her ability to get the faculty and staff what they wanted). This, though, is often the exception, not the rule. More likely, administrators are fortunate to get some of what they want in terms of positions, funding, and investments. As much as this is not an ideal situation, it, at least, can provide an administrator with some cover if she or he is unable to fund something or someone (e.g., "I'd love to be able to send you to this conference; however, the university[25] has made it clear that no one can attend conferences this year due to the budget."). At the same time, it can also make the life of an administrator much more challenging, for she or he will then need to make a decision as to what to fund and even what to cut. Since, in such situations, it is nearly impossible (if not completely impossible) to please all faculty and staff, as those who aren't funded accordingly can and probably will feel slighted, if not discriminated against, the best approach is a collective, shared governance approach.

A collective, shared governance approach to budgeting involves a number of important aspects. First, if possible, budgeting should be tied to an overall or specific strategic plan (e.g., for the entire college or university or for the specific unit or units an administrator oversees). For example, if a university- or college-level strategic plan priority is to increase enrollment as well as graduation and retention rates, then there is a clear case to prioritize the funding of new positions (and funding in general) in admissions, recruiting, graduation initiatives, and student support (as much as, if not more than, new faculty hires). At particularly healthy institutions, budgeting/funding recommendations may be made by a budgeting committee that can review specific proposals for funding (a proposal process and procedure can be created). After review, they can make their specific recommendations to an administrative manager/leader. These committees, though, rarely have decision-making power. While it is certainly possible to grant them this power, if one does that or if one is at an institution where they do have this power, one will probably be at the mercy of whatever decision the committee may make, a position in which few administrators long to be.

Regardless of whether they are a recommending or decision-making body, the virtue of such a committee is that it promotes shared governance, takes the pressure off an administrator, and helps promote the sense that faculty and staff are at least active stakeholders, if not equal stakeholders, in the shaping and prioritizing of their unit(s) as well as the college or university at large. However, at more dysfunctional (e.g., siloed or individualistic) colleges or universities, a budgeting committee can actually make matters worse by leading to intense fighting for resources, unresolvable conflicts, or unfounded recommendations that serve mainly to benefit the committee members personally or professionally. It can always be challenging to go against a committee's recommendation, especially if the recommendation is very strong and the stakes are significant. However, there will be times in which going against the recommendation may be the right thing to do and the best thing for the institution. If this seems likely to occur on an ongoing basis, it can be preferable to make some of the more important budgetary/funding decisions within a smaller, inner circle. However, if one does this, it may be seen as stripping away some level of shared governance and can lead to some institutional critique, even disdain.

In addition to tying budgetary/funding decisions to a strategic plan (or plans), it can also be helpful to tie these same decisions to student success-related initiatives/goals and student need (e.g., a certain amount of funding is contingent upon x and y increases in retention and graduation rates). By doing so, an administrator can be utilitarian by essentially connecting budgetary/funding decisions to how much it is likely to help students as whole. More specifically, she or he can also try to determine the amount of proverbial student payback a funding decision may or can have, given how large of an investment it may be. The amount of the investment will be a factor in the decision-making process, and it is also possible to fund certain programs or proposals partially as opposed to outright rejecting them. As those who are funded will be presumably content, it is very important to consider the feelings and possible responses of those whose funding proposals are (partially) rejected or not highly prioritized, especially since the evaluation process can never be completely objective. As much as it is possible and realistic to state this, let the related individuals know that their proposals can either be resubmitted or revisited. Especially if the proposals show some promise, one can also convey ways they can be made even stronger. Ideally, such feedback would be given either by a budgetary committee or by an administrator in a face-to-face meeting. Not only can it be dangerous to put this feedback in writing, but it can be misconstrued.

Budgeting at Different Administrative Levels

The previous section focuses on broad strokes approaches to budgeting. As budgeting can be clearer in the specific rather than the abstract, the following are some more examples of how to approach budgeting, pending the position, the kind of institution, and the culture that exists there.

Department Chairs and Mid-Tier Administrators

The good and bad news about being a department chair or mid-tier administrator (e.g., head of an administrative unit such as accessibility services or teaching with technology) is that, compared to many other administrators, they tend to have limited budgets and limited abilities to do much to allocate money. Faculty, staff, and administrator salaries or salary ranges are often determined by the state (in the case of public institutions) or by the dean, the provost, other senior-level administrators, or even the board of trustees or equivalent. In particular, the dean and provost are often the main hiring agents. While it is possible for chairs and mid-tier administrators to lobby for individual faculty raises or hiring salaries, this is rare (generally more common at elite institutions, where departments may have more autonomy as well as a larger budget, and where attracting "big names" can be important). Further, lobbying for individual faculty, staff, and administrators can be seen as a form of favoritism. Chairs and mid-tier administrators may have an easier time lobbying for faculty, staff, and other administrative salary raises for their entire department or unit if they can provide evidence of inequities with other departments or units, but this, too, is rare, as most senior-level administrators will be reluctant to grant salary increases to one department or unit for fear of either a domino effect or that they themselves may be accused of favoritism.

Chairs and mid-tier administrators may have the best chance of lobbying for individual faculty, staff, and administrator salary increases, especially if a convincing case can be made about equity and workload. While it is not the same as a literal salary increase, chairs and mid-tier administrators can be more successful in lobbying for course releases for faculty as well as stipends for additional work (e.g., to lead assessment or for work as an assistant chair, a contract for a staff member to teach a course each year or semester, which compensates her or him beyond her or his base salary). Other aspects of department or unit budgets tend to revolve around funds for operational expenses, sabbaticals, professional development (e.g., travel for research), books and materials, and so forth. Faculty and staff often look to chairs as their emissaries to lobby more senior-level administrators for additional departmental or unit funding, and the more one can be a successful advocate, the more likely one will be to be at least partially, if not completely, supported by one's department or unit.

Dean of a College or School or Senior-Level Administrator

Perhaps more than any other administrator, with the exception of the president or those who work in the advancement/development office, deans or their senior-level administrative equivalents (e.g., associate vice president of student affairs, vice provost for academic affairs) usually are either expected to fund-raise for their schools/colleges or to come up with creative methods to maximize and increase financial resources for their respective schools, colleges, or units. These individuals are generally the main staff or faculty-hiring agents. This is not to say that they are autonomous in that regard, as they often have to work with a human resources office (or equivalent) and their supervisors (generally high-ranking senior-level administrators such as the provost, the vice president for student affairs, the vice president for business and administration, etc.), especially if their supervisor takes a strong interest in financial matters. Deans and their administrative equivalents also usually have the ability to allocate funding to specific colleges, schools, and units, as well as the ability to take their funding away.

While they can never be completely transparent with all aspects of their budgets (e.g., unless it is a matter of public record, salaries cannot be revealed), a dean or administrative equivalent would be wise to appear as transparent as possible with her or his faculty, staff, and other administrators. Often, projecting the school, college, or unit budget in broad strokes at a school-wide meeting helps faculty, staff, and administrators feel that they are being entrusted and are part of an inclusive team. Some deans and their administrative equivalents also have specific formulas for funding colleges, departments, or units (e.g., funding based on full-time-equivalent students) or upon comparative workload. While such techniques can be helpful and useful, such administrators should be careful in revealing too much of what goes into the creation of a budget, not only because individual salary details cannot and should not be revealed to a public audience (even if they are publicly accessible) but getting into too much detail can lead to unresolved disputes (e.g., Why did you use that funding formula and not this one?). Further, getting too much into the proverbial weeds of a budget could turn a relatively brief meeting into a marathon meeting that complicates matters and resolves nothing. Moreover, even if they feel, for good reason, that decisions have been made equitably, faculty and staff naturally tend to be more concerned with their own colleges, schools, or units, and there isn't really a perfectly objective formula to follow when allocating funding or salaries.

Senior-Level Administrators

While senior-level administrators (e.g., provost, vice president for student affairs, vice president for business and administration, vice president for advancement) may be removed from the details of most individual salaries, they are generally the ones who have the greatest authority and ability to make wider decisions that can ultimately affect virtually all faculty as well as a considerable number of faculty, staff, and administrators at a college or university. How should schools be comparatively allocated? Should faculty and staff in certain fields (e.g., business, the STEM fields, information technology, advancement, and athletics staff) be compensated more than others, or should there be equity increases for some individuals or units? Which staff should be allocated to different colleges, schools, or units? How can or should faculty release time be determined? All of these determinations are certainly not made in a vacuum, as not only do senior-level administrators generally report to the president of the university, but for a college or university to function well, these individuals need to work well together. If they do not, it can lead to protracted debates and arguments about resources that can pit schools, colleges, and units against one another. Further, senior-level administrators need to be cognizant that some units, colleges, schools, or even individuals who directly or indirectly report to them may feel that the senior administrator exhibits favoritism. Widespread belief that a senior-level administrator exhibits significant favoritism, which has led to inequities, can lead to a host of serious problems, from a decline in morale, to interfighting, to even a mutiny against the senior-level administrator (which can manifest in an eventual termination).

There are things that can be done, though, if one is a senior-level administrator to, if not prevent these things from occurring, at least minimize their possibility. For instance, if one comes from a specific academic or administrative unit or school (e.g., the psychology department for a provost, residential life for a vice president for student affairs), those from other units or schools may believe that one is predisposed to be biased toward one's primary college, school, or unit. If it turns out that this home college, school, or unit is relatively overfunded compared to other schools or units, it is worth investigating whether other colleges, schools, or units may benefit from additional funding. As senior administrators are the ones who usually determine the dean's or administrative equivalent's budgets, it is imperative to build an administrative team with whom one can be transparent and who are team players and partners. If deans or their administrative equivalents do not feel their respective colleges, schools, or units are sufficiently supported (or if they feel they are not being sufficiently supported), one can be certain that will get through to department and unit chairs, and will trickle down to faculty, staff, and other administrators, as well as students.

These examples, I hope, illustrate the fiscal challenges and opportunities facing and open to administrators at various levels at colleges and universities. No matter what institution an administrator may be at, finances and budgeting will be important, and in some circumstances (e.g., for-profit institutions or budget-strapped institutions) paramount. Colleges and universities, like any other organization, cannot survive or thrive without money, but as stated earlier in this chapter, the presence of a significant amount of money (in terms of an endowment or through other means) does not necessarily make for an effective or vibrant institution. Without strong leadership, management, and vision as well as a culture of inclusion and a commitment to free expression (with some limits) and the pursuit of knowledge, a college or university will almost inevitably flounder. The next chapters engage with these equally important issues.

Chapter 3

Free Speech, Censorship, and Harassment

I want you to have all the academic freedom you want as long as you wind up saying the Bible account (of creation) is true and all others are not.
—Jerry Falwell

I don't believe in firing professors. They have academic freedom.
—Alan Dershowitz

The principle of academic freedom is designed to make sure that powers outside the university, including government and corporations, are not able to control the curriculum or intervene in extra-mural speech.
—Judith Butler

I t is a beautiful spring morning. The sun is shining, the birds are chirping, and you are hard at work on a meaningful, important new student affairs initiative. You think to yourself how lucky you are to have a job in student affairs, a unit you love, where you can help do so much to improve the lives of deserving students. You are, in fact, so immersed in your latest project that you haven't noticed the chanting going on outside your building. Now that the chanting has gotten louder, it has jarred you out of your focus and you can now make out some of what is being chanted: "Hey, hey, ho, ho. Racist pigs have got to go!" "A demonstration," you wonder, "but about what?" You don't remember being informed about a demonstration, and your staff usually keep you up to speed when there are upcoming public events, protests, or gatherings. As you continue thinking this over, one of your support staff comes into your office and tells you that you should look outside the main office windows, which offer a more panoramic view of the activity going on outside the office.

What you see is a group of about fifty students holding signs and placards, many of which are directed at a scheduled campus speaker for next week, a prominent conservative figure who has recently, pending your perspective, made inflammatory, bold, or blatantly racist comments. After the chanting subsides, students begin taking turns speaking at a makeshift podium outside your building. Student after student demands that the speaker's invitation to campus be rescinded, and that inviting this speaker to campus is tacit racism. When a student takes the stage and begins to defend the speaker, he is jeered, heckled, and called a racist. The crowd grows restless and loud. Your team looks at you for guidance. You try to avoid audibly sighing, as you know this will be your decision to make, and it will be a decision that will not escape intense scrutiny and critique, no matter what you choose to do. So, what will you do?

This is just one example of freedom of expression issues with which administrators engage at colleges and universities. The issue is much more complicated than inviting or disinviting a speaker. In this case, multiple students, from the student labeled as a racist for defending the invitation to the speaker to historically underserved students who may feel that their very existence on campus is threatened by the speaker, can and presumably will claim that their individual or collective freedom of expression or their right to be protected from incendiary or hate speech has been violated. In most circumstances, neither will be right or wrong, as the likelihood is that the contested speaker is not stating something that is indisputable hate speech or is threatening, such as "Death to all Muslims" or "*X* or *Y* are nothing more than dirty animals." While language and certain political positions can imply racism and even (potentially) incite violence, an implicit statement is often open to interpretation. As soon as the words "racist," "sexist," or "hate speech" is affiliated with an invited speaker or activity, especially if this designation gains momentum, goes viral, or has some substance, an administrator's decision will be mostly made for her or him—cancel the speaker or face the consequences, which involve the strong likelihood of being labeled a racist or sexist oneself, which could certainly lead to intense public criticism as well as possible or eventual demotion or termination. Canceling the speaker may invite the disdain of those devoted to the speaker's cause(s) or to free expression, but the consequences will probably be less severe (e.g., one might be called a biased liberal or a weak administrator who folds easily). In the circumstance detailed previously, the likely end result is the cancellation of the speaker's visit, if not because of a campus-wide need to repudiate the speaker's real or perceived viewpoints, then because of "public safety" concerns, which can be a convenient, seemingly nonpoliticized way to try to resolve the situation without taking a side or position.

This chapter engages with key academic freedom and freedom of expression questions and issues as they pertain to college and university administration. These issues have become increasingly important at colleges and universities, and now, more than ever, they may and often do involve issues of alleged harassment, censorship, and slander, as well as potential moral quandaries and legal consequences. To invite or disinvite a speaker? To respond or not to respond? To speak out or not? To critique or place sanctions on a faculty member, staff member, or student for something she or he wrote or said? To what extent can religiously affiliated institutions curtail (or even halt or silence) the speech and actions of faculty, staff, administrators, and students perceived to challenge specific religious beliefs or practices? These are just a few of the questions or general issues that can face administrators, and each is or can be a veritable minefield of perceived student rights, free speech, political correctness, hate speech, harassment, censorship, and academic freedom. In many ways, they are all intertwined in a potentially messy if not explosive stew that can change year to year, month to month, day to day, even hour to hour. No matter what kind of institution an administrator may serve at (public or private, religious or secular, large or small, residential or commuter, nonprofit or for-profit, etc.), (senior) administrators can never completely avoid these issues, as they have become part and parcel of college and university life.[1]

The Current Landscape of Free Speech and Expression in Higher Education

The issues of perceived student rights, free speech, political correctness, hate speech, harassment, censorship, and academic freedom have only increased in recent years with the enrollment of socially active and social media–savvy late-era millennials (or post-millennials), who appear to possess a collective and individual social boldness in how they (or a small vocal but visible group) are engaging with important issues of social equity, racism, sexism, and other social movements. This development has run parallel to the nongenerational and social media–driven #BlackLivesMatter movement, the #MeToo movement, teacher demonstrations, gun control demonstrations, and so on. Further, a growing number of faculty, staff, and administrators have found themselves criticized or even targeted by students, community members, or other faculty, staff, and administrators for either supposedly clamping down too much on free expression or for supposedly not doing enough to protect those who perceive themselves to be the target of language and content thought or deemed to be abusive, threatening, racist, or sexist.

Conversely, students and community members may feel likewise targeted by faculty, staff, and administrators if they express (especially in a public forum) ideas and beliefs that may be perceived as contrary to (perceived) campus inclusiveness. A simple word, an accidental slip, or an unfortunate choice of words can end up being enough to ruin the career if not the livelihood of an administrator, staff, student, or faculty member.[2] It can also bring notoriety and attention to these same individuals that can thrust them sometimes (unwittingly) into the public eye, simultaneously destroying and creating professional opportunities. A good example would be former University of Missouri communications professor Melissa Click, who achieved a kind of public notoriety after a video of her calling for "muscle" and pushing away a reporter circulated during a spring 2016 demonstration. While Professor Click was subsequently fired from her position at the University of Missouri, she was subsequently hired by Gonzaga University and has since become the subject of many essays and journal articles. The entire experience, it could be argued, while presumably quite personally upsetting for Professor Click, may have provided her with more professional opportunities by elevating her status (for better or worse) in the public arena.

While no one can convincingly claim that faculty, staff, or administrators currently have or have ever had complete academic freedom or the freedom of absolute expression (which no one really has), it is hard to dispute that, especially in recent years, college or university faculty, staff, or administrators are held (or attempted to be held) increasingly accountable for speech or actions deemed to be offensive or abusive. This can be even more pronounced at private or religiously affiliated institutions, which may promote certain viewpoints and lifestyles to the point, in more extreme cases, whereby faculty and staff have to sign religious and lifestyle commitment clauses or contracts upon hire, which they must follow while employed by the institution or in the position. Even private institutions that are not religiously affiliated can have a greater ability to clamp down on supposed "free speech," as they are not beholden in the same way that public institutions are to the federal or state government. Some view this development as an advancement in narrowing the power disequilibrium between faculty and students (or between administrators and staff) as well as between faculty and community members, who may regard faculty as arrogant, disconnected elitists who attempt to impress their largely liberal agenda upon their students. Others regard this as more of the continuing mollycoddling of students, generally (late) millennials, begun in primary school and continued through college and beyond. Supporting this claim, in *The Chronicle of Higher Education*, Catherine J. Ross cites a 2015 Pew poll, which states that "40 percent of millennials believe that society should prevent speech that offends minority groups." Further, she argues that primary and secondary schools tend to "teach that students should be insulated from upsetting ideas, intellectual conflict, and wounding words and images." She also suggests that primary or secondary schools "can't punish children who hurl racist and sexist insults at classmates unless the slur is accompanied by physical acts. If bullying consists of words alone—no matter how toxic—the speech clause usually protects the speaker and prevents the state from imposing punishment."[3]

While Ross is generalizing about all primary and secondary schools when there is certainly a distinction in terms of how public and private primary and secondary schools can respond to perceived hate or abusive speech, her points are relevant in that there is generally less distinction made between physical and verbal acts at the college and university level than at the primary or secondary school levels, especially as the vast majority of college and university students are adults (as opposed to minors) who can and are (or should be) held fully responsible for their actions. However, at all educational levels and at all institutions (public, private, primary, secondary, colleges, universities, secular, and religiously affiliated), teachers and faculty can be held responsible for their actions and language. If, for instance, a dean of a college or university receives a complaint from a student that a faculty member has made a racist or sexist comment (or comments) in class and, after an investigation, the complaint is found to have substance, the dean (and/or other administrators) will need to act, whether that is in the form of a written admonishment of the faculty member placed in a personnel file or, if the transgression is significant enough, suspension or dismissal. Failure to do so may result in the dean or even the institution being held legally and financially liable, should the student or students who feel wronged pursue it. In situations like this, while the response taken may be dependent upon the context and situation, an administrator should not proceed alone or according to her or his own perceived moral compass. There should be college or university policies and procedures for faculty wrongdoing, which should involve others (e.g., human resources, academic personnel, and/or a committee of peers) involved in the investigation and decision-making process.

This, however, can be more easily said than done, as it can be subjective as to what kind of speech may be considered offensive, injurious, or harassing. Further, in context with a class, for instance, with required racially, sexually, or violently explicit material, is a student justified in claiming that she or he is or will be offended by the material and should therefore not be required to complete the readings or be provided with an alternate assignment or assignments? However, how can a student know if any reading material will be offensive until she or he reads the material, by which time the supposed damage will already be done? Should the determination, then, be left up to the instructor? And if so, how can she or he know what will be offensive to students? If the material is not labeled as potentially explicit or identified with a trigger warning of sorts, does this mean that the instructor, and by extension the school, college, or university, is confirming that the other material is safe or appropriate to read? Certainly, there are all kinds of additional statements one can, for instance, put on a syllabus to try to bypass these, as of yet, unresolved questions, which have led to a host of responses and perspectives. Some instructors have chosen to flag certain readings or viewings with some form of trigger warning; the same instructor can include a note on the syllabus stating that this is only her or his subjective accounting, and that students will need to contact her or him if they have any additional concerns. However, each statement can lead to another potential grievance or objection (e.g., How does the instructor evaluate if a student's concerns are valid? What does she or he do if she or he feels that they are [or not]? How does she or he remain equitable in terms of any alternative work assigned to some but not all students?).

It may seem that I am suggesting that trigger warnings are not something a college or university administrator should support. However, I am not asserting that at all. Rather, in keeping with one of the primary goals of this book, of encouraging critical engagement with difficult, complicated, and often subjective issues related to college or university administration, in this case, I do not believe there are specific better or worse ways to address (or to not address) trigger warnings as they relate to course content, with the exception of the more an instructor gets to make this determination, the better. Not only is the instructor ultimately the best person to determine this question/issue, but she or he should take responsibility for the content and direction of her or his course. This being stated, administrators at a college or university with explicit conduct codes (e.g., a strongly affiliated religious institution) may feel more compelled to endorse target warnings or their equivalent. Further, if students have been vocally assertive about wanting these warnings and such issues have risen to the senior administrative, board, or community levels, there is an even stronger case to suggest that instructors adopt some kind of trigger warning (or its equivalent) into their syllabi. Doing so does not mean altering the course content or watering down the reading/viewing assignments to minimize any potential "triggers." Rather, it is more like putting a parental advisory sticker on a musical recording with explicit lyrics.

Trigger warnings are just one of the many freedom of speech or academic freedom issues with which an administrator may need to engage during her or his tenure at a college or university. Academic and personnel policies and procedures may be overly vague and insufficient to cover the various possibilities one may encounter. What should one do, if anything, if it is revealed to them that a faculty member who is a direct report is engaging in a relationship with one's assistant or with one of her or his former students? What if two faculty members who are direct reports begin to date each other, then get engaged, married, or divorced? Employee handbooks may define consensual and nonconsensual relationships, but they can be vague in what is potentially permissible, prohibited, or actionable. Even if such work relationships are allowed with no restrictions whatsoever, they can create a sense, if not a reality, of inequity, whereby a work "power couple" may be perceived to or may actually help one another at the cost of others.[4] However, unless there are explicit prohibitions against these kinds of relationships in an employee/faculty handbook, contract, or equivalent, there is little an administrator can or should do, except to make sure, as much as possible, that she or he treats everyone equitably and responds to complaints when and if they arise. In these circumstances, it is generally better to follow the advice of the Beatles: "Whisper words of wisdom: Let it be." Work relationships may be inevitable at most institutions, but they are only significant issues or problems if they form in contrast to contractual guidelines, if there's a clear power discrepancy involved, or if there are legitimate complaints. There is little to gain by digging into relationships and probing for potential conflicts or complaints if they do not directly or indirectly present themselves.

Campus Speakers and Free Speech

What, though, has become a larger, pressing issue for administrators (and, as alluded to with this chapter's opening situation) are planned or actual campus speakers who may hold controversial views (e.g., Milo Yiannopoulos at UC Berkeley, Charles Murray at Middlebury) or faculty who may teach controversial classes (e.g., Jeffrey Tobin's "The Phallus" class at Occidental College, Damon Sajnani's "The Problem of Whiteness" at the University of Wisconsin-Madison, Hugo Schwyzer's "Navigating Pornography" at Pasadena City College). The language and content of these speakers or classes may be deemed to be forms of hate speech, sexism, racism, or microaggressions. Whereas "racism," "sexism," and "hate speech" have been regularly used and identified for decades, the term "microaggressions" is more of a recent concept, and it is generally more nuanced, subjective, and vague. What are microaggressions? Writing for *The Chronicle of Higher Education*, law professor Geoffrey R. Stone describes microaggressions as "words or phrases that may make students feel uncomfortable or 'unsafe.'" To be certain, some argue that it is good to make students (or anyone, for that matter) uncomfortable and even (within reason) unsafe, and that this is part and parcel of the educational process. However, at what point do the seemingly strongly held perceptions or feelings of someone outweigh that of others, especially if the perception is that the specific individual feels unsafe, disrespected, unable to speak her or his mind, or is (re)traumatized by the subject matter or language? Should the strong concerns of the one outweigh the perspectives, preferences, or beliefs of the majority? These are among the most challenging issues facing college and university administrators (as well as, to some extent, faculty and staff).

While there is no concrete way to objectively demarcate what is hate speech or microaggressions from what is not, this doesn't stop certain motivated people from arguing that they have been or will be a victim of either hate speech or a microaggression (or microaggressions) if a specific speaker is allowed to come to campus during or after her or his speech. It can devolve into something like a battle of who feels the most aggrieved or who is the most vocal and visible about a grievance. The most vocal, visible (through campus administrators, the campus or local media, or other various social media platforms), articulate, and sympathetic will generally prevail. Still an administrator may be involved directly or indirectly in the decision-making process as to whether certain speakers are invited or disinvited to campus. Should a speaker who argues that women are in some ways less genetically/biologically capable than men be allowed to speak on campus? Should a speaker who argues that homosexuality is sinful and aberrant be allowed to speak on campus? How about a speaker who argues that there should be targeted profiling of Muslims? In each of these cases, some students and community members are bound to feel and argue that the college or university is sponsoring hate speech or harmful microaggressions, while others will argue that these speakers have the constitutional right to free expression, especially when the subject matter may be controversial or challenging. College and university administrators can become caught in the middle of these divided and often heated perspectives. It can be a verifiable Catch-22 whereby they can be held accountable if they approve of speakers deemed to be offensive or threatening (even if they do not personally agree with them) but also held accountable by free speech proponents if they do not approve or cancel speeches that have garnered negative attention.

In the case of campus speakers, to some degree, it can be easier to discern potential problems by investigating the potential speaker's public record. If one invites Ann Coulter or Milo Yiannopoulos to campus, one can safely predict the general or specific campus response (pending the campus and the region of the country). Sometimes student, faculty, or community groups arrange campus speakers (or begin the process) before campus administrators even know anything about it, whereas in other circumstances (and at some campuses or in some positions), campus speakers must be coordinated, vetted, and ultimately approved by a certain unit or individual[s]). However, is there any point at which an administrator should consider stepping in and canceling an event? This determination can depend on who coordinates the speaker as well as the potential likelihood of an incident occurring. If the speaker is being coordinated by a student-driven campus group, it is generally not a good idea to intervene unless there is either a clear indication that the speaker or potential speaker will engage in what most would consider to be hate speech, overt racism, or sexism (e.g., David Duke or Chris Cantwell, the main White nationalist leader in the 2017 Charlottesville "Unite the Right" event), or if there is a real physical danger (a true threat) to the speaker or community member(s). Regardless, there may also be a significant vocal and convincing groundswell of opposition to the speaker. As the latter can be difficult to gauge immediately, it is generally best to wait and make a determination about rescinding (or not) the speaker's invitation later, depending on the topic or content of the speech, the campus response, and potential or actual safety concerns.

There is often no ideal or morally correct action or answer for an administrator caught between the demand for free expression and the demand that the campus community be protected from injurious speech or actions. As much as possible, though, administrators should not attempt to make the decision of canceling scheduled events or speakers on their own, not only because it can be potentially detrimental to their professional career to do so but also because these decisions are rarely clear or easy, and there is a clear benefit from the collective wisdom engendered by inclusive debate and deliberation. Given how quickly situations and events can morph, escalate, or even turn violent, it is helpful to create a policy and procedure (or update an existing one) involving different campus constituents (including, most definitely, students, whose presence can signal that students have a voice and who can ultimately serve as campus emissaries) to investigate and ultimately approve or deny events or speakers who might be controversial, potentially disruptive, or believed to be injurious. In addition, if an institution does not have a clear, written grievance policy along with a procedure involving multiple levels of review, these should be put into place. As part of the process, an ad hoc or actual campus committee consisting of faculty, staff, and students who can evaluate campus speakers would be ideal and in keeping with the spirit of shared governance.

Usually, committees are best as either intermediate recommending bodies or even final deliberating bodies for challenging decisions. New college and university administrators, though, should be aware that other administrators, staff, or faculty may be more than happy for an administrator (or others) to handle difficult or potentially fraught cases on her or his own, but they may only have their own best interests in mind. In such circumstances, it is important to document communication(s) with any external parties (e.g., students, legal counsel, community members). As tempting as it may be to document the events of difficult situations with one's colleagues by emailing a distillation of the discussion and actions, this is not always the most effective technique. First, it can lessen or even eliminate whatever trust one may have earned from one's colleague(s) by putting them on record, because doing so will make one's own lack of trust clear. It can also lead to protracted arguments about what was or was not said. That being said, when the occasion is significant enough (or can turn significant), and if one feels the need to put someone or something on record outweighs the potential burning of a professional bridge, it can be worthwhile to do so. Even if it ends up not helping in this circumstance, it can send a clear message that one is not open to "off the record" discussions with that person (which, in the worst-case scenario, can be intimidating in nature, coercive, or misinformed). When it comes to classes and course content, it is generally wise not to become involved unless there are specific grievances and complaints. Faculty committees should vet courses, and ideally, there should be a faculty and staff grievance committee who vets complaints and makes recommendations to an administrator.

Complaints and Grievances

Still, administrators may end up having to weigh in if not decide what to do when presented with claims or grievances detailing hate speech or microaggressions. Some may argue that administrators should be uncompromising defenders of academic freedom in the classroom. For instance, Stone argues: "For a university to fulfill its most fundamental mission, it must be a safe space for even the most loathsome, odious, offensive, disloyal arguments. Students should be encouraged to be tough, fearless, rigorous, and effective advocates and critics."[5] This is an admirable yet ultimately unrealistic point of view. A college or university should not be a "safe space" for hate speech that actively targets a group of people or for speech that is without any form of intellectual merit (e.g., a speaker promoting a "flat earth" theory). If Stone were a college or university president or administrator and allowed an active member of a virulent neo-Nazi group to deliver a speech defending the Holocaust and encouraging violence toward ethnic minorities, he would be savaged by campus and external community groups, and would likely lose the respect of the campus community if not his position as well. As another example, if Stone were a college or university president or administrator and allowed a group of students to publicly ridicule a faculty member, staff member, or an administrator (or vice versa), that faculty or staff member (or vice versa) would have every right to sue the institution (if not Stone himself), and faculty, staff, and administrators might feel unsafe.

These challenging and difficult issues and decisions are enough to keep anyone's head spinning. If an administrator finds her- or himself in a position of trying to determine whether something is or may be (perceived) hate speech or harassment and thereby subject to censorship (potential or actual), she or he should try to avoid making a decision that is overly rigid and for which she or he bears complete responsibility. If she or he takes a hard line that promotes complete or near complete academic freedom and denies (virtually) any responsibility on the part of faculty for the content of their courses, she or he risks being directly or indirectly held responsible for their actions. If she or he insists (or strongly encourages) that faculty put trigger warnings in their syllabi, promotes the creation and use of alternative assignments for students who may object to course materials, or even promotes curtailing subject matter in the classroom, she or he will probably lose the respect of most of the faculty, who may push back strongly. Rather, if an administrator receives complaints from students (unless these complaints are immediately actionable, such as sexual harassment, or if the complaints are especially egregious), it is generally better to bring them up with faculty in an individual meeting[6] and ask them what they think may be the best way to address them. Even if the faculty member seems resistant to change or take action, an administrator can still make recommendations and present her or his point of view but make it clear that the ultimate responsibility lies with the faculty member her- or himself. Most faculty want to be liked and appreciated by their students. Certainly, at many institutions, student evaluations are crucial in determining renewal, promotion, and tenure. Working collaboratively with faculty, an administrator may find a way to address their concerns and the concerns of the students at the same time. If not, she or he may ultimately need to make a decision that is unpopular with one group or the other.

While complaints and grievances may not quite be the bread and butter of an administrator's daily working life (with the possible exception of those who work in the areas of student affairs or human resources), they can certainly occupy a more significant amount of time and effort than they do for faculty. Ideally, an administrator's goal is to investigate or adjudicate complaints or grievances in an equitable, deliberative, and thoughtful fashion. However, it is not possible to consistently please all parties all (or even most) of the time. In fact, it is rare to complete an investigation in which all parties feel that they have been treated equitably and are content with the decision(s) made. This does not mean that an administrator should give up on striving for equity, but it does mean the virtual inevitability of being disliked, critiqued, and even possibly disrespected on private, semi-public, or even public occasions (in some cases, virulently so).

In the end, more than likely, an administrator will have to make decisions that can and will be unpopular for certain individuals and groups or that can have negative repercussions (sometimes simultaneously with positive effects) for the college, university, or the administrator her- or himself. I have never known or seen a senior administrator who did not have her or his share of critics (and her or his supporters).[7] In fact, I would argue that any senior administrators who appear to be universally adored are either not doing their jobs adequately or have created an environment where free expression is not encouraged. In the end, anyone who is thinking of going into college or university administration should not be overly in need of personal and professional validation, and should have at least somewhat of a thick skin (or the ability to grow one). This thick skin may be harder for faculty to develop (unlike with students or with student evaluations, administrative and staff colleagues generally do not disappear at the end of the semester, and some can be especially forthright, articulate, powerful, and persistent), in that there are generally beloved faculty[8] who may receive widespread acclaim from students and administrators alike without needing to grow a particularly thick skin.

If an administrator does not have or cannot grow a thick skin, if she or he cannot become reconciled with being disliked or critiqued, potentially in a hurtful and sustained manner by colleagues, she or he will probably not succeed as a college or university administrator or she or he will probably end up being miserable in the role. That being stated, sometimes it will be hard to distinguish if it is the role, the institution, one's supervisor, or just the time period that makes one unhappy or even miserable in the role. If an administrator is more or less certain that her or his position isn't a good fit, then, by all means, she or he should consider moving to a different kind of position (or even another institution). However, if she or he is new to the role or the institution, or if she or he may just be going through a rough patch, it makes sense to stay the course or at least give it time before making any significant, potentially life-altering decisions. It is common for administrators to have difficult days, months, and, in some cases, even years, in which they are less than happy in their positions, with their supervisor, or at a certain institution, but these things can change gradually or suddenly with a change in leadership, a reorganization, or a new institutional focus. The wisdom is discerning what can be changed along with the likelihood of such change from what will not change or what is not likely to change.

This wisdom can be easier to glean than apply, especially when it comes to individuals who critique or dislike college or university administrators. Pending the situation, the extent of the critique, the culture of the institution, and the individual(s) involved, there are different factors to consider before determining whether to respond and how to respond if one decides to do so. If the aggrieved parties are students, and there is more than a slight possibility of the issue becoming part of the public record, if not public fodder (e.g., student protests or coverage in the student paper), or getting to a direct or indirect supervisor, then it is appropriate and sensible for an administrator to meet either with a group of students or hold a town hall meeting. At the same time, while town hall–type meetings can be especially effective in promoting transparency and communication, they can also be wildly unpredictable, leading to ambushes, protests, and accusations. If it appears likely that any of these could occur, it is generally better not to hold one. That being stated, if this does occur, it is paramount to be cool, calm, and collected, even if and when others are heated, accusatory, and wildly inaccurate. Additionally, it is better not to engage in a public argument, as the aggrieved other party is not likely to be converted by logic and reason even if one feels both are on one's side. Rather, when possible, it is better to acknowledge some part of the argument of the aggrieved (e.g., "That's a good point. I understand what you mean. No one wants to raise student fees." Or "This is an important issue to add to the ongoing conversation."). As much as possible, if a town hall meeting is held, one should try to arrange to be accompanied by the administrators, staff, faculty, or even other students involved in the decision-making process, as it is much easier to vilify and critique one person than a whole group of people.

If the aggrieved individuals are faculty, staff, or other administrators, there are many related factors to consider. Since faculty, staff, and administrators are employees of an institution, they are all bound (or should be) to certain employee standards, guidelines, or rules. As such, one may be able to use employee regulations to curtail or prevent certain individuals from making potential or actual injurious statements in general, or specifically toward any other individual or group. Yet, this can be a dangerous path, especially if the faculty, staff, or administrators are direct reports. In these situations, where it can be viewed as an abuse of power to curtail critique, it is generally better to not become involved unless the accusations are severe (e.g., racism or sexism) or if the situation threatens to blow out of proportion. If an administrator develops a strong reputation at her or his current institution, minor allegations generally fade away or are rebutted by others who respect, value, and trust the administrator. Pending the individual or individuals making the claim, one can consider speaking to them directly, but this can always carry the risk of making things worse. If the aggrieved individuals are peers, while there is the option of going to that person's supervisor (who may be one's own supervisor), this should generally be the last option, as the supervisor will probably not want to get involved and may end up resenting that it was even brought up at all. If the supervisor does address it, one's relationship with the aggrieving individual(s) will undoubtedly suffer. Instead, it is better to not engage, try to de-escalate with humor, or voice concerns directly in an objective, respectful, and preferably non-emotional manner to the aggrieving individual(s), as they generally won't want matters to escalate.[9]

It can, however, be considerably more challenging when a supervisor or someone in a supervisory position is the aggrieving party. In those situations, an administrator has to be especially careful, as reporting a supervisor to his or her supervisor (e.g., if she or he is the president of the institution, there is nowhere else to go other than human resources, the chair of the board of trustees or equivalent, or perhaps the chair of the academic senate, should the institution have especially strong shared governance) can ultimately backfire and erode if not destroy whatever trust may have been built up thus far. This can have short- and long-term consequences in terms of one's current job stability as well as potentially compromising one's ability to move to another position. It is more like the nuclear option, especially if one does not have a tenured position to fall back upon. Generally, it is better to gently address the issue with one's supervisor in a way that she or he should not find off-putting (e.g., by posing questions and directly or indirectly bringing up alterative ideas), or, if it is significant enough, it can be better to just not address the issue and start looking for another position elsewhere.

The aforementioned are mainly examples of critique that may be directed toward an administrator. The vast majority of administrators are supervisors, and, as such, they are generally in positions to evaluate others. No matter what college or university one may be at, there will always be a hierarchy and a power disequilibrium between individuals who work there. That being stated, there is a wide range of organizational structures in higher education, and these structures may change with new administrative leadership or with major events (e.g., a budget shortfall or a budget surplus) at the institution. This range can be anything from an institution that functions more or less like a representative, highly participatory democracy to an institution that functions more or less like a virtual monarchy or oligarchy. Generally, the latter can occur more often at a private or for-profit college or university that does not have unions and public regulations (beyond regional accreditors); they are more apt to be driven by (potentially) unchecked senior administrators and a board of directors or trustees. Public colleges and universities, on the other hand, do not lend themselves as easily to more dictatorial organizational structures and have to make a good deal of their operations accessible to the public.

Practical Examples of Academic Freedom, Free Expression, Engagement, and Censorship

Some administrators regard the twin areas of human resources and student affairs to be the proverbial dank and dangerous cellar (or dungeon) of a college or university, where so much can be fraught with potentially dire consequences, and where an administrator's career, integrity, and livelihood can be literally on the line. While many administrators who begin as faculty do not move directly into student affairs and human resources, both areas are often a part of or allied to most administrator's portfolios, whether he or she is a provost, dean, department chair, or something analogous. Whereas many decades ago, both areas (human resources and student affairs) might have been tiny outposts at most colleges and universities (if they existed at all), overseen by what, from today's standards, would probably seem like a skeleton crew, they are now among the most important but also the most potentially volatile areas of college or university administration.

Further, these areas have branched into more specific subdepartments. Some colleges and universities (especially if they have a sizeable student population) have their own stand-alone Title IX staff who specifically investigate gender-based discrimination and related issues. There are often multiple staff in a dean of students' office, from caseworkers to honor code administrators to counselors and disability and accommodation officers. Much of these developments, it can and has been argued, have helped the college or university become more responsive to student needs as well as a more accessible and equitable institution. Indeed, it is hard to disagree that the addition of professional counselors who can and do help students with learning challenges (e.g., dyslexia, attention deficit disorder) have helped improve the environment and relative accessibility of higher education. However, it can also be argued that these developments have come at a cost (e.g., a decrease in tenure density) and have been overly prioritized. Still, even with the presence of these support staff, whose focus may be on protecting students, other faculty, staff, and administrators, as well as the institution itself (when, in reality, their focus might be more on protecting themselves), administrators must be mindful of potential minefields they can walk into from not addressing student grievances effectively (and this can be based solely on perception, not reality), to being held liable for supposed neglect of an issue, to demands on the part of students and parents for specific perceived remedies or responses. The best way to examine these issues critically, I believe, is by analyzing real-life examples and considering the range of possible responses available to an administrator as well as the potential or probable consequences for the various responses.

A Parent with Strong Political or Institutional Connections

Suppose a parent with strong political or institutional connections calls or emails, insisting that his or her child has been discriminated against and is in need of greater academic accommodations. The parent insists on action. What should be done?

College and university administrators new to their position (especially those coming from the faculty ranks or from outside higher education) may initially respond with a certain amount of incredulity that some parents of adult-age college or university students not only try to become involved in their child's or children's education but may also want to be the primary communicative front between their child (or children) and the college or university. There are a number of theories for this growing phenomenon, including the rise of so-called helicopter parents, the perceived delayed adolescence of millennials (and post-millennials), the growing desire on the part of the public to hold colleges and universities "accountable," and the growing sense on the part of that same public that if they or their families are paying money, they are the customer, and the college and university is beholden to provide responsive customer service. The extent to which parents may be involved or try to become involved in their child's or children's education can certainly vary from institution to institution, but smaller, lesser-known or lesser-reputed institutions, as well as institutions that have financial/enrollment issues, may be in a weak position to say no or at least to dismiss parents of students. At the same time, even established institutions without these problems have come to value the importance of cultivating relationships with parents as a tool to recruit and retain students, as well as cultivate potential donors. This is evident in the posting of positions on the popular academic job search site higheredjobs.com such as "Alumni/Parent Programs Officer," "Director, Alumni and Parent Relations," "Alumni and Parent Relations Coordinator," "Associate Dean for Parent and Family Engagement," and "Director, Visitor and Parent Services" at schools such as Carnegie Mellon University, the UC Berkeley, the University of Puget Sound, Boston College, and Curry College, respectively.

Does this mean, then, that if a parent calls or emails on behalf of a current or prospective student, the university or a specific administrator needs to or should respond? The answer is a cautious no, but the ultimate decision to respond or not is a much more complicated and nuanced one, depending on a number of factors. First, what may be common sense to most administrators who have been in their position for some time but may not be as apparent to newer administrators is that in order for any college or university employee to speak with a parent or guardian of an adult student, the adult student needs to complete a written form indicating her or his approval. This approval form is often called a FERPA form, named after the Family Educational Rights and Privacy Acts, which protects the privacy of student records while acknowledging that family members (in this case, parents, may, with approval, be provided with access to these records). If a student completes such a form, indicating, for instance, that her or his parents can have access to her or his academic records, then if the parents request these records, they should be provided. However, FERPA issues are not always as cut and dry as that. Sometimes parents may want to act as assertive advocates for their child or, especially with issues where their child feels she or he was wronged or treated unfairly, parents may want to take the lead in confronting the instructor, corresponding administrator, or the university itself. Additionally, FERPA does not apply to prospective students, so admissions, recruiting, and financial aid offices often feel freer to contact parents, and those parents may not be happy when that contact or responsiveness is taken away or reduced after their child matriculates (which can and does occur).

One's first instinct as an administrator may be to avoid conversations with parents as well as any potential confrontations, and, indeed, there isn't anything obligating an institution to respond to parents or guardians, even if they are listed on a signed FERPA form, beyond releasing specific records to them if they are so designated. However, ignoring them can carry risks. Often, especially at smaller institutions, if a parent is assertive enough to contact an administrator or her or his administrative unit, if she or he does not receive a reply, or if she or he is dissatisfied with the response, there is a significant chance that she or he may contact an administrator's supervisor or, in more extreme circumstances, even go public to a campus or community newspaper. If one's supervisor either feels that administrators should engage with parents or does not want to deal with any perceived community aftereffects (e.g., loss of potential revenue if this is or could be a donor, loss of reputation, decrease in enrollment), then not only may it be necessary to engage with a parent or parents (who may already be predisposed to not respond kindly if they feel their initial request has been ignored or if they feel dismissed or disrespected), but one has also disappointed one's supervisor.

The best path to take, in general and depending on the institution and its culture, is to engage with the parent just enough to make her or him feel that she or he is being heard or the issue is being heard but not enough to let her or him feel that there is an open line of communication. To do this, it can be helpful to cite FERPA regulations, especially and certainly if the student has not submitted a FERPA form. Even if a student has submitted such a form, there are still additional options. First, as long as it is accurate, one can state that it is the policy of the department, school, college, or university to engage with students directly. Alternatively, an administrator can state that she or he cannot engage with the parent(s) unless the child/student submits written authorization to do so. This may depend on the level of detail on a FERPA form. Many such forms only refer to records. If, as the aforementioned example details, a parent claims that her or his child has experienced discrimination, that may not be covered by an existing FERPA form, in which case it is much better to obtain written authorization from the student to engage with a parent or parents before deciding whether or not to do so. If one is thinking of or is being pushed toward going down this road, it is also possible to require that a student be a part of any conversations or meetings one may have with parent(s). In this case, an administrator would have to do that or meet with the student her- or himself (or have someone else meet with the student) in order to get her or his account of the supposed discrimination. In the end, the best option is usually to respond to the parent(s) but involve them as little as possible.[10]

Several Students Insist on Meeting with an Administrator at the Same Time

What should an administrator do when several students insist that they all meet with her or him at the same time to discuss a serious issue?

This is a challenging question and issue, which may depend on the administrator's position as well as the existing culture or kind of institution (public, private, shared governance heavy or more autocratic, etc.) at which the administrator serves. Denying a meeting with a specific student or students can lead to a larger (public) complaint and can also give the impression that an administrator does not care about students. At risk of being accused of stating the obvious, one does not want this reputation, as it can lead to detrimental effects, hampering one's ability to accomplish much, and it can seriously stain one's reputation. At the same time, it can be dangerous for administrators to be too available to students. If, for instance, a department chair, dean of students, or a dean of social sciences has an open door policy, she or he can be inundated by students (as well as staff and faculty), some of whom may try to monopolize her or his time and efforts, make unrealistic or unrealizable demands, or attempt an ambush.

One option is to hold ongoing office hours for faculty, staff, and students (for all at once or separately). It is not a significant time commitment to be available for a couple hours a week for drop-ins. However, doing so can have both negative and positive results. Being more accessible to others can make it appear that one genuinely cares and is actively interested in hearing from others. At the same time, an administrator who does this can open herself or himself up to a host of complaints and grievances, with which she or he might not otherwise need to engage if she or he does not hold open office hours. For instance, staff may come to open office hours with complaints about other staff, relatively minor in nature (e.g., feeling disrespected or insulted by the supposed tone of an email), which might otherwise resolve themselves but which they now will want to be administratively resolved. At the same time, it is true that offering more direct access can work to help settle festering issues before they become larger problems. The truth of holding office hours as an administrator is that there will be occasions in which they will be helpful and other times in which they will make one's job and position more difficult. It is worth trying, though, to see if the pros ultimately outweigh the cons. If it does not work, an administrator can always stop holding them. (Even though she or he may be questioned as to why, and assumptions may be made that she or he does not care as much about what others have to say or think, these same assumptions can be made if office hours are never held at all.)

In this hypothetical circumstance, though, an administrator can have a formal or informal policy or procedure that details that she or he will only meet with students, faculty, and staff individually (not as a group) unless a compelling explanation is provided to meet with them collectively. Multiple students, faculty, staff, or other administrators who request a meeting without fully disclosing the details may be looking for a way to pressure an administrator into action or, in a worst-case scenario, may be trying to ambush her or him into either stating something she or he will later regret (which she or he would have trouble disputing if more than one person can verify it) or even claiming that she or he said something that was never said.[11] (With more than one person present in a meeting, and if multiple witnesses claim something was said that was never said, an administrator will be in a much more difficult position than if only one person did. If an administrator ends up being recorded visually or orally, she or he will have very little to no ability to respond.) This being stated, meeting alone with individual students (or staff, faculty, or other administrators) can also carry risks, since one would have no way of confirming if something occurred or not. If one feels that the meeting may be contentious, it makes sense to reach out to human resources (or analogous office) to see if a staff member from their office may be present. Alternatively, one can ask a trusted colleague who has a vested interest in the matter to be present. Lastly, if having another person present may not be appropriate or if there's no compelling reason to do so yet one still has concerns about what might be said or done in the meeting (or what might be reported later), one can leave one's office door open and try to have someone trusted (e.g., one's assistant) sit nearby, within earshot of the meeting.[12]

A Faculty (or Staff) Member Complains about the Quality of the Institution

What should an administrator do when a faculty or staff member complains about the quality of the institution and a perceived lack of administrative vision or leadership?

While it may or may not be true that faculty and staff are more often malcontents than administrators, the former are usually more apt to voice critiques than the latter, who are not generally in positions of power and who usually are less apt to stir the pot (at least publicly). Still, it is not unusual for faculty and staff to complain about an institution, if only to one another. On some occasions, they may be completely justified in their critiques, and one may share their concerns as well. In other circumstances, their critiques may be hyperbolic, unsubstantiated, or politically motivated. Administrators, at least to some degree, represent the institution, and as such they need to be careful in what they state or acknowledge. The best strategy in situations like this is to listen and ask questions, conveying interest and sympathy while avoiding direct agreement or acknowledgment. Usually it is a good sign if a faculty or staff member comes to an administrator with concerns, as that signals a comfort and trust. (At the same time, an administrator may be approached because she or he is believed to be relatively weak or apt to take direction, and the faculty or staff member may feel that she or he stands the best chance of getting what she or he wants in this manner.) Even if the faculty or staff member makes a direct or indirect critique of an administrator's performance or abilities, it is important to avoid being defensive or argumentative.

In situations like this, ironically, sometimes flattery works. If someone suggests that the committee one is leading is not functioning effectively, the complaint can be addressed by asking questions about why and what might work better (even if one does not agree with the critique). This can put one in better stead with the person making the critique, who may then feel heard, respected, and included. Whether or not one ends up taking her or his advice or suggestions is another matter and depends on how strongly one feels about the situation, behavior, or actions, as well as how much changing course may affect an administrator's professional relationship with the person making the critique, and the unit, school, or institution. If the person complains about the quality of the institution, one can probe for how she or he thinks it could be improved. If she or he complains about a lack of (effective) leadership, one can ask her or him for what she or he would like to see or for an example of when she or he saw effective leadership on campus.

Repeated Reports from Faculty and Students about Inconsistent Grading

An administrator hears repeated reports from faculty and students that certain instructors, particularly a few, are extremely easy or difficult graders, with either too little or too much rigor. What should an administrator do?

It is not uncommon for faculty to gauge themselves against one another in a way not dissimilar to how students evaluate faculty informally and formally through sites such as ratemyprofessors.com. While determining and evaluating "rigor" can never be completely objective, it is true that certain instructors will ask more of their students than others, and certain instructors have higher or lower grade distributions than others. Although it may be tempting for administrators who evaluate faculty to look for and use objective data such as grade distributions and student evaluation ratings, it is important to only consider these items as one of many things one can look at in order to complete a thorough review of a faculty member. In some way, shape, or form, faculty will be subject to evaluations, although the extent to which they are and the intensity of the evaluation varies from institution to institution.

If an administrator's institution does not have a clear process to evaluate faculty, one should be put in place as soon as possible. Part of this process should involve what materials are evaluated (e.g., syllabi, assignments, student evaluations). If these materials are scrutinized, and there is a clear and equitable process in place for evaluations, promotion, and tenure (should that be awarded) at the institution, issues of rigor and grading may be mostly handled at that level. If not, or if the procedure is not sufficiently clear, there are different choices an administrator may have in order to address issues of rigor and grading. As part of the review process, faculty can be required to submit grading distributions, or, better yet, working with someone in the area of institutional research, an administrator may be able to generate comparative data about grading and student evaluations, which can then help put instructors and their grading distribution in context with other instructors and classes. Schools and departments can also set baseline standards for classes in terms of assignments and requirements.

What should be avoided, though, is singling out individual faculty for supposed issues of rigor and grading based on hearsay from other faculty or based on where they may fall compared to other faculty in terms of grades and evaluations. To be sure, data outliers can be addressed, but faculty will generally not respond kindly to any administrator who suggests that they are too rigorous or not rigorous enough. Not only will this probably be taken as an intrusion on their perceived academic freedom, but it will probably create ill will on the part of the faculty member toward the administrator. What can result may either be a subsequent decrease in rigor or blame cast upon the administration (e.g., the faculty member telling her or his class that she or he has to be tougher with grading because of the administration). Faculty who have low grade distributions can be challenged to come up with ways to improve student success while still maintaining rigor, and faculty with high grade distributions can be challenged to push their students to accomplish even more.

Harassment

A student, faculty member, staff member, or an administrator reports harassment by another student, faculty, staff, or administrator. What should an administrator do?

There is no disputing that issues of harassment, whether it is degrading, abusing, sexual, or aggressive action, behavior, or language, have become significant issues at colleges and universities, just as they have at most workplaces. Whereas decades ago, if one had a colleague or supervisor who acted inappropriately, the general advice (sadly, especially for women, historically underserved groups, or others in a position lacking power) was to do one's best to act professional or to try to grin and bear it (or leave the organization), thankfully there are now considerably more employment regulations in place to protect the rights of workers. Overall, this has been an important and positive development, and has also caused a significant shift at colleges and universities and with administration. If a campus community member (including an administrator) witnesses what may be perceived to be harassment, and, most certainly, if she or he receives a harassment complaint, she or he must act as quickly as possible. This does not mean she or he has to rush to judgment, and the action(s) may depend on who is making the grievance against whom, the nature of the grievance, and college or university policies. In cases of harassment grievances by staff against other staff, a college or university's employee handbook or human resources (or analogous office) should provide guidance, and an administrator should report the instance to them immediately. In cases of harassment grievances by different groups (e.g., students grieving against faculty or staff, staff grieving against faculty or students, faculty grieving against staff or students), an administrator will probably need to reach out to other offices (e.g., faculty affairs or a specific college or department if the incident involves a faculty member) along with human resources.

However, pending the seriousness of the grievance, an administrator may need to act immediately in conjunction with human resources (unless the administrator works in human resources or analogous office). For instance, if one works in student affairs / residential life and one receives a grievance from a student claiming that another student has sexually harassed or abused her or him, one will have to act by either issuing a no-contact directive, removing the accused student from the accuser's environment, or, in most circumstances, refer the matter to public safety or campus police, even before an investigation has begun, let alone completed. In less severe cases or in cases in which the accuser has power over the accused (e.g., a faculty member claiming harassment by a student), an administrator may be able to (again, along with human resources) engage in mediation efforts, pending the seriousness of the accusations and pending what the accuser wants to pursue. In some circumstances, all an accuser may want is a verbal or written apology, while other times the accuser may want the accused to be terminated, expelled, or even arrested/imprisoned. It is important, whenever one is involved in these cases and investigations, that one remains neutral, even if one party appears to be more trustworthy than the other. In this (and most circumstances), an administrator's task is to be an impartial evaluator and to try to come up with an equitable and just resolution.

The aforementioned are just some examples of potential issues (even potential minefields) administrators can face in the areas of free speech and academic freedom as well as perceived harassment and censorship. It is important to recognize that these issues can emerge at any time and in any place, and if they are not addressed adequately or properly, it can not only damage an institution but devastate an administrative career. It is also important to recognize that there are disagreements on the best way to handle these issues, and the way one handles them can and should be dependent upon the culture at an institution, the personnel involved, and the nature of the institution itself (e.g., secular or religiously affiliated, public or private, nonprofit or for-profit). When there is a campus action deemed to be at least potentially racist or sexist, some segments of the campus community may demand immediate and forceful action, whereas other parts of the same community may argue for a more measured approach that allows for what they believe to be due or fair practices.

As much as an administrator may want to immediately act (and sometimes he or she should), it is important to be deliberate and to not be caught flat-footed during a campus issue, lest it become a crisis. Even if one does not feel ready to condemn a specific individual or individuals because there does not seem to be enough information to do so yet, the act can still be generally or specifically condemned (e.g., "We, at —— University, have no tolerance for behavior or actions that demean or disrespect any groups."). Working with different groups (e.g., students, staff, faculty, and other administrators) to come up with an equitable and appropriate solution is also important, as well as holding campus events that either promote community or promote inclusion. If one is in a senior role as an administrator and one is not visible and vocal in controversial issues of free speech, academic freedom, or professional behavior, one's perceived lack of response will become part of the conversation, and one could end up being the target of an angry community. In order to avoid this and maximize one's potential as an administrator, it is important to have strong presentation skills and a strong and compelling vision for one's units and for the institution. This is the focus of the next chapter.

Chapter 4

Vision, Strategic Planning, Branding, and Image

The most pathetic person in the world is someone who has sight but no vision.
—Helen Keller

Vision without execution is hallucination.
—Thomas Edison

The Vision

So, what's your vision for our department, school, unit, or institution? College or university administrators, especially at the senior level, are likely to be asked this question frequently or be expected to articulate it frequently in different contexts or on various occasions as well as in short blurbs and in longer speeches. It is natural to recoil a bit during the first several times one is asked about one's vision, as it brings to mind something vaguely mystical or messianic, and it may tempt one to ask the questioner for a pack of tarot cards. "My vision," one might be anxious to say in response to the tenth or so time of getting some variation of the "vision question," "My vision, in all honesty, is a time in the not-so-distant future when I will not be asked these loaded, amorphous questions anymore!"

In all seriousness, though, despite its implications and the tendency of those who answer the vision question to respond in vague, clichéd terms or with unrealizable expectations, it is extremely important to have inspiring but realizable short- and long-term goals and objectives. Further, the manner in which an administrator conveys her or his vision is close to, if not equally as important as, what is said. Enthusiasm, energy, and optimism can help lackluster visions, goals, and objectives seem much more exciting and vibrant, as can engaging language and imagery. In contrast, visions with significant and valuable content can fizzle if they aren't delivered with enthusiasm and optimism or if they aren't broadly shared and embraced. Toward that end, an administrator should be a skilled communicator who can convey ideas to a broad audience (including community members, staff, faculty, and even students) and an effective leader/manager who can get a wide swath of the campus community behind her or his vision itself so that it becomes a shared or collective vision (which should be the ideal goal).

This, though, is often easier said than done. When it comes to a specific vision, the challenge is in creating and utilizing something nongeneric and realizable but still ambitious and noteworthy while not being controversial or overly complex. The vision should be specific but not so overly specific that faculty, staff, or community members have little or nothing valuable to contribute to the vision. If this occurs, the vision can seem like a command from a select person or persons above (e.g., the president or senior staff). At most colleges and universities, this is not likely to galvanize the campus in any significant or long-lasting manner. Visions that are constructive or offer the campus community an opportunity to contribute or apply it is much more effective, long-lasting, and inclusive. In the end, people who ask a vision question or who seek a vision statement are mainly looking for the following: (1) an inspiring and optimistic portrayal of the future; (2) a sense of priorities, which will generally be evaluated on the basis of the listener's priorities; (3) something that provides distinction to the department, school, or institution; and (4) something that will benefit listeners personally or professionally.

While strong vision statements cannot or should not, of course, ever guarantee or promise success, weak or absent vision statements can doom a college or university administrator from achieving anything of significance.[1] As an example, while these are worthwhile goals, no one will be especially inspired or impressed by a vision that merely revolves around an increase in student success (e.g., increases in retention and graduation rates as well as in student satisfaction indexes), as these are goals of virtually all colleges and universities. On the other hand, although it may be inspiring to some in the campus community, it is not effective or realistic to create outlandish vision statements— for instance, that a lesser-known, financially struggling, religiously affiliated, liberal arts institution in a remote corner of North Dakota will become a preeminent and highly ranked liberal arts college, producing top-notch global scholars—unless one is confident of being able to, at the very least, receive an extremely significant influx of capital.

At the same time, there is a case to be made that one should go bold (although not *too* bold) when crafting visions or vision statements, even though doing so will inevitably carry some inherent risk. As an example, consider Elon University in North Carolina. For decades, Elon was a sleepy, somewhat religiously affiliated and financially challenged private institution in a small North Carolina town. However, as detailed by George Keller in *Transforming a College* (2004) and continuing with the bold leadership of President Leo Lambert, Elon University rapidly became a top-notch teaching and research-based liberal arts university. The campus administrators convinced its trustees and stakeholders to invest heavily in its infrastructure and in the recruitment of more academically prepared students who might otherwise have chosen another liberal arts college or university. The end result was a complete campus makeover, from student services to academics. What followed was a significant increase in applications, additional gifts to the university, the recruitment of top-notch faculty, and a quick ascent in the academic rankings (e.g., *US News and World Report*).

Soka University in Aliso Viejo, California, followed a similar model of bold and substantive infrastructure investments that ultimately paid off in terms of national (and international) recognition. Soka, which opened in 2001, is, as of 2018, according to *US News and World Report*, ranked first for faculty resources among liberal arts colleges as well as top in the area of foreign student factor.[2] Additionally, according to *US News and World Report*, Soka is ranked second among national liberal arts colleges in ethnic diversity, seventh as a best value school in this same category, and is tied for thirty-ninth overall in the category of national liberal arts colleges.[3] How did Soka rise so quickly in the rankings? For the most part, the answer is simple: money, investments, and clever marketing. Soka appears to be willing and able to spend money in order to increase its reputation, evident not only by how it waives tuition and fees for students whose family income falls below a certain threshold (as of 2018, that threshold was $60,000 per year) but also in how it self-promotes. What makes Soka more unusual, however, is that it has a sizeable endowment, greater than many private colleges and universities.

Perhaps even more important, Soka has been willing to invest and spend at least some portion of its endowment and has done so in a clever, self-promoting manner. For instance, in recent, printed recruitment materials, the university asks the question: "What does a small Liberal Arts College do when it wants to support students interested in the health fields?" Soka answers this question itself on the flip side of the brochure with the following: "Think $60 million, 12 top faculty recruits and a new Life Science Concentration . . . opening Fall 2020." Time will tell whether this marketing technique and campaign works, but if Elon's example holds true for other institutions, Soka's academic and cocurricular rankings may continue to rapidly rise. Bold visions can be important and even crucial to achieving success, but without a funding commitment and a willingness to invest (in addition to a willingness to take some probable initial losses and possibly fail), a bold vision will almost undoubtedly be unrealizable.

What, then, separates strong from weaker visions or vision statements? In addition to being financially realizable, which is, of course, considerably easier at financially robust or healthy institutions, effective vision statements are generally holistic and apply to the whole unit, school, or campus while also being distinct. In the *Chronicle of Higher Education*, Daniel Seymour suggests that a strong vision statement "should create structural tension between an actual state (where we are) and a desired state (where we want to be)."[4] This is well put, but the challenge is trying to get a sense of where most faculty, staff, and students want to be, as many will have different ideas and perspectives. Moreover, there is no way to achieve anything that will not have its fair share of dissenters, and another part of the challenge of crafting a strong vision statement is trying to navigate competing preferences and assuaging the desires (if they can be, without compromising something integral) of those people or units who want to be prioritized. Vision statements that are specific to one's own desires as an administrator will probably not work in the long or even short term because in order to make a vision not only a reality but also meaningful, effective, and long-lasting, one has to have the support of a large swath of the campus community. Also, in order to make a vision effective, an administrator must be able to inspire a significant portion of the campus community to share her or his ideas and enthusiasm. This can mean being (somewhat) flexible to change and involving others in the vision-making process.

One danger in formulating a vision statement is making it too rigid and complete without involving enough constituents.

While it is likely that an administrator will be asked to provide her or his vision for a department, school, or institution during the interview process, visions can and should be modified after one begins a position. In fact, an administrator can create a wide-ranging committee to develop or create a vision or to help shape a vision for a unit or an institution (perhaps at the same time as a strategic plan or plans) so that she or he may gather or gain wider support and collective ownership. After all, others will be more invested if they feel this is their vision, too. In the end, if an administrator involves more (capable) constituents, her or his vision will probably, if not certainly, be improved. This being stated, there can be danger in having too many people involved in the process. As there is no way to involve all constituents in the process, the best general model is a representative democracy, whereby a single person (or maybe two or three at most) represents a unit or department or school on a committee. This may mean, though, being open to presenting a somewhat half-baked or incomplete vision—or being open to change. Doing so may be challenging because it can make one seem less adept or decisive, but the alternative (appearing or being impulsive, not deliberative, or not inclusive) can be even worse in terms of gaining sufficient support.

As an example, imagine that an administrator wants a college, school, unit, or the entire institution to have a specific global studies and sustainability focus. In this circumstance, it may make sense to hold back on some more specific elements of one's vision (e.g., specific international partnerships, curricular changes, reorganization of departments, reallocation of resources). Ideally, an administrator would want her or his desired focus (global studies and sustainability) to emerge from below (e.g., from colleges, the school, and units via faculty, staff, or administrators). However, if one just lets the college(s), school(s), or unit(s) come up with their own focus, the specific focus one wants may not emerge. An administrator can present them with specific possibilities revolving around the areas of global studies and sustainability (e.g., international education, human rights, campus community environmental partnerships). Alternatively, she or he can present the direct or indirect benefits of adopting a global studies and sustainability focus with the hope or confidence that others will be convinced to support this focus or approach. This strategy is usually better if one feels confident that one's ideas and the general or specific direction will be well received. It is possible, though, that an administrator may not end up knowing whether her or his ideas are being well received, even if it may seem (initially) that they were when first presented or discussed with others. Perhaps one was convincing or perhaps others appear to be convinced only because of the power of one's administrative position. Of course, the former is better than the latter, although sometimes, especially if an administrator strongly believes in a specific vision or direction, she or he may have to settle for the latter. If, as is often the case, one is unsure, a more prudent practice is reaching out to specific faculty or staff who have a strong interest in the field(s) and asking them to take the lead on developing ideas[5] or initiatives (presumably through a subcommittee of those who are also interested or invested in the field[s]). Involving the community, board members, alumni, and students in the planning process can also be very fruitful. If they feel invested in the forming of the vision, they may be more likely to contribute (financially or otherwise) to the department, school, or institution.

Strategic Planning

After completing or presenting a vision or vision statement, the next step is often to formulate a longer-term strategic plan. Developing a vision or vision statement can be done simultaneously with the development of a strategic plan. It may also be done prior to beginning a strategic plan. The danger in doing the latter is that it may seem that the end result has already been identified before the process even began. The danger in doing the former is that there may seem to be no guiding principles shaping the strategic planning process. While much can depend on the institution and the administration, faculty, and staff there, it usually begins with a general vision before proceeding with the strategic planning process, and one should be open to refining the vision during and at the conclusion of the strategic planning process. This would also allow the campus community to have an opportunity to shape and take some ownership of the (hopefully) collective vision. This vision should guide the actual strategic plan itself, which is generally a compilation of the major goals and objectives of a unit or institution, along with the specific ways to accomplish those goals and objectives within a certain period of time. It is not difficult to write a strategic plan, and it is not difficult to generate one with attractive and noteworthy goals, although there can be variance in the extent of the plans, the extent of detail, and the extent to which the campus community is involved in the process. The challenge is in the utility of the strategic plan. Not only can it be challenging to accomplish the goals of the plan, but it can also be challenging to get the campus to use a strategic plan consistently and regularly. Too often, administrators beginning their new position dash out a strategic plan only to shelf it for the next several years, until the time period for the strategic plan elapses and a new one needs to be created (or until a new administrator takes over). Understandably, this can create a great deal of skepticism about the strategic planning process, not to mention a reluctance on the part of many campus constituents to invest much time (if any) in the process.

Ideally, a strategic plan ought to consistently guide an institution's future and priorities; it should also (ideally) result from research, discussion, and deliberation concerning the current status of an institution, its desired future, and how the institution can get to that desired future. That, though, is easier said than done, especially at larger institutions with a wide variety of colleges, schools, institutes, departments, and units. Depending on one's administrative position and the relative size of the institution (as well as whether strategic planning occurs at the institutional, college, school, department, or unit levels), a strategic plan may be more or less specific or expansive. Regardless, it will be impossible to include all constituents in the strategic planning process. Ideally, one would want a committee structured rather like a representative democracy, whereby a representative from each major unit covered by a strategic plan is at the literal and metaphorical table, and is included (directly or indirectly) on a steering committee.

Still, even if an administrator arranges such a committee, she or he will need to decide if she or he will start more from the proverbial top or bottom. As one option, which tends to be more applicable to larger institutions, subcommittees can develop their own strategic plans first, which can then be presented to the larger campus-wide committee. For instance, an academic affairs division that has six colleges and four units could ask each college and unit to develop their own strategic plan (which could, even further, be subdivided into the departments) first. This plan could then be presented to the campus-wide committee and integrated into the division's own strategic plan, which encompasses all six colleges and four units. The challenge with this approach, though, is that it can lead to a phenomenal amount of paperwork (e.g., in this case, ten separate strategic plans) that needs to be folded into one. This does not mean that the approach cannot be used, and the benefit of using it is that it will be more collaborative and inclusive. If it is used, one way to manage the paperwork and to increase the efficiency of the synthesis is to limit each unit to about a page of specific measurable goals or objectives (e.g., one could limit them to around five to seven) along with very brief descriptions of how to reach these goals or objectives with target completion dates.

Whatever option an administrator chooses, one technique that is likely to help is reaching out to specific faculty or staff with a background or strong interest in the area(s) that she or he wishes to promote or that end up being the main focus of the strategic plan (e.g., environmental studies and international education for a global studies and sustainability focus). If one is able to get faculty and staff on board with one's vision, or, better yet, if they take ownership of a vision that aligns with one's own, it can effectively remove administrative direction and presence (which is ideal, even though it may still remain as a largely invisible guiding force) from the picture. In so doing, an administrator will have effectively seeded the groundwork for her or his vision to become a reality in the strategic planning process. Since others will have taken ownership of this vision, though, one faces the risk that one's original vision or visions may morph into something other than intended. If this possibility, if not probability, is acceptable, then there is little to worry about. However, if an administrator is dead set on a specific focus or vision, she or he will need to be involved in the process on multiple occasions, unless she or he has a very committed and devoted cadre of faculty and staff. If an administrator does end up needing to do most of the proverbial heavy lifting, she or he should still aspire to a significant level of campus involvement and inclusivity, and she or he would be wise to not be overly assertive, as that may be taken as imperial and imposing, which can be detrimental to the strategic planning process, let alone the successful implication of the strategic plan itself.

After the structure of the strategic planning process has been determined, the next step is to consider how to start. As mentioned earlier, some colleges and universities begin the strategic planning process from the proverbial ground up. In these circumstances, a campus-wide strategic planning committee may be more or less composed of unit heads (and, in some cases, community partners, alumni, or students) who create, distribute, and discuss their own strategic plans. A leader, or leaders, of the campus-wide committee subsequently integrates them into a larger campus plan. Even if this is done, one place to begin, especially if the process is not guided by the formulation of a vision statement, is with an examination of the institution's mission. While there can be overlap between an institution's mission and a vision, there are two helpful, general distinctions to make. A mission focuses on the entire university, whereas a vision may be specific to a division (e.g., academic affairs, student affairs). A mission also tends to focus on the present, whereas a vision is focused on the future. Although a mission can be formulated and accepted without a specific vision, a vision should take into account an institution's mission. If this is not done, it can risk either the creation of an unrealizable vision or a vision that conflicts with a mission. Any such conflicts ideally would be vetted before a vision is promoted; otherwise, it is almost inevitable that a chasm will quickly develop between those who support the mission and those who support the vision. As a mission is already an accepted part of a college or university and has been presumably vetted by the campus community, including the board, it is likely that a vision not aligned with a mission will be unsuccessful (or will, at best, be partially successful). While it is certainly possible to use the strategic planning process to revise the mission, it is important to consider it as a guiding post for the planning process. It can always be revised at the conclusion of the strategic planning process.

Mission

College and university missions (which are sometimes accompanied by values or identity statements) tend to be short and vague, but they can be effective starting points for both a new or revised vision statement and the strategic planning process itself. To examine further, consider four mission statements from distinct universities: an elite private institution (Yale University), a public institution (the University of Mississippi), a lesser-known, religiously affiliated institution (California Lutheran University), and a community college (El Camino College). First, Yale University's mission is "Yale is committed to improving the world today and for future generations through outstanding research and scholarship, education, preservation, and practice. Yale educates aspiring leaders worldwide who serve all sectors of society. We carry out this mission through the free exchange of ideas in an ethical, interdependent, and diverse community of faculty, staff, students, and alumni."[6] But how does one get from Yale's mission statement to a strategic plan? One way may be parsing the mission into specific areas: research/scholarship, diversity, preservation, practice, leadership, world improvement, ethics, and academic freedom. Then, the primary strategic plan or subcommittees could expand on these areas with specific goals, activities aimed to achieve the goals, and ways to measure success. Another approach is to work on revising the mission before even beginning a strategic plan. This can be the best way to go if, for instance, Yale seeks to have a significant change in direction or focus, such as an emphasis placed on public service and social justice.

Alternatively, one could also divide or interpret the language in the mission. For instance, the first sentence of Yale's mission states, "Yale is committed to improving the world today and for future generations through outstanding research and scholarship, education, preservation, and practice." From this sentence, it seems clear that a goal of the university is to improve the world, as nebulous as that may be. Part of the strategic planning process, then, could be arranged around the actual or potential global impact of university practices, which could be pared down to the unit level, followed by specific goals and ways to measure global impact. The third sentence of Yale's mission, "We carry out this mission through the free exchange of ideas in an ethical, interdependent, and diverse community of faculty, staff, students, and alumni," could lead to two additional focuses: community and communication. To expand upon the former for a strategic plan, one could examine the ways in which the university's units could engage more with ethics, interdisciplinarity, and diversity. The latter (communication) may be much more challenging to include in a strategic plan and could end up being subsumed by a focus on community (which, if it is functioning well, involves "the free exchange of ideas").

Yale's mission and possible strategic planning process undoubtedly generated from and relates to its position as a preeminent private university. In contrast, the public research- and teaching-focused University of Mississippi's mission is the following: "As Mississippi's first comprehensive, public university and academic medical center, the University of Mississippi transforms lives, communities, and the world by providing opportunities for the people of Mississippi and beyond through excellence in learning, discovery, healthcare, and engagement."[7] While there are definite similarities between this mission and Yale's mission, in that both focus on either "transforming" or "improving" lives, the University of Mississippi's mission is understandably more focused on the public and the state. In addition, its mission clearly identifies a focus on "healthcare" and an "academic medical center." This language, in itself, would or should motivate anyone working on a strategic plan to devote a significant amount of time to these areas or units, which are presumably in the state's and public's interest. In addition, given its public mission and statewide focus, a strategic plan for the University of Mississippi could have a community-based focus; that is, it could be prioritized by ways the university could improve specific areas in the state. It also states nothing about technology, social justice, diversity, career preparation for the twenty-first century, or becoming a premier research institution.

In that, sometimes it is just as important, if not more important, when looking at mission statements to consider what an institution leaves out. In this case, the University of Mississippi's ambitions seem pretty modest in comparison to other, more cutting-edge public research institutions, such as Arizona State University, which not only emphasizes "advancing research and discovery of public value" but positions itself as "assuming fundamental responsibility for the economic, social, cultural and overall health of the communities it serves."[8] The University of

Mississippi, on the other hand, does not appear to take responsibility for anything in the state or community. It could be argued that by doing so, the University of Mississippi is being more realistic. After all, it is just a university; unlike the state legislature, it does not drive policy or enact it. ASU may be ambitious in the language of its mission, but does it really take responsibility for failures in community or state healthcare or increases in unemployment, and what does it mean to take this responsibility? If the unemployment rate in the Phoenix/Tempe area goes up (or in Arizona at large), for instance, is ASU partially to blame, and if so, what should the consequences or repercussions be?

Unlike ASU, California Lutheran University, a more teaching-oriented, holistic, and religiously affiliated institution, has a university mission more focused on building the individual character of its students. CLU's mission is "to educate leaders for a global society who are strong in character and judgment, confident in their identity and vocation, and committed to service and justice."[9] There is nothing in its mission about a specific social function, community, or group. Undoubtedly, CLU's focus on "service and justice" and "character and judgment" relates to its identity as a Lutheran-affiliated institution, but these terms are nonreligiously specific, and the university's focus on "global society" allows it to appeal to a wider, more secular audience. Since enrollment and recruitment are significant issues at lesser-known, teaching-oriented, religiously or culturally affiliated institutions, it is not surprising that CLU's mission is vague and inclusive. Any strategic plan, though, that CLU would develop should stress globalization, leadership, personal growth, and ethics, or the mission itself should be altered. The challenge for CLU and other religiously affiliated institutions (especially those that are more strictly affiliated) will be the extent to which the board or its religiously affiliated constituents may set the parameters of its mission.

As one might imagine, community college missions tend to be as expansive and inclusive as possible, since they are generally open enrollment and indiscriminately (at least in theory) serve the surrounding service area. As one example, El Camino College's (which is located in the Los Angeles metropolitan area) mission is the following: "El Camino College makes a positive difference in people's lives. We provide excellent comprehensive educational programs and services that promote student learning and success in collaboration with our diverse communities."[10] A person beginning the strategic planning process at El Camino College might consider focusing on the following areas: student learning and success, diversity, comprehensive educational programs, and cocurricular services. It is striking that there is no mention of any specific academic program, no emphasis on globalization, and, perhaps in part because of its location and its status as a community college, it is the only one of the four institutions to focus on diversity in its mission (although El Camino College uses the word "diversity" in reference to demographics of its surrounding service communities as opposed to a commitment to be more inclusive as an institution). Indeed, it is interesting that El Camino College chose to qualify its communities with the descriptive word "diverse," as opposed to making some aspect of diversity and inclusion a more active goal. If El Camino College were engaged in revising their mission, they might consider whether they want to modify the language and content to reflect how the institution would directly benefit its diverse communities (instead of just collaborating with them).

The mission of a college or university can be the beginning and end point of a strategic planning process. That is, one can use an existing mission to chart out a vision and then a strategic plan or one could begin by potentially revising the mission itself. The latter may be the best approach to take if there is already a specific vision widely accepted by the campus community but not yet (fully) reflected in the mission. A result of the strategic planning process can also be a revision of the mission. Regardless of which approach is taken (if any) as part of the process, one should present a strategic plan to a committee (or committees) and the larger campus community. While it is true that engaging the larger campus community can carry risks, especially at larger institutions, at the same time, doing so can promote a community spirit of teamwork and transparency. There are many ways to engage the campus community beyond huge convocation-like events in which direct engagement cannot really occur because of the size of the audience. Engagement with smaller, targeted groups generally works best in fostering healthy, productive dialogue as well as buy-in to ideas, an identity, a strategic plan, or a mission. Not only can the strategic plan be presented to the campus community after it has been vetted and approved, but it can also be presented at the conclusion or beginning of each year, noting what was accomplished or not accomplished in the previous year and making adjustments to the overall plan accordingly. If this is not done at the campus level, it can, at least, be attempted at a smaller level (e.g., with the senior staff, the strategic planning committee). If the campus and senior staff do not bring the strategic plan back for revision and discussion at a key point (or points) in the academic year, it will likely languish until the next senior leader or leaders (e.g., president and senior staff) take the reins and presumably develop a new plan.

Branding

So what happens, then, after a collective vision, identity, or strategic plan for a department, school, or institution has been determined? For most institutions, the next step is branding. Most administrators will be involved (perhaps heavily so) in questions of institutional identity, or, more specifically, branding. This marketing term, to which some faculty and staff (and even other administrators) may recoil due to its business and consumer connotations, refers to concretizing an identity while increasing the visibility of an institution's identity and reputation. Reputation is crucial, for why would one want to brand mediocrity or something generic? Branding is a relatively new development for colleges and universities, and is largely a product of the late twentieth and twenty-first centuries.[11] Branding efforts have become an important facet of colleges and universities due to competition with one another, increased tuition costs, and the public's desire for accountability. If branding has more or less become ubiquitous at colleges and universities (or at least ones that are struggling with enrollment or who want to distinguish themselves), one challenge is the time it takes for a "brand" to solidify. A complicating factor is that by the time the brand solidifies, torpor may set in, or a new administration may take over and may be interested in taking the institution in a different direction. The main challenge is for a college or university to come up with a brand that expresses the core value(s) and significance of the institution. Another challenge is coming up with a brand that is or will be at least relatively long-lasting, while leaving enough space for important, productive, and enthusiastic future developments.

A good example of a brand like this is the University of Central Florida's "This is big," along with its accompanying subbrand "And the best is yet to come." Usually, extremely large institutions like the University of Central Florida (its 2017-18 enrollment exceeds 65,000) have to combat the perception that in higher education extremely large institutions treat their students like numbers and are overall like mass-producing factories. UCF's brand flips this negative assumption into an attribute, emphasizing all of the positive aspects of being at such a large institution, from research production, grants, and community impact to the wide variety of academic and cocurricular opportunities available to students. Further, UCF's brand is largely nontemporal, as it will presumably continue to be one of the nation's largest universities for the foreseeable future. At the same time, it is vague enough, leading one to wonder: What is big and what will be coming in the future? Virtually everything can be big in virtually infinite ways, pending one's definition, and if the best is yet to come, then whatever big that is coming will be even better than now. Due to this vagueness, for the most part their brand does not risk alienating alumni, donors, and board members, who may see other bold brands as a radical departure from the institution to which they were previously committed.

Generally, branding is more important for institutions that are not particularly well known or that have unstable enrollment patterns or finances. Branding can also be important for established institutions, in that an effective new brand can help catapult the institution to greater national attention, to greater gifts, improvements to its infrastructure, and subsequent ability to attract and retain better faculty, students, and staff. This, in turn, can lead to a positive reinforcement loop, whereby the better faculty, staff, and students lead to even more national attention, which leads to even more gifts, and so on. Still, it is hard to imagine that elite universities like Princeton, Stanford, or UC Berkeley need to spend much time on branding (given the brand they already have), as opposed to more teaching-oriented private and tuition-driven public institutions such as Kentucky State University, Nevada State College, Presentation College (South Dakota), Earlham College (Idaho), or University of the West (California). The last three institutions mentioned are private. While it is true that state-supported schools can have their own challenges in terms of how much they are funded by the state as well as state and system bureaucracy, in contrast to Jeffrey R. Docking, president of Adrian College and author of *Crisis in Higher Education*, who claims private institutions do not need to have branding or be branded anymore because a private school brand is "solid," I would argue that private colleges and universities (many of which struggle with enrollment management) can have an even greater need for branding because they are not at least partially subsidized by the state.[12]

College branding often involves an attempt to create something memorable, important, or worthwhile. The brand of one of my previous institutions was "The leader in global education" at a time in which the terms "global education" and "globalization" were academic buzzwords. While the institution did offer study-abroad programs and had a global presence (including an international campus), it did not have a global studies major or minor and only a struggling international studies major within a history and political science school. Yet, the brand fit with the institution's emphasis on diversity and its close proximity to New York City, a quintessential global city. Some staff defended the brand by claiming that the institution was one of the first universities to have a notable online presence, yet this was a specious argument. At the same time, many students came to the institution because they felt kinship with the institution's brand, even if there wasn't much substance to the brand itself. However, perhaps because no overt promises accompanied the brand or perhaps because of the relative torpor of the institution, the brand continued until the institution's next reaccreditation review, when it became apparent to faculty and staff that they could no longer justify the brand.

Even colleges and universities that do not want to engage in branding may find that they are branded (to various degrees by incidents that occur at their campus, or by students, faculty, staff, or administrators who get significant attention, especially online). This, of course, can have significant implications for a college or university, from precipitous dips or significant jumps in enrollment and fund-raising, among other possible end results. Peter Schmidt, writing for the *Chronicle of Higher Education*, argues that "colleges' marketing and public-relations departments recognize that prospective students and their parents go online to get much of their information, and seldom look past the first page or two of search results."[13] Consequently, colleges and universities sometimes enlist external help to downplay negative press and to "push links to positive publicity to the top of search results." For institutions that experience widely publicized racist or sexist acts, this can be detrimental. If an institution does not have a strong brand, explicitly or implicitly (e.g., a very strong academic reputation), then it is especially challenging to weather difficult social media storms, thus increasing the need for a strong brand.

There is, though, debate about the relative importance of branding as well as the need and value that it may bring. If something is branded, then, by definition, it is something that will last, if not become permanent. Further, the longer the brand exists, the more entrenched it can become and the more difficult it will be to rename it. Some faculty and staff see branding efforts as symptomatic of a larger problem: the increasing corporatization of the modern university and the decline of its educational focus, most notably apparent in the nationwide decrease in tenure density at colleges and universities and the growth of professional and for-profit institutions. In *Academe*, Rudy H. Fichtenbaum argues that we must push back against branding[14] or any movement toward the corporatization of the university, as anything otherwise treats colleges and universities as "a commodity" when they should be viewed as "a public good, meant to serve the interests of society as a whole and not simply to train compliant workers for corporations that serve the 1 percent."[15] However, higher education has always been, to some degree, a commodity, and it is hard to identify how colleges and universities were more specifically a force for the "public good" in the past (unless one considers the training of White male clergy to be a force for the public good, as that was the purpose of the majority of colleges and universities in the past), and how they have lost that focus, if they indeed have.

Others see branding as an effort to decrease the individual and collective power of the faculty. In the *Chronicle of Higher Education*, John Quiggin argues that "branding" represents the "desire to subordinate the efforts of individual scholars in research, extension, and community engagement to the enhancement of the corporate image." Quiggin concludes that brands are "nonsense," which bear "no correspondence to reality."[16] In a sense, he is correct. It is accurate to state that branding relies on promoting images and phrases without deep analysis, and aesthetics without the promotion of critical thinking. It is also accurate to state that brands seek to convince readers or viewers for insubstantial reasons. However, it is important to understand the purpose of brands, which are not to hoodwink faculty (and staff) into corporate subservience, as Quiggin might argue, but rather to bring focus, attention, and resources to the college or university, which, at least in theory, can benefit all who work or attend there (or those who live in the surrounding community, state, or even nation). Branding, which may be done simultaneously with a strategic plan or when a new leader or leaders take charge, can be instrumental in changing both the internal and external perceptions and focus of an institution. It could be argued that almost everything else, from funding to staffing decisions, stems from a brand. Good brands, such as the UCF brand discussed earlier, can also flip what might commonly be seen as a negative into a positive. Smaller, struggling institutions, for instance, can benefit from branding their small size as an attribute and, pending their finances, by going even smaller by increasing their quality (making their admissions process more competitive). More rural or "remote" colleges and universities could try to use their location in their branding by emphasizing institutional community, sustainability, and the surrounding beauty of nature.

Thus far, the discussion of branding has mainly been focused on the institution, when in reality branding can take place at the college or unit level, especially at larger research universities where certain colleges and departments may gain a reputation for strengths in certain areas. Some argue[17] that, especially in the social media–dominated twenty-first century, branding now occurs significantly at the individual level and is, more or less, unavoidable. In other words, all faculty, staff, are administrators are brands, whether they like it or not, or whether they actively construct one for themselves or not. This brings up the question of whether a brand is distinct from an identity or reputation. We all have identities, but there can be a significant difference between a reputation and a brand. While one can have some control of a brand, there is usually little control over a reputation. In fact, brands can counteract reputations that exist or could exist. To illustrate this further, the following is a practical, real-life example.

Identity, Aesthetics, and Reputation

When I was a newly hired assistant professor, I had a fellow junior colleague who frequently wore a T-shirt and shorts (or jeans during the winter months) to the math classes he taught. His style of dress gave him the appearance of being a laid-back, easygoing professor, although he was actually very rigorous and demanding. He tended to receive uneven student evaluations and had a disproportionate number of in-class disciplinary issues, perhaps because his unintentional brand (derived from his style of dress) clashed with the reality that he was a rigorous and challenging instructor. While I never had any evidence one way or the other, I always suspected that this had something to do with his style of dress as well as his youthful appearance, which clashed with his teaching style and subsequent reputation.

As I looked similarly young, was correspondingly rigorous in the classroom, and wanted to avoid in-class behavioral issues, when I was a faculty member, my standard uniform was pretty strictly business casual: slacks and dress shirt (later morphing into business formal when I became a faculty-administrator). Indeed, when I first started teaching at the tender age of twenty-two, I had a senior colleague who recommended that I wear a suit to class every day to counteract my (at that time) youthful appearance. Yet, this was (and continues to be) most definitely not the faculty mold. I generally followed the faculty mold with my business casual dress, while I quickly realized that I could identify the (senior) administrators or wannabe (senior) administrators (like the person who recommended that I wear a suit) by the manner in which they dressed (a suit or a shirt and tie for men and executive formal wear for women). (Senior) administrators generally dress as business professionals, whereas faculty and other staff tend to be more casually dressed. This is the norm at most colleges and universities to the point that one can safely state that the aesthetic brand of college and university administrators is business professional. On the surface, this may not matter, but metaphorically it represents the frequent divide between the more powerful administrators/managers and the "managed" faculty and staff.

While dress and appearance may seem relatively minor and the preceding observation unsurprising to most anyone who has worked in higher education, it does illustrate how image is of greater importance in college and university administration than it is for faculty. "Image," though, is an expansive term and does not relate to just physical appearance. It can also relate to a person's accomplishments and degrees (e.g., a PhD from an Ivy League institution, the quantity and quality of publications, a certificate from a prestigious university, the procurement of a sizeable grant or gift). It also has communicative dimensions (both oral and written) and extends to the relative size of the department, school, or university that one oversees or where one is employed (generally bigger is more impressive). In the end, an administrator's collective image or brand can be integral to her or his ultimate success, even if some (or most) of it is largely superficial. Does one want to be known as the ethical leader? The academic leader? The creative, innovative leader? The skilled fund-raising leader? If an administrator does not know, or if she or he does not devote time to ponder these questions, for better or worse, she or he will become whatever her or his audience believes based on appearance, actions, and behavior. To be sure, all human beings are three-dimensional and complex, but administrators (in large part because of the power they hold or that their position holds) may be viewed at times as one- or two-dimensional, based on appearance, behavior, or actions. If one does not manage these things, they may ultimately manage one's future as an administrator.

Whereas for faculty members, substance and content tend to reign supreme, for administrators, there are multiple, competing areas of importance, which are often aesthetic in nature. Being a clear and convincing communicator is definitely important to being a successful administrator, as is having a commanding or inspiring presence. This being stated, there is a danger in appearing too autocratic. However, there is no clear litmus test or objective measure to determine how much assertiveness is too much. In fact, it can depend on the institution and the culture there, even the specific situation, the individual(s) involved, and the administrator her- or himself. Just as some people have a more naturally imposing or assertive public presence, others have a more naturally laid-back and minimal public presence. The former often have to work on toning down their presence, while the latter often have to work on amplifying their presence. In addition, personal engagement, storytelling, humor, and empathy can also help make for a successful administrative leader. This means "not indulging in self-revelation, but unveiling just enough of your inner core that your listeners feel connected to you and start pulling for you" (55),[18] according to Sylvia Hewlett, author of *Executive Presence*, a monograph that utilizes survey-based research of successful executive and administrative leaders.[19] An administrator would be wise to project that she or he is a (relatively, albeit not overly so) knowledgeable, secure, and successful human being with an interesting history and personal life (whether one feels this is actually true or not). For faculty who move into administrative roles, this should seem familiar, as it is also applicable to classroom teaching. However, for administrators, one's personality and professional style, perhaps even more than the content of what one does, can be a significant measure, if not the ultimate determinant of success.

One way that many administrators connect with faculty and staff is by complimenting them directly and engaging with them. Senior administrators often acknowledge and thank people for attending events, and at those events, they may methodically spend a good amount of time directly interacting with participants (possibly more time with those perceived to be the honorees or the perceived VIPs) while striking (or attempting to strike) a delicate balance of bringing attention to themselves and inquiring about the professional interests and personal lives of the attendees (e.g., their family and, in particular, their children) so they feel appreciated and included.[20] Even though an administrator's private or personal life should not be relevant to her or his success, it can, in fact, matter, although it can matter in ways that are hard to discern. While perhaps not consciously, faculty and staff may be less apt to get behind an administrator who appears to be personally guarded or who is single or a divorcee, even if she or he does not have children. There is almost definitely a gender difference here, in that women who fit this mold may be more likely to be described as cold, standoffish, or uninspiring, as women tend to be unfairly evaluated on perceived emotional qualities more than men.[21] That being stated, regardless of gender, having a family can humanize a college or university administrator, can make her or him seem more secure, and can provide a common point of interest and discussion with others, just as it can for other political or cultural leaders.

It is no accident that when announcements of new college and university administrators are made, it is typical for family members to be mentioned (e.g., Dean Smith eagerly anticipates moving to Springfield with her husband, eleven-year-old daughter, and six-year-old son).[22] Subconsciously or consciously, faculty, staff, and other administrators may read this and feel more secure in their new leader (who has now been humanized) and even empathize with her if she has children, as opposed to if the blurb just read that Dean Smith eagerly anticipates moving to

Springfield with no mention of a family whatsoever. Is there something wrong with her, faculty and staff may wonder? Did she fail in her personal life? How do we know that she will succeed in this role if she hasn't succeeded in her own personal life? To be sure, none of these questions is fair, and while, presumably, no one will ever articulate them verbally, they will be considerations (consciously or subconsciously) or they may affect the way Dean Smith is perceived (at least initially). In the end, though, there is very little one can do about these perceptions. One's personal life is what it is, and while those who have what appears to be a robust and stable personal/family life may have an advantage in terms of getting administrative positions or having a more significant "honeymoon period," this will only last so long and in the long run, ability and accomplishments generally prove more important and long-lasting.

This is not to suggest that faculty members do not cultivate their own brands or images, and some of the aforementioned items (e.g., professional pedigree and publications) apply to faculty as much as they do to administrators, if not more. However, unlike administrators, faculty tend to be evaluated (at least by their peers and supervisors) based on their teaching, scholarship, and service, the vast majority of which are content specific.[23] While I cannot state with any degree of certainty that no one has received tenure based solely on the institution where she or he received her or his degree alone (e.g., Harvard, Yale, Princeton, Stanford), if this has occurred, it is or should be a relatively isolated incident. Still, in this era of online evaluation websites such as ratemyprofessors.com and similar platforms, faculty and administrators may have become increasingly aware of the relative importance of image and presentation (or at least students have made them aware of this). While nonmanagerial staff may not be as concerned with branding or aesthetics, they, too, live in an era in which social media has become ubiquitous and important, as has visual literacy. It has become part and parcel of many if not most young Americans' growth cycle to learn how to visually present and promote themselves in order to stand out in some form or forms of social media.

Still, image and appearance can be even more important for those who move into senior-level administrative positions.[24] While faculty may have a virtual image established by their research, scholarship, and teaching, college and university administrators generally have more visual and behavior-based images or brands based on their social and personal styles as much as their professional style, which they may cultivate to gain respect, admiration, or even obedience. In this, knowing oneself is crucial. As with teaching, what works for one person may not work for another. This does not mean that an administrator should just conclude that she or he is what she or he is. It is important to push oneself to change (holistically or publicly) if one's image, brand, or style doesn't seem to be working. That might mean, for instance, trying to be more extroverted (e.g., embracing public speaking opportunities and taking more opportunities to engage with people) or if one tends to be more talkative and assertive, controlling the amount to which one socializes or dominates discussion.

Chapter 5

Management, Leadership, and Ethics

People buy into the leader before they buy into the vision.
—John C. Maxwell

A leader is best when people barely know he exists, when his work is done, his aim fulfilled, they will say: we did it ourselves.
—Lao Tzu

A leader is a dealer in hope.
—Napoleon Bonaparte

A leader takes people where they want to go. A great leader takes people where they don't necessarily want to go, but ought to be.
—Rosalynn Carter

Defining Leadership in Higher Education

During a regional accreditation debriefing session at one of my previous institutions, the site visiting team publicly stated, as part of the institution's commendations, that I was a "great leader." As a highly self-critical person who also questions authority by nature, I regarded the site team's praise with a certain amount of skepticism. While it was true that I took the lead in the accreditation process at an institution that, at the time I was hired, was significantly out of compliance and in a general state of decline, I generally thought of myself less of a leader and more of a diligent and organized worker who created systems and structures, who attempted to hire and retain the best possible employees, and who then led efforts to create and implement a number of policies and procedures that the institution needed but did not have in place. However, I hardly thought that what I was doing was inspiring, let alone displaying great leadership skills. Yet, what I discovered was that, at least in college and university administration, leadership is not necessarily about what one accomplishes individually; in fact, to many faculty and staff, individual accomplishments may denote a self-interested academic leader. Rather, successful administrative leaders tend to be those who help lead successful, inclusive community and collaborative efforts and initiatives. They also can make others feel good or better about themselves, their unit, or their institution while promoting respect, trust, and confidence, which can lead to inspiration.

While there is certainly no objectively accepted definition of a leader or the qualities of effective leadership, in many professional or political roles, a leader is an *individual* who inspires *others* (emphasizing others and deemphasizing her- or himself), who has ideas and thoughts that she or he expresses (articulately) that influence and guide others. A leader may provide direction, guidance, and vision. When considering political, philosophical, and military leaders, such as Martin Luther King Jr., Mahatma Gandhi, Alexander the Great, George S. Patton, one does not generally think of, let alone know anything about, those who helped support them, and often those who collaborated, supported, and followed them are viewed as part of an indistinguishable mass, if they are considered at all. Unlike these kinds of individual leaders, being a "great leader" in college and university administration can be somewhat of an oxymoron, in that while it may be important to be identified as an individual, it can, in many ways, be counterproductive to stand out as one. Those who actively try to do this may be viewed as arrogant and self-serving by faculty and staff, who may want to be viewed as stakeholders, if not exemplary individuals (as they, too, may have strong egos). In that, successful administrators are more like skilled facilitators, if not master manipulators, than conventional leaders. The "leading" an administrator does is often conducted behind the scenes, in individual meetings with other constituents, in a manner similar to that of a House majority (or minority) whip. Further, leadership for administrators can be a matter of aesthetics and presentation in addition to, if not more than, the actual substance.

This does not mean that college and university administrators have to contend with a unique environment, nor does it mean that the organizational structures (which can vary from institution to institution) there do not exist elsewhere. While there is some truth to the assertion that colleges and universities are distinct and perhaps unusual (although not unique) organizational entities, there is a wide range of hierarchical structures and power centers at colleges and universities depending on the size (small, medium, or large), the nature (public, private, religiously affiliated, elite, open enrollment, etc.), and the culture (inclusive, hostile, top-heavy, faculty-focused, etc.) of the institution, which is subject to change. In *The Essential Academic Dean or Provost*, Jeffrey L. Buller asserts that in higher education, "no one is ever #1—not really."[1] Although it is true that there are various amounts and levels of checks and balances at colleges and universities that may restrict a singular individual (e.g., a president or a chair of the board of trustees) from exerting too much individual power, at some colleges and universities, a singular individual (e.g., an especially effective, charismatic, or autocratic president at a small institution) can wield an enormous amount of power, especially if, as was the case at one of my previous institutions, she or he has essentially handpicked most of the board and senior administrators. Buller claims that the most significant and "essential principle" for senior-level academic administrators, especially deans and provosts, is that "all leadership entails leadership from the middle." While it is accurate, Buller suggests, that "everybody reports to somebody,"[2] this does not mean that everyone has an equal amount of power, nor does it mean that all supervisors grant the same level of relative power to their direct reports. Further, some managers barely manage whereas others can be extremely micromanaging, controlling, and even threatening. Others can be selectively micromanaging pending the subject, the individual, or the time period.

Decision-Making

For college and university administrators, as with business executives, especially at institutions in which there is a slow-moving bureaucracy or in which there is a pervasive fear of upsetting others, being decisive or at least being perceived as being decisive is often considered part of being (construed as) effective. Faculty are notorious for laboriously debating ideas, policies, and assertions ad nauseam. In fact, some faculty build their entire scholarly career on refuting or challenging widely held academic ideas, theories, or suppositions. At the same time, faculty and staff may be reluctant to want to make difficult decisions about one another or in general. This can be and often is where an administrator steps in and makes the decision(s) that others seem unwilling or reluctant to make. That being stated, there should be some degree of discussion and debate in the decision-making process. If there is not either and a decision is merely made by someone or a small group of senior administrative leaders (or even a singular administrative leader), it will likely be viewed poorly by faculty and staff. There may be times in which an "executive decision" needs to be made quickly with minimal to no consultation, but this should be the exception rather than the rule.

Any administrator who does not appear to support at least the idea of shared governance is likely to not be strongly respected or valued by many staff and certainly by most faculty. At the same time, any administrator who does not get specific results is also not likely to be strongly respected or valued. The challenge is in striking the right balance between being decisive and still employing (or at least being perceived as still employing) aspects of shared governance. This balance can vary from institution to institution, from position to position, even from unit to unit. Some administrators may call the attempt to foster shared governance while trying to get what they want "guided discovery." Through the process of "guided discovery," faculty, staff, and other administrators can be encouraged to reach the same conclusion that the administrator has or wants them to reach through (as much as possible) an invisible guiding hand (e.g., through a certain agenda in a meeting, certain choices presented, placing and coaching a "confederate" in the audience, or through other means). When "guided discovery" works, it can establish collective buy-in and support of an administrator's idea(s), but when it does not work, it can spectacularly backfire with not only the administrator not getting what she or he wants but with faculty, staff, and other administrators losing significant trust and respect for that same administrator.

While being decisive is important for an administrator, even one who strongly supports shared governance or guided discovery, I am not suggesting that decisiveness is something unique or specific to administrators as opposed to faculty and staff. Faculty and staff who appear indecisive or who appear to lack personal or intellectual confidence may not be considered effective by their students, peers, or supervisors. At the same time, appearing decisive is only one part of being an effective administrator; an equally if not more important aspect is the process and content of the decisions one makes. An administrator can be extremely decisive, but these same decisions can be construed as misguided, unilateral, impulsive, retaliatory, and generally ineffective. Faculty may be viewed in a similar manner by students (as can staff by students as well as other staff or administrators), and disaffected students and staff may grieve against faculty or other staff who they view as making unfair or unreasonable decisions. Being decisive while being nonauthoritarian means acknowledging other positions in a nonaggressive manner with respect, calmness, and poise. Most faculty who have taught for a (significant) period of time learn the importance of not being emotionally affected too much by difficult students or situations (or become at least somewhat hardened to these students or situations). Similarly, most staff who have been employed in different positions, who have worked for multiple (challenging) supervisors, or who have worked with a wide variety of staff, administrators, and students can also develop a considerably thick skin, which is ultimately essential for administrators.

Engaging with Others: Diplomacy

There is a difference, though, between faculty and administrators in their ongoing professional engagement. While faculty hold power over the students they teach, and staff often hold little to no power, administrators engage with a number of colleagues, supervisors, and community members as well as their own direct reports. These direct reports may hold more power (or have access to greater resources) than students, who tend to be fully employed (and may have the strength of the union behind them) by the institution and under an administrator's purview for an indefinite period of time as opposed to just in a faculty member's class for a semester. Whereas a faculty member might, for instance, compose and send a lengthy rebuttal to a student's claim of unfair grading[3] or a peer's review of their scholarship, an administrator needs to be more careful with her or his wording and her or his response, even if the claim made is personally insulting or has no substance. In a way, college and university staff who move into administrative positions have less of a learning curve than faculty, as staff may bring with them years of experience working with other administrators and have gotten to know a wide variety of other staff (whose positions they may eventually oversee). They may also be more accustomed to withholding or muting especially strong opinions or critiques (which is not common and often does not come easily to faculty).

Toward that end, less is often more in administrative writing, and, when possible, unless it is clearly to a person's benefit (as in cases where one wants to put someone on record in writing), it is generally better to not put anything in writing when dealing with potentially fraught situations. Instead, it is often best to meet in person and to either have a colleague present as a witness (if needed) or, if necessary, capture the content of the meeting by writing an email afterward. Aggressively pushing back against or even attempting to demolish a colleague's argument may make one feel better temporarily (and may be more of the traditional faculty approach), but in the long run, it can lead to disdain from colleagues, who can spread negative rumors or accounts, or who may want to retaliate. Further, it will probably do little to change attitudes or perspectives. Instead, whenever possible, an administrator should strive to acknowledge the other person's perspective/argument and present an alternative case in an objective, nonthreatening way. This more diplomatic approach provides colleagues with an opportunity to change their mind without feeling that they are losing face. However, it may involve biting one's tongue and not stating or masking what one may truly think and feel (especially if those thoughts and feelings are negative). In fact, doing so may ultimately be the best way to achieve one's desired results.

While faculty members may find these same diplomatic skills useful for their respective positions, they have a more selective need (if it is even a need) for diplomacy—for instance, when they teach and when they interact with colleagues or administrative supervisors if there is something they may want (e.g., promotion, tenure, research release time, a specific course, approval of a curriculum). Further, faculty, when they teach, generally have a captive audience of students who are generally interested in impressing them, if only in order to get a better grade. Thereby, the odds are perpetually (at least during the time they have the students in class) stacked in their favor. In contrast, administrators (and staff) may be directly or indirectly engaged with other people (in meetings or presentations) each and every day, some who are direct reports or colleagues and others who may be external to the institution. Further, even when administrators are not technically on, they may be directly or indirectly interacting with colleagues, subordinates, supervisors, or community members, who may be evaluating them consciously or subconsciously at any point. In each of these settings and with each person or group of people, a different approach or style may be used or adopted. The ability to engage effectively with others is a skill that generally comes easier to extroverts over introverts. Extroverts usually have a much easier time navigating interpersonal relationships, which are often critical for (senior) administrators. However, this is not to suggest that extroversion is a definitive asset for an aspiring college or university administrator. Extroverts may become overconfident in their abilities to engage with others; they can get bogged down in conversation at the cost of their work and can come across as arrogant and demeaning to faculty and staff, whereas introverts may come across as more efficient and better, more caring, and trustworthy confidants and leaders.[4]

Ultimately, while the work and results of administrators may override most everything else, likability or popularity can be extremely important. Faculty and staff generally want someone in a senior administrative role who they can see as a role model or as someone inspiring. At the same time, they want to be made to feel personally important and valuable (as do most employees). In addition, they may want someone who will be willing to support them through difficult issues and who is willing to take on difficult issues (e.g., difficult student issues) that they may not want to deal with themselves (or not on their own). In the end, faculty and staff generally want administrators who will make their lives better, easier, and even more prestigious, whether that is through material gains such as salary increases, course reductions, public acclaim, and flattery, or by taking on difficult issues for them. At the same time, faculty and staff generally respond less favorably toward overly assertive or (perceived to be) arrogant (senior) administrators or those who take too much credit for collectively completed work. Too much focus on oneself as an administrator as opposed to collective or individual focus on other faculty, staff, and students can be detrimental to one's standing and general regard.

Toward this end, one of the best pieces of advice I ever received when beginning my career as a college administrator was to withhold, selectively present opinions, and at times even "play dumb," especially when it comes to leading or even engaging with some faculty. While, of course, no one ever wants to appear stupid, and "playing dumb" is hyperbolic, there are occasions when an administrator may want to feign ignorance—for example, so that she or he does not get caught in an unwinnable argument or allow others (especially faculty) to feel that they know more, even if they do not. At times, there can be a great deal of value in reining in one's views, insights, and knowledge, and either drawing others out or projecting competency rather than brilliance. This is especially the case if an administrator is in a position of power over faculty, in which case they may feel reticent to voice their own opinions or they may be compelled to blindly agree with her or his ideas, even if they do not really support these ideas. If participants feel valued, respected, and appreciated, they will be more apt to contribute significantly (and form a solid, highly productive team) as opposed to if they feel they are just working to help make an administrator shine brighter.

In areas where faculty take significant interest (e.g., curriculum, content analysis, policy development), an administrator may be able to play along with faculty expectations—namely that, as C. K. Gunsalus contends, "an academic who takes on an administrative role loses twenty I.Q. points."[5] In areas where faculty are not particularly invested (e.g., assessment and program review), an administrator wouldn't need to consider tempering her or his competencies, except if they get in the way of efficiency, which is the main concern faculty will have if they aren't invested in the area or task. While feigning incompetence will almost certainly not be helpful, being modest, unassuming, and appearing more or less intellectually competent or reasonably strong can help faculty, in particular, feel more confident in their own abilities as well as in their own sense of superiority.

Like most people, faculty and staff in higher education can have fragile egos, want to feel valued, and want to believe if not see that they are just as important, if not more important, as administrators. If an administrator appears too slick, too accomplished, too eager to dismiss the ideas of others, and too egocentric, it can turn many faculty (and staff) off. Consequently, administrators also need to be cognizant of not appearing too imposing or intimidating while also not being overly demure or introverted. Toward that end, it is important to take the time to engage faculty and staff in their particular interests and even, to some degree, in their personal lives. Doing so helps show that an administrator cares, and if she or he shares some personal information in a compelling manner, it can make staff (and faculty) feel privileged and important. At the same time, there is no easy answer as to how much one should engage with faculty and staff regarding their personal lives. In part, it will depend on the individual. Some faculty and staff are considerably more private and guarded than others. What one person may see as concern and interest, another person may see as intrusive. Generally, if a faculty or staff member brings up personal matters, it can be safe to assume that she or he will take positively to one's personal inquiries. For more extroverted administrators, establishing personal relationships with faculty and staff outside the office may not only help solidify connections but can also breed loyalty. However, doing so comes with some potential drawbacks, if not pitfalls. Not only can it open an administrator up to perceptions of favoritism, but becoming friends with direct or indirect reports may lead to actual bias or conflict and disappointment.

Accessibility, Management, and Leadership

Of course, as much as possible, an administrator should want to avoid disappointment and should want to minimize conflict, although, in the long run, both are more or less inevitable for any administrator who is in her or his role long enough. While this may occur, it is important to consider the majority's viewpoint, as there is power in numbers, even if those numbers are coming from the administrative middle or from staff, faculty, or students. If leading from the middle is important in terms of getting things accomplished (as I believe it is), a significant part of the importance lies in the sheer number of people in the "middle." It is also hard for any administrator (let alone politician) to resist something that is coming from a vocal and sizeable group. In particular, if the vocal and sizeable group is composed mainly of students, it can be challenging to ignore their requests or demands. While student requests, it can be argued, may not be as well informed or convincing as that of faculty and staff, colleges and universities (especially teaching-oriented institutions) exist mainly for students. Ignoring or not addressing the desires of students in favor of one's own priorities or preferences as an administrator can be professionally dangerous, even if it may seem clear that it is the right thing to do. These are precisely the kinds of things that if captured on video and uploaded to social media can go viral and provoke immediate debate, discussion, and change (including personnel changes).

For these reasons, it is not uncommon for faculty and administrators to enlist students to join their side in any ongoing debate or difference of opinion. As one example, faculty and administrators trying to gain traction for a new initiative or additional funding may bring a group of students to an open meeting (e.g., faculty senate). These students, especially if they are sufficiently impassioned and use social media platforms, can be especially effective in helping faculty or administrators succeed or fail. Doing this, though, can be risky for several reasons. First, if the attempt is not successful, not only can the students direct their dissatisfaction toward the person or persons who they may believe led them to failure in the first place, but others may view the faculty, staff, or administrator as manipulative and untrustworthy. Even if the attempt is successful, it can create an expectation that in the future, students can come with their respective issues and ask (if not demand) administrators (and faculty) take up their cause(s).

In a related, hypothetical but quite possible situation, an administrator could become too accessible to students. Buller claims that an "essential academic leader is accessible," but I would qualify his assertion with the phrase "selectively accessible."[6] An administrative leader can drown in minutiae and meetings if she or he makes her or himself too accessible. Further, she or he can then be held captive by the numerous and sometimes competing desires of others if she or he is too accessible. Administrative leaders can be selectively accessible (or regularly accessible) for those who directly report to them, and they may hold general office hours for drop-ins (although if they do this, they must be prepared for any issue or demand that may come their way). As a general rule of thumb, being in meetings more than half or two-thirds of any given day on average is probably too much, just as holding more than a couple of office hours a week (if one holds them) is about as much as an administrator should consider doing. This, though, is just a suggestion, not an actual rule, as there are or will be some days in which serious issues emerge that require immediate and complete (even round-the-clock) attention. For the most part, especially at the senior level, administrators simply do not have enough time to do all that they want or even need to do in a given day or even over an extended period of time. Under "normal" circumstances, what can an academic administrator do with all of his or her projects, tasks, competing demands, or requests, which cannot all be completed, at least not promptly? How can one say "no" or "not now" in a way that is not perceived as being dismissive or lazy?

In that, especially when and if there is a flood of work, it can be effective for administrators and their support staff to think of their units rather like emergency rooms in hospitals and them as screening staff performing a daily (or sometimes even hourly) triage. Determining which items, meetings, or tasks are more important than others and when they should be completed is one of the most critical tasks of an administrator, especially if she or he has a significant number of programs, units, or personnel under her or him. For some administrators, especially those in the most senior of positions, this is precisely one of the most important tasks for her or his executive assistant or chief of staff. An especially effective executive assistant or chief of staff not only can arrange one's schedule and answer or address immediate requests, but she or he can be on the front lines, saying yes and, more importantly, saying no to those who request meetings or attention. Some administrators, though, like to do as much of this work themselves as possible, and in circumstances when one has an executive assistant, chief of staff, or administrative assistant who is not that reliable or effective, it can be sensible to take on this responsibility (or at least part of it) oneself, at least until the staff has stepped up or new, more efficient staff have been hired and are in place.

Administrators also have to determinate how much time they want to spend writing and responding to emails, calls, paperwork, and other requests. While it is uncommon for those at the very top (e.g., presidents and vice presidents) to respond to emails, calls, and other requests promptly (unless the requests come from those who hold power over them or the issue is clearly urgent), some administrators, generally not quite this high on the academic totem pole (e.g., deans, associate vice presidents, department chairs, directors), consciously make a point of responding quickly (if not almost immediately) to emails and calls. In some circumstances, especially if the person responds during off-hours (e.g., early morning, at night, or over the weekend), doing so can give the impression that the person is extremely hardworking and devoted. In many cases, this behavior does represent diligence and commitment, but in other cases, the person may purposely be trying to project that she or he is a completely devoted and extremely hard worker, when either she or he may not be efficiently completing her or his other work or she or he may not be profitably using her or his time during "regular" business hours. As a case in point, I once knew an administrator who vocally boasted about how, when he was in a previous administrative position, he would regularly go in early and leave late, which gave the impression of great diligence. What most didn't know, he confided, is that he was regularly using the institution's gym for upward of four hours each day.

There is a danger, though, on the flip side. Administrators who do not regularly respond to emails, calls, or other requests, or who do so in sporadic or tardy fashion, may not gain the confidence of faculty and staff. While there may not be a perfect balance of how much time one should spend before responding, another good rule of thumb (especially for email, which is how most official university communication is conducted and where there is a time stamp as well as a permanent record) is not to be more than a week behind. This can depend on the institution and the culture there. Some institutions or groups of administrators clearly value prompt (digital) communication, while others are more ambivalent or even lackadaisical. At the former kind of institution, the expected maximum reply time may be more like a day or two (or even shorter) rather than a week. Of course, it can also depend on the nature of the issue or request, some of which may be more time-sensitive (or perceived as more time-sensitive) than others.

While one does not need to respond to each and every email or call received, it is important to recognize that if one does not respond, the other person will likely feel slighted (and she or he may persist with additional emails or calls). Sometimes it is better for this to happen than to put something potentially problematic in writing (although, in such circumstances, it is generally better to call). However, if the real reason an administrator is not responding to emails or not responding to them promptly is because she or he is truly overwhelmed with work in general or if she or he is working on a specific time-sensitive project, it is important, if possible, to communicate (or have one's assistant or chief of staff do so) with a quick message indicating that a response will be forthcoming. One could also consider offering an apology and explanation if it ends up taking a long time to get back to someone. To a large degree, faculty, staff, and other administrators will be more sympathetic and understanding if they know that a person is working hard on a time-consuming project (e.g., accreditation, an audit). However, anyone's patience may run thin if this reason/excuse is used too frequently.

While administrators need to be engaged digitally at least to some degree, there is no objective answer as to how much they should engage with peers and subordinates in person. To be sure, there should be some in-person engagement with others, but as with digital contact there is a fine line between too much and too little in-person engagement. If possible, it is helpful to have regular meetings with unit leaders/direct reports, but how frequently these meetings are held can be determined on the basis of how often the unit leaders/direct reports want to meet, the extent to which one needs to be involved in their units, and how much time and other competing high-level priorities one may have. Consulting with unit leaders is important in this regard. Some will jump at the opportunity to meet as frequently as possible, while others will avoid meeting unless one makes them. It is largely pointless to force frequent (even sometimes regular) meetings with unit leaders/direct reports if they are resistant or if there is no apparent or immediate need in doing so. Those who strongly resist or avoid meetings can often be doing so because they have something to hide or because they want to be autonomous. They may also be overly autocratic, or they may not (fully) respect administrators or the power of administrative positions. In any case, these are usually one's most (potentially) problematic direct reports. Although an administrator does not have to meet the desires of unit leaders/direct reports, their desires can be taken into account. If one does meet with some unit leaders/direct reports more frequently than others, one can risk being accused of favoritism. However, this may not be a large risk to take, and it can be worth doing if the benefits (maximizing time and efficiency) seem to outweigh the drawbacks (unnecessary meetings, inefficiencies, and possibly appearing to display favoritism).

In addition to meetings, it is important for administrators to have a wider physical/in-person presence, but it is debatable as to how much of a presence is too little or too much. Buller asserts that essential academic leaders "manage by walking around,"[7] and that they "have impromptu conversations with students and faculty members wherever they meet them, eat regularly in the dining halls, attend campus events, and create a culture of openness that keeps them informed about the key issues in their programs."[8] Buller's assertions definitely have merit, in that "invisible" academic leaders, no matter how much they may accomplish, may be perceived as aloof, uncaring, or not invested. This can especially be the case for college or university presidents, who should have some level of ongoing campus visibility, albeit not too much, lest the campus start wondering why she or he has so much time on her or his hands. However, midtier and other senior-level administrators may not have the same need or desire to be especially visible.

Further, there can definitely be such a thing as too much visibility for administrators. When I was a faculty-administrator at a small college, the president made a regular habit of periodically and frequently walking around at unannounced times. After some time, many faculty and staff started to become uncomfortable with these unannounced visits, which could sometimes be stilted and awkward, not only because the generally socially awkward president would attempt to engage individuals in sometimes-stilted conversation but also because power can make people in a subordinate position feel anxious or uncomfortable. After all, virtually everyone at a college or university wants to impress the president, or at the very least not embarrass him- or herself in front of her or him. At the same time, faculty and staff began to wonder how the president had the amount of time he appeared to have in order to do this on a weekly and sometimes even daily basis. Some also thought these visits to be evaluative in nature. With time, it became somewhat of a running joke about the president "walking around." Whenever word got out that the president was about to enter a specific building or had already started "walking around" in the building, many, if not most, faculty and staff did their best to scatter into the proverbial wind.

More charismatic, extroverted, and generally engaging administrative leaders can often use informal conversations with faculty and staff to inspire confidence and to get more of a holistic view of their institution, as well as to gather ideas. Indeed, I have seen another president do exactly this. Buller suggests that "the best administrators are those who can make each person they meet feel as though they have all the time in the world just to interact with that one individual."[9] While this is, at least, somewhat of a hyperbolic claim, since any administrator who consistently does this will have trouble accomplishing her or his work, there is truth to the assertion that administrative leaders who demonstrate what appears to be genuine care and concern for faculty and staff are more apt to earn their trust, respect, and admiration. Being enthusiastic, uplifting, and positive can also help. Buller also asserts the importance of "quiet confidence" and having "a relaxed demeanor."[10] However, there are times in which such behavior may be viewed as being timid, disaffected, or glib. When there are significant moments or times of crisis (e.g., dealing with a deadly occurrence on campus or dealing with a racist act), the campus community expects strong emotion or strength from their administrative leaders. In fact, if neither is seen (or not sufficiently demonstrated) in these critical moments, it can lead to a gradual or immediate loss of confidence in the leader(s).

Ultimately, leadership at colleges and universities is as much, if not more, about making other people feel included, respected, and valued as it is about what one may or may not achieve. Certainly, individual professional achievements can matter, and they certainly bear importance when one is being considered for a position, but they are generally only as important to faculty and staff at a college and university in the extent to which either helps them personally or if they feel as if they played an acknowledged role in these accomplishments (which they can then also claim as their own accomplishments). At the same time, being an effective administrative leader can differ, to some degree, depending on the size of an institution, its selectivity and focus, and whether it is a public or private institution. In *Saving Alma Mater*, James C. Garland suggests that it is easier to make decisions at private institutions than public institutions.[11] He argues, "Public higher education is an unhappy family. The family members are governors and elected officials, trustees, regents and governing boards, college and university presidents and chancellors, professors and administrative staff members."[12] However, private colleges and universities can have many similar kinds of stakeholders (e.g., mainly business professionals, prominent community members, and religious affiliates), and these same stakeholders may hold a disproportionate amount of power at a private institution compared to a public institution, where there are usually a greater number of checks and balances. This can potentially make it both easier and more challenging to make decisions at private institutions. There may be a shorter or even nonexistent bureaucratic process at such institutions, but if the most powerful constituents are not on board with an administrator's ideas, it can be extremely difficult, if not impossible, to put her or his ideas into action.

Management and Leadership Style(s)

Even if it is challenging for an administrator to make decisions, this does not necessarily mean she or he is hamstrung as a leader or that she or he should adopt a specific leadership or management style. Ultimately, as alluded to in the previous chapter, it is important to become the type of leader that matches one's personality and style. If one is introverted and soft-spoken, for instance, one will probably not feel comfortable adopting an overly social and assertive leadership style or managerial persona. An administrator should not force a personality or managerial change, as it will probably seem fake and she or he will be or become uncomfortable or miserable acting in a way that is contrary to her or his personality. At the same time, there will be occasions when one may need to step out of one's comfort zone. For instance, if an administrator is a conflict-avoiding, soft-spoken introvert, she or he will want to push herself or himself to act (on occasion) in a more assertive or gregarious manner, especially when particularly assertive faculty, students, staff, or other administrators push back or act overly aggressive, or in important social situations.

Not all faculty and staff, after all, respond to the same managerial style. It is important, though, that style is not confused with standards. While an administrator can have different goals and approaches with direct reports, she or he should have equitable standards. One can be more prescriptive and assertive with some, though, who have not earned one's trust and confidence. For instance, one can push back assertively against claims direct reports may make and set specific due dates for them. One can also insist on seeing their work before it is finalized, and one can meet with them more frequently, among other things. While some may be turned off by a more assertive, autocratic style or manner, others may only respond to managers who are more assertive, if not autocratic.

Adjusting style to audience is important as well as knowing that administrators will have multiple audiences (as well as distinct direct reports and peers), especially when beginning a new position. When doing so, the best thing one can do is listen and learn how to interpret the personality and professional styles of one's supervisor and colleagues as well as direct and indirect reports. Certain cues may provide initial assessments. For instance, those who pepper their sentences with first names tend to be more assertive and domineering. One would be wise, in conversations with them, to do the same and to respond strongly to assertions they may make; otherwise, one may cede too much power to them. Those who speak forcefully, in absolutes (e.g., "We must . . ." or "We have to . . ."), may not be doing this because they are especially wise or knowledgeable but because they do not want anyone, including most definitely an administrator, to challenge them or to push them to change. Those who ask about family or who interject personal anecdotes may be more extroverted. It can help to ask them questions about themselves, but it can be dangerous to allow them to dominate the conversation with their questions or personal anecdotes too often. While one wouldn't want to engage with them too often (as that can quickly eat up too much time), one should be ready to share stories and experiences; otherwise, they may try to dominate the discussion and, ultimately, an administrator's authority, or they may feel that she or he is detached, inauthentic, or overly guarded. Those who detail their accomplishments upon the first encounter (and especially those who continue to tout their achievements) are generally the most insecure and often the least competent but also the most potentially dangerous because they will generally be focused only on themselves.

Ambition, Leadership, and Management

Being an effective college or university leader, though, does not mean nullifying one's own self, needs, and desires. In *Leadership as Service*, Kent A. Farnsworth argues that "when one chooses to be a college leader, one should elect to become professionally selfless. The principle of "service first" should apply to all leadership."[13] This advice sounds noble enough, but it is overly simplistic and misguided. First, no one can ever be fully selfless, and any administrator who tries to do so could be used, blamed, or thought to have no real vision, creativity, or ability to innovate. In addition, she or he may not rise professionally or may be thrown under the proverbial bus at some point. One may try to appear as professionally self-effacing or self-minimizing as possible, and this is generally good advice to follow. However, one can still be ambitious without appearing arrogant or condescending by considering what impact one's decisions may make on one's professional or personal life. As a general rule, it is good for an administrator or any other professional worker to be ambitious, even though there is a definite danger in displaying that ambition too often to others, as they may interpret it as arrogance or they may become overly competitive. As with faculty, administrators who grow complacent or content with the status quo tend to accomplish less than those who are hungry for advancement and success.

Generally, personal or professional ambition is not something frequently valued in an administrative leader (at least not if it is nakedly displayed). Rather, faculty, staff, and other administrators more often value administrative leaders who appear to be transparent, trustworthy, inspiring, positive, and enthusiastic. One of the best ways to display these traits or characteristics is by sharing challenging information, displaying vulnerabilities or humanity, and by acting in what appears to be a selfless manner (even if it is not entirely selfless). Farnsworth claims that "leaders must be open to bad news. In fact, they must develop an atmosphere that encourages it to come to their attention. Few things are more destructive to trust than rumor or discontent that is allowed to fester beneath the surface."[14] I would go a step further. Generally, "bad news" at a university or college means decreased enrollment, a decreased institutional reputation, or decreased funding (or a combination of these things). If "bad news" exists or is on the horizon, it is likely that faculty and staff already are at least partially aware. Ignoring the issues will only make things worse. Being transparent, honest, and inclusive about actual or potential bad news will not only earn an administrator respect and trust, but faculty and staff may be more apt to work harder because they feel that they are all in it together.

Finances and Aesthetics: Size Matters!

Being the bearer of bad news often means being the bearer of a reduced budget and marking certain areas or even faculty and staff for cuts. As established in an earlier chapter, money or the pursuit of money is or often can become preeminent at a college or university. If an administrator brings in a great deal of capital, she or he may significantly increase her or his value, the currency of which tends to be power. Further, if that same administrator is instrumental in helping establish, select, and maintain the composition of the college or university governing boards, she or he can end up becoming more autocratic, if not monarchical. While I would be remiss to state definitively that if an administrator brings in a significant multimillion-dollar gift, she or he is set for life at that institution, that is not far off the mark. An excellent recent example is Dr. Carmen Puliafito, former dean of the University of Southern California's Keck School of Medicine, who reportedly engaged in illicit drug use and other nefarious activities. Largely because Dr. Puliafito brought in sizeable gifts and world-renowned researchers, the institution, at least initially, may have looked the other way at his behavior. Much to the chagrin of administrators who do the proverbial heavy lifting at an institution, such individuals can end up spending most of their time wining and dining current and prospective donors. Although this chagrin may be understandable, as much as possible, it should not be displayed, not only because those who bring in sizeable monetary gifts often become very powerful, but many administrators will be expected to bring in monetary gifts themselves and can be evaluated on their ability to do so. Generally, bigger will be better, although this can depend on whether the gift or gifts are unrestricted (preferable) or restricted (and, if restricted, to what).

This is not the only instance in which the job performance of administrators may be evaluated based on quantity, not quality. College and university administrators who look for other positions, for instance, may find that experience at a smaller institution that has less faculty, staff, and students is not as highly regarded as experience at a larger institution because of a general but widespread belief that larger institutions are more complex or complicated than smaller ones. According to this belief, the transition from a smaller to a larger institution is especially challenging. Rarely does one see the contrary belief—that it is more challenging to move from a large to a small institution. However, both assertions have truth to them. While it is true that larger institutions tend to have more complicated bureaucracies and a more complex division of labor, there can also be more nuanced, smaller institutions that often require administrators to take on a wider scope of responsibility and to finesse their interpersonal skills because there are simply fewer people there and sometimes no other option but to work with others with whom one does not get along, relate to, or respect. Still, the size of a staff managed and the size of a budget overseen as well as the overall enrollment at an institution matters to many administrators just as much as, if not more than, what one accomplishes at an institution. This is not to suggest that one should only pursue administrative positions at larger institutions, but it does mean that administrators at smaller institutions may have a more challenging time moving to other (larger) institutions, should they so desire.

Beginning a New Administrative Position: Staffing and Restructuring

At some point in their career, college and university administrators (or, for that matter, any supervisor of a sizeable staff) will have to deal with ineffective faculty, staff, or other administrators. While the common wisdom may be that inherited ineffective faculty, staff, and administrators are easier to deal with because one didn't hire them and therefore one doesn't bear any direct responsibility for them, these individuals often turn out to be the most difficult direct reports one will have. Not only is it likely that they have a network of existing support among other staff, but they may have grown adept at making themselves appear indispensable by not having other staff cross-trained in their area. At the same time, while faculty, staff, and other administrators who one hires may have a certain loyalty to the person who hired them, not only can this loyalty shift, but these direct reports can expect more or may grow disillusioned if the culture they join appears to be or is not sufficiently collegial or supportive. Still, even if this occurs, the likelihood is that there are significant issues at the institution, which is beyond one's control. One may be working to improve them, or one may be looking to move on to another position.

When beginning a new position, especially at a new institution, an administrator will inevitably inherit whatever her or his predecessor did or did not do, his or her staff (or at least the ones who don't leave at the same time as her or him), and the culture and financial status of the unit(s) and the institution itself. An administrator may have an option to alter some or all of the above, but even if all options are on the table, the more significant question to ask is: What is worth doing and in what order? The first several months of an administrator's new position will be key in determining the extent of what one may be able to accomplish in one's new position. Within a year, if not sooner, an administrator will have a pretty clear sense of what can and cannot be accomplished in the position and at the institution beyond what has already been accomplished. Fortunately, this is often also the so-called honeymoon period, in which one generally encounters goodwill and friendliness, and is usually offered some time to adjust to the new position and new responsibilities. However, it is important not to be lulled into what might end up being a (relative) false sense of security. The good work an administrator encounters may be her or his colleagues and staff either trying to determine whether the administrator will be an ally or adversary, or them trying to get on her or his good side.

It is generally a good idea not to make any rash staffing decisions or to restructure when first beginning a new position, even if it appears pretty clear very soon that one's units may be better suited with a different structure or staff. Not only can these developments be determined by the budget(s) one has, but it is not always so simple to make staffing and structure changes. In fact, it is usually better to postpone at least some change(s), especially when structures and staff have been in place for a long time. Too much change too quickly (or even just the perception of this) may lead others to view an administrator with suspicion, fear, or distrust. Organizational culture, especially at large institutions, can change very slowly, and the wisdom is in trying to determine what is most pressing to change and what the aftereffects may be, and building a coalition of support for the change(s) before acting.

Hiring and Managing Faculty, Staff, and Administrators

While an organizational restructuring may not be a viable option, one way all administrators can affect if not change a unit and institution's culture and effectiveness is through new hires.

Indeed, one of the most important decisions (if not the most important decision) administrators make is who to hire. To a large degree, this part of the position will be new to faculty members moving into an administrative role, and it will also be new to most nonmanagerial staff. Even if faculty or nonmanagerial staff have served on job search committees for open faculty and staff positions, they are not typically the ones hiring and overseeing the faculty and staff. Hewlett suggests that as a supervisor, one should "surround yourself with people who are better than you."[15] However, some college and university administrators have a tendency to hire those who will appear to be productive (but not overly productive to the point of raising expectations or taking too much of the spotlight away from others), seemingly not difficult to manage, and personally and professional compatible. Although it is possible to gauge the relative competencies and potential of applicants for a position during the hiring process, it is not really possible to conclude whether someone is "better than you" based on application materials and the interview process. Further, if an administrator hires faculty, staff, or other administrators who believe they are "better than you," it is likely that there will be managerial challenges or these hires may regard their position as little more than a (hopefully brief) stepping-stone to something better.

Hiring professional, accountable, reliable, capable, and trustworthy faculty, staff, and administrators is paramount, but personality and fit do matter, especially for staff and administrator positions, where so much time is spent in the office. Because hiring the best possible people one can is paramount, administrators who are in the position of hiring those who directly support them should try their best to advocate for the highest salary range possible (within reason). Investment in personnel cannot really be overestimated. Hiring the wrong people or hiring ineffective people can drain financial resources; it can also drain an administrator's energy and motivation as well as that of her or his more competent faculty, staff, and administrators.

At most colleges and universities, hiring is a multilevel and inclusive process involving different levels of review, recommendation, and approval before a person is hired. If an administrator is the direct supervisor of the person to be hired, it is likely that she or he will have veto power over a committee and be the primary hiring agent. This, however, is not always the case. Department chairs, for instance, technically oversee faculty in their department, but deans, not chairs, are the ones who generally hire tenure-track faculty (although chairs generally hire part-time faculty and support staff). If one is the final decision maker in the job search process, though, it is important to gather significant feedback from the job search committee and the campus community. One may also get specific recommendations from the committee or vested others. If the feedback clearly favors one person and is ultimately convincing, it should be relatively easy to proceed with the job offer. If, however, one has reservations about the strongly preferred candidate, one must weigh the concerns with the viability of the other candidates as well as the potential or actual fallout from one's (soon to be) unpopular decision. Conveying the reasons for one's choice is important, especially if those reasons may convince others to change their mind (e.g., a falsification in a candidate's CV or résumé, racist or sexist comments made during an interview). One does need to be careful about sharing this information too broadly (generally just the search committee or others invested in the job search process), as wide release may provoke dissent from others.

In some circumstances, an administrator may be torn between multiple candidates and the recommendations of others. In these and other circumstances, it is helpful to get a sense of how the candidate might be as an employee. One will probably not be able to ascertain that by contacting the applicant's references, though, as she or he probably already prescreened those references. One can ask the applicants for additional references, but those, too, are likely to be prescreened. The best option is generally to do one of two things: (1) ask the applicant(s) if one can call off the list or (2) ask the applicant(s) to identify and contact their existing or previous supervisor(s) if they are not already listed as a reference or references. Doing either is especially important when it comes to hiring staff and other administrators since faculty are more or less like independent contractors who are not managed in the same manner as staff. Even if the applicants say no to the requests, or if they hedge, that, in itself, can raise enough concerns to lean toward (if not eventually choose) another candidate. This being stated, there can be instances in which applicants work for difficult supervisors who might be tyrannical or unreasonable. That, in fact, may be one of the primary reasons why the applicant wants to leave her or his current position. So, it is important to take the feedback received as just that: feedback and not necessarily the truth.

Another reason applicants may be interested in a position, of course, is that they desire a higher salary. While there is nothing intrinsically wrong with seeking a position because of its salary, of course, if salary seems to be the primary reason an applicant is interested in a position, that should raise a significant red flag. This being said, salary matters, and low salary ranges can and most definitely do prevent quality applicants from applying or accepting a position. This is unfortunate, and not what an administrator wants. While it may seem to be an easy decision to raise a salary range by a certain amount (e.g., $5,000, $10,000, or $15,000), doing so can sometimes be one of the most difficult things an administrator can attempt to do. In some cases, it can be because an institution (or an institution's human resources or analogous office) is overly frugal and assertive; it can also be due to existing factors, such as the current salaries and ranges of other staff. Although equity is important when it comes to salaries, an administrator's objective and focus should be on hiring the best person for the position while maintaining some kind of equity within her or his units. She or he is not responsible for what others may receive in other nonreporting units, and she or he is not responsible for ensuring equity (or something approaching equity) across campus (with the possible exception of administrators in the general area of human resources). At the same time, especially since an administrator should not want to upset those who have the power to make these kinds of decisions, it is important to acknowledge and be sympathetic toward those who may make this argument (e.g., in human resources), even if one does end up pushing back against it. If this is done, the best technique (depending on the institution and the people) is to be gently persistent and willing to compromise if need be. One will presumably need to work with them again in the future, after all, and it is better not to burn those bridges if at all possible.

While hiring adept and engaged individuals is one of the most important responsibilities of an administrator, it is just the first step in the process of keeping staff committed, cohesive, and, within reason, content. To do this, it is important to praise those who do a good job while making them feel that they are valued contributors and stakeholders. If an administrator builds up quality employees, they are more apt to want to remain in the position. This means making sure one praises faculty, staff, and other administrators while giving them credit for their contributions and generally minimizing any public recognition of one's own contributions. It also means creating opportunities for these direct reports to contribute to discussions and to the decision-making process in general. This does not mean an administrator has to concede complete power, and, in fact, this can never really be done, because college and university administration, like all kinds of administration, can never function as a pure democracy. If an administrator is able to set up an agenda or framework of questions or items to be discussed in advance of a larger meeting (as long as those questions or items are things that do not have to be answered in a specific way), it can provide her or his direct reports, at the very least, with the illusion of control or participation and, more often than not, some input into the decision-making process. The end result is often an improved product or products and (more) widespread, collective buy-in.

Performance Evaluations and Engaging with Direct Reports

Setting and adjusting salaries, of course, can only do so much in encouraging strong employee morale and performance. Beyond hiring, successful college and university administrators are not only adept at retaining quality faculty, staff, and other administrators but also in mentoring and constructively evaluating them. Depending on the kind of institution an administrator is at, her or his ability or options to manage and set clear performance standards may be extremely limited or quite variable. Some institutions have well-defined performance reviews that must be completed in a specific time period and in a specific manner, while other institutions have unclear, intermittent, or even a total absence of performance evaluations. If and when possible, it is important to have clear standards. While the format and regularity of the evaluations may be predetermined by human resources or its equivalent office, there may be, at the very least, additional ways to improve the process so that direct reports receive feedback that is constructive and does not come to them as a surprise.

A best-case scenario for evaluations is to make one step (usually the first step) in the process for faculty, staff, and administrators to self-evaluate. It is much easier for employees to change if that change comes from them through self-identification of viable areas for growth and improvement. Having faculty, staff, and administrators complete self-evaluations prior to their "official" evaluation can help toward this end. However, some will take self-evaluations as an opportunity to self-promote and detail their work using the most effusive language possible while not admitting any real or significant area or areas for growth. These will almost certainly be the most challenging direct reports to manage. Asking them to set up yearly goals can help at least push them into objectives that can be later measured and evaluated, but in the end, it is not uncommon for administrators to have some challenging faculty, staff, and administrators under them who are overly assertive or aggressive, who are hypersensitive to any form of critique, or who are mostly or completely incapable of accepting criticism. While it is usually helpful to couch criticism in the context of either positive reinforcement or the desire to help the individual grow, for some faculty, staff, and administrators the only kind of feedback that can conceivably work is clear, direct, and unfiltered critique. In such circumstances, the behavior may only change if the direct report feels there may be significant or real consequences for her or him (e.g., demotion or termination).

Evaluating faculty can be more distinct, especially as there are usually promotion or tenure guidelines, which provide, at the very least, vague standards in the areas of teaching, scholarship, and service. While it is unlikely that there is only one person evaluating faculty, pending her or his position, an administrator may hold the primary or final determining factor as to whether faculty are tenured, promoted, or retained. If an institution does not have a clear or effective process to evaluate faculty, a revised or new policy should be put in place as soon as possible. Part of this process should involve what materials are evaluated (e.g., syllabi, assignments, student evaluations, scholarship, evidence of service contributions). If these materials are scrutinized and there is a clear and equitable process in place for evaluations, promotion, and tenure (should that be awarded), faculty who are high performing should be retained and non- or lower-performing faculty should not.

When considering how to address behavior or performance for all direct reports, not just faculty, it is helpful to explore specific situations. Consider, for instance, a student affairs staff member who works late hours regularly but who is also accessible (too accessible) to students and staff, and who spends too much time socializing with them and getting involved in other college or university matters that are not particularly germane to her or his position. In this circumstance, pending the individual and the institution, it can be helpful to commend her or him on her or his work ethic and institutional commitment but also clearly state general and specific job responsibilities that could be completed more efficiently and effectively. Consider, in another circumstance, an academic affairs staff member who insists that she or he is too busy to take on an initiative that her predecessor used to handle and insists that an administrator defend the perceived boundaries of her or his office and the scope of her or his position. In this case, an administrator can work with the direct report to prioritize her or his work. To do this, an administrator can probe more for an account of the direct report's major responsibilities and then provide clear guidance for work prioritization.[16] Alternatively, or if this does not work, an administrator can still assign specific initiatives to her or him within the parameters of her or his job description. If she or he does not rise to the occasion, one will then have more material with which to act upon in the future, should reassignment, demotion, or termination be considered. In the end, if these issues are not directly, clearly, and unambiguously addressed, it is safe to presume that the behavior(s) will continue unchecked.

To get more information and collective input from faculty, staff, and other administrators, one can ask a sampling of them directly, in (private) meetings, or indirectly, through an anonymous poll (I would advise doing both), for their perceptions of performance reviews. Further, while it can bring with it problems (e.g., for those who do not receive them), tying merit increases to performance reviews can give direct and indirect reports additional incentive. It can also soften the blow if one is at an institution where performance evaluations are mostly perfunctory and where one has an interest in making them (more) rigorous. Doing so can also help an administrator accomplish one of the best things a leader can ever do: create a number of other effective leaders with whom she or he works.

Ethics and Ethical Leadership

In order to create and maintain an institution that has high-functioning administrative leaders, there needs to be an ingrained and valued ethical culture, which an administrator needs to help foster and nurture. This being stated, most college and university administrators are middle managers (with the middle spanning from those who only oversee one individual to those who oversee hundreds, indirectly or directly). As such, they will inevitably have competing demands and interests from above and below (as well as from colleagues and peers). Sometimes the decisions will be easy or relatively easy if the preponderance of support is on one side or the other. However, one must always weigh the consequences of one's actions even if those consequences are based solely on optics. Does one want to terminate an insubordinate staff member who is extremely well-liked by the vast majority of his or her coworkers? Does one want to follow the budgetary recommendations of one's supervisor, even though one may have a significant difference of opinion from her or him? Should one grant a request for research release time from a difficult faculty member who used to be a prolific and esteemed researcher/scholar but who hasn't published anything in more than ten years?

The aforementioned examples are just a sampling of the difficult choices and decisions college and university administrators can face. These decisions sometimes or even often cannot be made by merit alone, nor can they be guided by a binary ethical idealism that perceives mainly right and wrong choices. There is a reason why going into college and university administration is equated to joining the proverbial "dark side," because administration can be a morally shady, even dirty, business. The challenge is to keep one's moral bearings as intact as possible while keeping two primary goals in mind: effectively doing one's job and protecting oneself. Protecting oneself as an administrator means securing allies and work friends. It may also mean, at times, being ingratiating or being selective in responding in kind to coworkers who are or can be incompetent, lazy, or hostile. The less they know and the more they believe that one is their ally, even if one is not, generally, the better. This does not necessarily have to be as morally dubious or vacant as it may appear. For instance, one can always be personally friendly with coworkers, supervisors, or direct/indirect reports, even if one thinks very little of them professionally (or personally).

While college and university administrative work can sometimes be morally shady or dark, it need not be that way. As with many professional and leadership roles, college and university administrators can and do struggle with ethically gray areas. Additionally, it is generally true that, as with any other profession, the higher a person rises in any organization and the greater the amount of power that person possesses, the greater the opportunity, if not the likelihood, for corruption. For some administrators, there is often little worse than those who see things in dichotomies—good or bad, wrong or right. In fact, during an interview for an administrative position, a senior administrator to whom the position reported once asked me how I am with gray areas. The right answer, it was immediately clear to me, was that I should be open to them, should the time and circumstance arise (or if I were to be asked by the senior administrator to "bend the rules" or "consider extenuating circumstances").

Just as in the contemporary United States, at colleges and universities, there is a growing dichotomy between those who champion the importance of ethics and ethical leadership and those who ignore or trounce upon ethics. When I began as a college administrator/department chair, I was generally more Kantian in my approach to ethical issues. It seemed, especially in cases of management, evaluation, curriculum, and petitions for exceptions (which can so often be the job of a department chair), that Kant's categorical imperative to never act upon anything unless as a maxim was a good framework to use. At that time, I did not think that a utilitarian approach in college or university administration could ever work, because there are times in which the best decisions can be unpopular ones (e.g., raising tuition and fees or terminating or demoting a well-liked but nonperforming staff member). As time went on, I gravitated more toward pragmatism, although there were times in which it became apparent that I was not willing or able to do the pragmatic thing, because I thought it was not the right thing to do. In the end, I have found that the best approach to college and university administration is a kind of pragmatic realism or moral relativism. This means, in a nutshell, trying to consistently do what one believes to be the uniform or universal right thing but recognizing that reality and consequences can often impinge upon idealistic desires, thereby leading one toward making what some might argue to be morally questionable decisions because those decisions appear to hold the best chance of improving or resolving the situation. While the ends do not always justify the means, especially if the impact will be on people (e.g., termination), sometimes they do.

So, before coming to what seems to be the ethical conclusion that all applicants ought to be treated exactly the same, no matter what, it is important to consider whether race, ethnicity, gender, or class should matter in the application process, and if so how much. It is also important to consider what should be done when asked by a high-ranking administrator at one's college or university (perhaps even the president) to "consider what you can do"[17] for the son or daughter of the university's most significant donor and alumni. Is it worth it to dig one's heels in and stick to a Kantian categorical imperative in all circumstances? Sometimes, in these circumstances, the best thing to do is find some middle ground that does not sacrifice one's ethical integrity but also is responsive to the specific demand, which will inevitably have a range of possible responses as well as pros and cons for those responses. In this case, the answer might be to accept (grudgingly) the applicant as a "nonmatriculating student." Consider another circumstance in which a provost wishes to set a higher standard for promotion or tenure than is currently established at certain colleges. The majority of the faculty at those colleges are strongly against this, and those at the other colleges do not seem to care too much, but the provost feels it is the ethical and equitable thing to do. If the provost took a utilitarian approach, she or he probably would not do anything. However, if she or he takes an ethically pragmatic approach, she or he would consider how important the issue of equity really is, what the aftereffects might be, and how both might affect the university as a whole (as well as the provost's own position and career). In the end, the provost might end up compromising by gradually or incrementally increasing standards in some schools, about as much as possible without going over a proverbial tipping point, resulting in too much pushback or critique.

To be sure, there is subjectivity in ethics both at the theoretical and the practical levels. The aforementioned example is of what a college or university administrator might do or consider doing in a practical situation. There is an even more complicated gray area in which a college, university, or organization may profess to be ethical when it actually is either self-serving or attempting to police a certain kind of behavior or even thoughts. For instance, writing for the *Chronicle of Higher Education*, Maria Brandt describes how she was reported on her college's "anonymous ethics hotline" for assigning overly political texts. While the particular complaint was dismissed, Brandt argues that "as we move into an ever-more-contentious political climate, administrative processes have begun to encourage faculty and staff to complain quietly about philosophical differences rather than engaging in healthy, open dialogue." For her, it is an example of "just one of many ways our academic freedom and culture of academic discourse are under subtle, persistent threat." Or is it? If, as Brandt's university described it, an "ethics hotline" is a system that "enables college employees and associates to confidentially report activities that may involve unethical, illegal, or inappropriate activities," what is wrong with having an avenue for whistleblowers who may fear consequences?[18] There is no intrinsic problem with an ethics hotline or any other means of reporting potential ethically dubious behavior. In fact, in theory at least, having something like this, especially at institutions that do not have an ombudsman or equivalent, can lead to important revelations that can and should be investigated.

Some faculty and administrators argue that ethics should be, but currently is not, central to university or college life. In his essay "Practice What You Teach," Boston College faculty member James Keenan argues that since most faculty, administrators, and staff have "no training in professional ethics," they consequently "do not promote a culture of ethical consciousness and accountability."[19] Supporting his argument is the fact that there can be no disputing that recently, some administrators, faculty, and staff at colleges and universities have displayed an appalling lack of ethical behavior, from the sham classes at the University of North Carolina at Chapel Hill (to safeguard student athletes) to certain for-profit institutions (e.g., the Corinthian Colleges) that have been closed due to their practice of preying upon students and lenders to get as much money as they can. However, how does one increase ethical behavior in such institutions, departments, or units? It is unreasonable, of course, to insist that all administrators, staff, and faculty have some background or "training in professional ethics," although a case could be made for the need to have some kind of college-level ethics requirement as part of a college or university core curriculum or general education. While such a requirement might conceivably help, it certainly could not prevent significant ethical transgressions, just as writing and math requirements cannot promise or guarantee proficiency in either. What could?

While there may be no clear answer to this question, without sound, ethical leadership at the top of any organization, whether it is a college or university or anywhere else, it is likely that the organization will be more susceptible to ethical transgressions.[20] Leaders are ultimately responsible for the culture in their unit or organization, and they may affect the culture directly or indirectly (consciously or subconsciously) by setting an example, for better or worse. If leaders in a certain organization act in sexist or even racist ways, that behavior is likely to infiltrate other units and encourage similar behavior in other employees. It is, of course, easy for an organization to state that they are devoted to ethical leadership, but it is hard to measure and evaluate whether it truly demonstrates ethical leadership or whether its leaders demonstrate it (although egregious examples of ignoring violent, sexist, and racist acts or statements can clearly indicate serious ethical issues and lapses). An additional challenge may be defining "ethical leadership." Although there may be no precise definition for ethical leadership, emeritus professor Donald C. Menzel suggests that "there are three basic ingredients: being an ethical role model to others, treating people fairly, and actively managing ethics in the organization."[21] He also suggests that ethical leadership is akin to "leading with integrity," which he defines as being "honest, truthful, and unwilling to compromise values or principles for advancement or personal gain," as well as "taking personal responsibility for errors one may commit, and recognizing and crediting others for their work and contributions to the organization's mission."[22] This, though, may be easier said than done, and a good case in point is how an administrator deals with direct orders.

One of the most significant ethical dilemmas or difficulties an administrator may face is when she or he is asked to do something by her or his supervisor with which she or he does not agree. In such circumstances, it is usually better to tread carefully by acknowledging the supervisor's point of view, even when one does not believe it has (much) merit, and present one's viewpoint more as concerns and questions rather than in an overly assertive fashion. Doing so does not, of course, guarantee success, but it allows the supervisor to consider changing her or his mind without feeling that she or he will lose face or that his or her authority may be diminished. It also may help an administrator get to a point at which she or he is ready to make some kind of compromise to her or his position, which, while not ideal, is (grudgingly) acceptable. Still, there will be times when an administrator may feel bound not to follow a recommendation or even a directive from a supervisor. The main reasons to do so are either because of moral considerations (e.g., terminating someone who one feels does not deserve to be terminated) or because the personal or professional fallout for oneself is simply too significant (e.g., if one is asked to take the front lines in dismantling tenure).

Make no mistake, though, saying no or standing up to a supervisor can carry grave risks for an administrator's short- and long-term professional career, let alone her or his employment status (especially if an administrator does not have faculty retreat rights). At the same time, it can also earn an administrator the respect and admiration of others. Hewlett claims that "the higher you go in an organization, the more impressive you are when you have the spine to share your convictions."[23] However noble it may feel to "speak truth to power," in Hewlett's words, the truth can often be relative and this "courage" is only good insomuch as it achieves results.[24] It can be beneficial for an administrator to present her- or himself as independent from her or his supervisor(s), but it is also important not to imperil this relationship, either. Therefore, one should be selective in deciding when and how one pushes back against requests, recommendations, or even orders from supervisors, that is, if one wants to have a long and successful career as a college or university administrator.

Certainly, when an administrator begins a new position, and periodically throughout her or his tenure, she or he may also be tested by colleagues or staff to determine how strong of a leader/manager she or he may be, how autonomous she or he can or should be, and how much she or he might be able to get away with doing or not doing. Administrators will inevitably encounter some bothersome things (e.g., certain support staff coming to work consistently late or leaving consistently early), but before rashly acting on those bothersome things, she or he should try to objectively prioritize one's most important tasks and leave other tasks for another time. It may not be right that one staff member comes in ten or fifteen minutes late and another staff member is consistently early, but is it worth addressing, especially if the one who comes in late consistently performs better than the more punctual employee? In the end, an administrator should keep her or his eyes on the prize, which is that once an administrator builds up a high-functioning, cohesive, and collegial team, not only will it be pleasant to be at work, but her or his workplace will become something like a well-oiled machine that needs little direction or management. That, as it turns out, is one of the biggest ironies of management: over time, those who end up managing the best are the ones who need to manage and lead the least.

Chapter 6

Diversity, Inclusion, and Religious Affiliation

Ultimately, America's answer to the intolerant man is diversity, the
very diversity which our heritage of religious freedom has inspired.
—Robert F. Kennedy

The next time some academics tell you how important diversity
is, ask how many Republicans there are in their sociology
department.
—Thomas Sowell

The lack of diversity in higher education is a problem we as a country
must tackle if we're going to live up to our promise.
—Wendy Kopp

You are sitting in a rather stuffy enclosed amphitheater, surrounded by fellow colleagues, faculty, administrators, and
staff, some of whom are dressed in traditional caps and gowns
while others wear normal business attire. At the lectern is the
recently appointed university president, who is speaking about
campus values and her vision for the future:

> We at —— University believe that diversity and inclusion aren't just words. It is the very foundation of who we are and who we want to be. It is a daily commitment to ask ourselves what more we can do to make our campus inclusive. It means equal access for all; it means maintaining a rich and welcoming learning environment for all, one that can help our graduates succeed in a global and intercultural world. It means that we believe there is power in our differences, that our differences are what make us special and unique . . .

You look around at the predominately White audience, some of whom are intently listening and periodically clapping, while others are raptly involved with their smartphones. Others are staring blankly into space, while some roll their eyes at key parts of the president's speech. They know what you know—that the student body is more than 80 percent White and the faculty are nearly 90 percent White. This has not really altered in decades. What makes this president any different from the others? You would like to think she is, but you are skeptical. You tell yourself you will wait to see if anything changes in a year or two, and then, well, what can you really do?

What Do Diversity and Inclusion Really Mean?

It has become ubiquitous at colleges and universities to express a deep commitment to diversity and inclusivity, to the point that it is hard to find a college or university that does not make diversity or some synonym (e.g., multiculturalism, inclusion, equity) part of its mission or focus. If diversity or a related word or phrase is not part of the main college or university mission, the likelihood is that the institution has a separate diversity statement, mission, or public commitment. This is a recent development at colleges and universities, which, certainly, prior to 1970, if not 1980 or 1990, would be more likely not to mention diversity as a priority, let alone include it in its mission. Yet, years later, diversity, in all its components (gender, race, ethnicity, religion, socioeconomic class, etc.), is and continues to be a significant issue at contemporary colleges and universities. To what extent is a college or university diverse enough? How is "diversity" determined? What steps should a college or university take in order to have a sufficiently diverse environment? Even if specific diversity metrics are met, what other steps or actions can an institution make or take to promote an inclusive, equitable environment? How can it be determined if an institution really has an inclusive, equitable environment?

These are all difficult, fraught questions, but they are nonetheless important, even though they cannot be objectively or conclusively answered. It may be easy enough to get campus constituents to agree to a spirit of equity, equal access, and inclusion, just as it is easy for any college and university to express a commitment to diversity. However, evaluating to what extent one has achieved or can ever achieve a desired level of diversity and inclusion (let alone whether such a thing is possible) as well as determining how to improve either or both are the truly significant tasks in front of any college or university administrator, faculty member, or staff member who is earnestly devoted to furthering social justice and equity in higher education.

The easiest measure of college or university diversity is a statistical analysis of enrollment demographics. However, these kinds of statistics can be misleading, and using something akin to a quota can backfire and in some cases be legally challenged.[1] Further, if one uses enrollment demographic statistics as the primary or even just one of many measures of success in (campus) diversity, should one consider the statistical breakdown of race, ethnicity, and gender nationwide, statewide, or locally as a statistical measure of success? If local or state demographics are used, then an institution like Dartmouth College should be content with being more than 80 percent White (the demographic of Hanover) or more than 90 percent White (the demographic of New Hampshire) as opposed to 61 percent for the entire United States.[2] As it turns out, Dartmouth's demographics more clearly represent that of the United States, with a total population of 48 percent White,[3] and I cannot imagine that they, their student body and their alumni, as well as the vast majority of Dartmouth faculty and staff, would be content with a demographic that mirrors Hanover or the state of New Hampshire. As a private institution that enrolls students from all over the country (as well as internationally), Dartmouth may feel that its demographics should more closely represent the larger United States, which it mostly does.[4]

Still, other private universities may not feel as beholden to diversify their student body if their institutional mission has a narrower or more specific focus. A good case in point is Yeshiva University in New York City. While New York City is undoubtedly one of the most diverse cities in the United States and the entire world, Yeshiva University, which is reportedly 94 percent White, is anything but ethnically diverse ("Yeshiva University Diversity"). However, as Yeshiva University is religiously affiliated with Orthodox Judaism, which is overwhelmingly White, it can be argued that Yeshiva should not be beholden to any local, statewide, or national diversity demographics but rather to its mission and religious affiliation. Yeshiva, it can be argued, reflects the lack of ethnic diversity in the Orthodox Jewish community. If Yeshiva were a public institution in New York City with the same or similar demographics, there would understandably be a public outcry of racism and discrimination.

It is important to recognize, though, that students at private institutions (nonprofit and for-profit) still benefit from some forms of federal and state aid (e.g., Pell Grants, Direct Loans). Therefore, to a much lesser degree, the public still supports sometimes nondiverse or arguably exclusionary private colleges and universities, even if they do not support their mission. Although specific regional and disciplinary accreditation agencies can (at least in theory, if not in practice) hold private colleges or universities accountable for their diversity initiatives or the lack thereof, this rarely occurs with religiously or culturally affiliated institutions, as to do so, it could be argued, could be viewed as an infringement of the institution's general rights as well as their right to religious freedom. As of now, the only means of external assessment to determine whether a private institution is eligible for state or federal aid is through accreditation, and accreditors and the federal government seem to have little appetite to hold many institutions' (especially private institutions') feet to the proverbial fire when it comes to diversity and inclusion. Further, when it comes to religiously affiliated institutions, regional accrediting bodies may be wary of recommendations that signal anything approaching religious intolerance or secular bias. In extreme cases in which there appears to be overt institutional racism or sexism, diversity and inclusion may become an issue for accreditors, but this is rare. Overall, there is no reason to believe that private (especially religiously affiliated) institutions will be held any more accountable for efforts toward diversity and inclusion in the future, unless there is a major leadership and culture change in the Department of Education and in regional accrediting offices.

Independent of regional accreditation, state entities may hold public institutions accountable for their enrollment and demographic statistics, because, after all, they provide funding to the institutions. Consider, for instance, the University of Wisconsin-Madison (UW). The city of Madison has a reported demographic of 75 percent White, 7 percent Hispanic, 7 percent African American, and 9 percent Asian American, with the remainder Multiethnic or Other.[5] The state of Wisconsin is even less diverse overall, with more than 81 percent of the population White, 7 percent Hispanic, 7 percent African American or Black, and 3 percent Asian American, with the remainder Multiethnic or Other.[6] UW's undergraduate population, meanwhile, is approximately 75 percent White, 5 percent Hispanic, 9 percent International/Nonresident, 6 percent Asian American, and 2 percent African American, with the remainder listed in other categories, including International Students.[7]

Based on these demographics alone, it could be suggested (and it no doubt has) that UW could do more to increase the diversity of their historically underrepresented undergraduate student body, but how much more? Would it suffice to have around 6 percent African American students instead of the current 2 percent? Is it largely acceptable that the percentage of White students at UW generally mirrors that of the city and the state as opposed to the nation at large? While one can argue that these statistics are not very meaningful in themselves to gauge real equity and inclusion at a college or university, they can, do, and should matter—the real question is how much. If, for instance, it was revealed that UW's undergraduate population was more than 95 percent White, it would invite (rightly so) calls for investigations of probable, if not obvious, racism or discrimination. Would this work the other way, though? What if UW was a majority-minority institution? Would it be (and the state of Wisconsin) heralded as a nationwide success story, or would there be claims of reverse discrimination? Undoubtedly, both claims would be made, with a good number of claims made somewhere in between.

The probability that claims of reverse discrimination would be made, though, itself reveals a lack of equity if one considers the opposing example of Mississippi and its flagship University of Mississippi at Oxford. The demographics of the state of Mississippi are: 57 percent White, 3 percent Hispanic, 38 percent African American, and 1 percent Asian American, with the rest Multiethnic or Other. The demographics of the University of Mississippi are: 77 percent White, 3 percent Hispanic, 13 percent African American, and 3 percent Asian American, with the rest Multiethnic or Other.[8] While it is true that there are several historically black colleges and universities (HBCUs) that serve the African American community in Mississippi (although they are not funded proportionally to the University of Mississippi), there can be no denying that the University of Mississippi's flagship institution is not proportionally serving the African American community or communities in the state of Mississippi, yet where is the statewide or nationwide outcry? Where is the analogous court case for a *Fisher v. University of Texas* (i.e., an African American student versus the University of Mississippi)? The University of Mississippi professes on its website a commendable commitment to diversity, as noted by its statement: "As an institution with a marked history of struggle with racial diversity, the University of Mississippi today realizes its unique obligation to educate and lead the state with unquestionable and unwavering commitment toward the goal of embracing all aspects of diversity."[9]

Toward that end, the university also has specific administrators who are focused on increasing its diversity and inclusion efforts (e.g., a vice chancellor for diversity and community engagement) as well as a specific action plan for diversity. The University of Mississippi may indeed be earnestly devoted to increasing campus-wide diversity, but this does not mean that doing so is a significant statewide priority. Without sufficient state resources as well as attention (statewide) to institutional racism, unconscious bias, and inequities between the White and African American communities within the state, the university and state may (continue to) fail its African American constituents, who may not have the political power of White constituents, who, had the roles been reversed and they found themselves marginalized, would likely have politicized the issue considerably or used their significantly greater political agency and capital to effect change.

The demographics of diversity can and do become even more complex in states with a more diverse population (e.g., California) and where certain ethnic groups (e.g., Asian Americans) may be demographically overrepresented statewide at public institutions (e.g., the University of California system). As of 2010, the US Census Bureau has determined the ethnic demographics of the state of California to be: 37 percent White, 39 percent Hispanic, 15 percent Asian American, and 7 percent African American, with the rest Multiethnic or Other.[10] The University of California (as a whole), meanwhile, is 30 percent Asian American, 21 percent Hispanic, 25 percent White, 4 percent African American, and 16 percent International, with the rest Multiethnic or Other. Statistically, Asian Americans are overrepresented in the UC system when considering the demographics of the state, with African Americans, Hispanics, and Whites, perhaps surprisingly, underrepresented. Should this matter? It certainly does to some, especially those who are rejected from specific UC campuses, although those with the best resources to contest this are generally those who have the most fiscal and cultural capital (e.g., Whites) or those who are already technically overrepresented in the UC system (e.g., Asian Americans).

Like many institutions or systems that have been in existence for decades or even centuries, the University of California has a distinct history of alleged and actual discrimination against specific ethnic groups given its demographics. Reportedly, the UC system discriminated against Asian Americans in the 1980s, which, it has been suggested, helped lead the system to end its affirmative action efforts in the mid-1990s, as some in the state argued that Asian Americans suffered from the results of affirmative action, when the reality was that Asian Americans were mainly competing against White students for admission.[11] Further, beginning in 2009, the UC system reduced "the number of students guaranteed admission based primarily on grades and test scores, and expanded the overall applicant pool by a projected 40 percent through revisions such as the scrapping of the requirement that students take the SAT subject tests." This had a reported effect of decreasing the Asian American population throughout the UC system while increasing the White population, with the Hispanic and African American population remaining mostly stable.[12]

Indeed, many in California do not consider Asian Americans (in the state or even nationwide) to be part of an underserved group or community, with the possible exception of Asian-Pacific

American or Asian-Pacific Islander. Further, some have come to believe that Asian Americans are now overserved at elite higher education institutions.[13] Still, it is hard to imagine anyone at these institutions arguing that there is a nationwide bias that favors Asian American students over all other students (including White students). While there may be some cultural basis in certain Asian American communities to promote education and knowledge, the same could be asserted for other communities (e.g., the Jewish American community), and those communities are not being singled out like the Asian American community has been, possibly because it may be easier to visually identify Asian Americans as the proverbial Other as opposed to a group like Jewish Americans, who are not generally separated from White students, unless they are not White themselves (additionally, there is, generally, a greater cultural sensitivity to anti-Semitism as opposed to the often "invisible" prejudice or racism directed toward Asian Americans). Although it could be argued that the category of "Asian American" is too large and unwieldly, and ultimately not reflective of the social, cultural, and class differences among different Asian American communities or groups, even if one breaks down the ethnic group of Asian Americans into subcategories such as Pacific Islander, Hmong, Japanese American, Chinese American, Filipino, and so on, there would still be at some Asian Americans who could be discriminated against in the college admission process.

This issue becomes even more complex when considering the following. While many public and private universities have significantly more White students than the demographics of their respective states, one doesn't often hear of complaints (e.g., the previously mentioned example of the University of Mississippi) that White students are overrepresented at public colleges or universities, even though they are in a number of US states, and it is not really possible to deny that White Americans are the most privileged racial or ethnic class in the United States. Therefore, while it can certainly be argued that more efforts could or should be placed on serving historically underserved groups (e.g., African Americans, Hispanics), it is challenging to morally justify restricting any other ethnic group beyond White students unless there is clear and substantive evidence of campus-wide or state-wide cultural bias in favor of Asian Americans. It is hard to imagine a case that can be made successfully that Asian Americans have an unfair advantage over White students, merely based on ethnicity.

Demographics and (Personal) Equity

Issues of diversity at colleges and universities, of course, go well beyond the ethnic demographics of the undergraduate population. There are many other areas to consider, such as gender, graduate education, the subcategories of specific schools or departments, socioeconomic class, and so forth. Gender is an especially important area to consider. Not long ago, men comprised a significant majority of undergraduate and graduate students in the United States. This statistic, though, has flipped in recent decades to the point that, statistically, women outnumber men at US colleges and universities by a significant amount.[14] Many possibilities and reasons have been proposed for this gender gap, from a greater culturally mediated belief in the importance of college on the part of women, to gender-specific cultural emphasis placed upon studying and obeying authority for women, to a reluctance on the part of men to enter traditionally female-dominated degree programs and professions such as education and nursing.[15] The likelihood is that the answer is a combination of these factors. How much should this matter, though?

As with White students, men in the United States have benefited in direct and indirect ways from their gender, whereas women have been subjected to (and continue to be subjected to) inequitable pay and are more likely than men to be the subject of harassment or abuse. Similar to ethnic demographics, there may be a tipping point beyond which the male-to-female ratio at colleges or universities will become a significant nationwide issue. If, for instance, the percentage of women at US colleges and universities skyrockets to 70 percent, 75 percent, or even 80 percent, it will be hard to deny that something institutional or cultural exists that limits men from pursuing higher education. However, while the difference between women and men at US colleges and universities is significant, it is not significant enough to be considered a major issue—yet. Gender can be an issue, though, when drilling down to the school and department level. Science, technology, engineering, and mathematics (STEM) programs, for instance, tend to enroll a disproportionate number of men in their programs, and some STEM disciplines have been accused of bias or even sexism.[16] Another issue bound to become even more important in the twenty-first century is how transgender students are classified or regarded. In the future, will there be additional gender designations beyond male and female? Or, will students just be asked to select the gender with which they most identify—male or female? If any of these changes are made, it could affect, if not skew, gender gaps or ratios.

While these questions have not yet been resolved, for certain, a comparative well-distributed diversity demographic does not mean that the institution has been successful in achieving equal access for all students and in promoting inclusion. Of course, statistics alone cannot be enough to demonstrate that a college or university is sufficiently devoted to diversity and inclusion. Nevertheless, as mentioned earlier, demographic statistics should not be ignored, either, but considered one tool of many (i.e., a baseline figure) to gauge diversity and inclusion efforts. In fact, there is danger in what appears to be a trend of not considering statistical demographics when it comes to efforts aimed to increase equity and inclusion. The emphasis, for some, especially those in historically served or overserved groups (e.g., Whites) is to emphasize the individual over the group or community. As Jonathan Zimmerman notes in his monograph *Campus Diversity*:

"Earlier generations of protesters often rooted their claims in social effects and injustices. . . . But today's students typically emphasize the effects of prejudice on *them*, particularly on their supposedly fragile psyches."[17] While these claims are generalizations and do not take into account how the larger #BlackLivesMatter and #MeToo movements were driven by collective, social media–driven grassroots political organizations, there is ample evidence, from the demand for trigger warnings in classes to supposed microaggressions, that the personal not only has become the political, but it (the personal) may be dwarfing the collective in terms of importance.

Increasingly, college and university administrators have been called on in significant ways to address what Zimmerman describes as the "psychologizing of campus politics." As established in an earlier chapter, not only have campus or community groups (or even individuals) placed demands upon administrators to invite or disinvite speakers, but they have also supported (or disavowed) trigger warnings. They also have insisted that the institution take "appropriate steps" when perceived or actual acts of racism or sexism occur and have pressured administrators to increase attention and energy placed toward equity and inclusion. Indeed, in the twenty-first-century higher education landscape, any administrator who does not at least profess a commitment to diversity, equity, or inclusion (let alone provide evidence that she or he has been successful in her or his efforts in these areas) will probably have a very short tenure in her or his position (understandably so). With few exceptions, administrators will be expected to work toward reducing equity gaps while increasing campus diversification and inclusion. Any administrator who does not at least give these efforts tacit approval will run the risk of being labeled racist or sexist. Yet, words can just be words. Enthusiastic embracing of campus diversity and inclusion may be just rhetoric without a clear plan for results. The real question is: What specific initiatives can be put in place to increase diversity and inclusion, and how can these be assessed?

It is easy, of course, for any unit, college, or university to point to anecdotal information that supposedly attests to a commitment to diversity and inclusion, but this cannot and should not be enough. What, though, are some meaningful steps that college and university administrators might be able to take in order to increase diversity and inclusion at their respective institutions or within their respective unit(s)?

Some institutions have taken successful steps to increase the diversity, retention, and graduation rates of historically underserved groups. These efforts include creating peer and community mentors, improving advising, launching predictive analytics that identify courses with high failure rates that can be addressed and improved, and establishing cohorts, among other initiatives. While establishing cohorts of students in residential facilities by major or by interest is not controversial and may help in building community and support, more controversial methods such as creating cohorts predominately for specific historically underserved groups or for less academically prepared students have also been tried to some success. Some institutions, such as Virginia Tech, devote specific dorm room floors to underrepresented students (e.g., women in the engineering college), while other institutions, such as Ohio State University, the University of Texas at Austin, and Wesleyan University, have created gender-specific or ethically specific (e.g., a Malcolm X House) residential communities.[18] It can certainly be argued that such approaches are exclusionary in nature, but historically (and currently) underserved students, it can also be argued, not only have every right to build or inhabit such spaces, but doing so may promote solidarity and community. Additionally, in an effort to encourage faculty and administrators to take ownership of and to improve equity gaps, some institutions (e.g., some California State Universities) have created dashboard and course-specific breakdowns of grade distributions by ethnicity, then asked faculty, department chairs, deans, and other administrators to identify and act upon ways equity gaps can be decreased or even eliminated.

Taking the lead on diversity, equity, and inclusion has become the job of multiple administrators. In recent years, at the institutional level, various colleges and universities have created administrative positions such as chief diversity officers (CDOs), whose main purpose is to build inclusive communities.[19] In fact, it has been reported that "nearly two-thirds of chief diversity officers (CDOs) at colleges report they are the first to hold that role at their school."[20] Of course, merely hiring a person in this role does not mean that an institution will become more inclusive. While studies that surveyed more than eighty CDOs suggest that a majority (68 percent) believe that "expectations and institutional buy-in were right for success when they started," these studies also suggest that "only 16 percent say the institution [had] a clear diversity and inclusion plan in place from the outset."[21] Although it may be that most CDOs feel generally supported in their role and position, as the aforementioned statistics illustrate, a relatively sizeable minority (approximately one-third) of CDOs do not feel this way. Further, the vast majority feel that they pretty much had to build their portfolio and office from scratch, as there was no foundation in place when they began their position.

Building Campus Diversity and Inclusion

While some institutions have placed more money and resources into diversity and inclusion with widespread campus support, that support is not always ubiquitous. Some faculty, administrators, and staff criticize the attention that colleges and universities are placing upon diversity and inclusion efforts, which they feel have come to override other campus priorities (e.g., hiring tenure-track faculty). One such critic is Johns Hopkins professor Benjamin Ginsberg, author of the anti-administration monograph *The Fall of the Faculty*. To Ginsberg, colleges and universities who devote significant resources to diversity and inclusion efforts are essentially bowing down to "a left-liberal agenda" and kowtowing to the "demands of organized groups of minority students" for fear of being labeled or ousted as racist. Ginsberg believes that administrators focused on diversity, who he calls "equity administrators," are power-hungry bureaucrats who are "constantly on the lookout for opportunities to wield influence, secure larger budgets, and take on more staff," by "the promulgation of new rules that create new offenses to police and more potential offenders to investigate."[22] As an example, Ginsberg details how "in 2015 the City University of New York's Title IX coordinator issued rules prohibiting the use of gender identifiers such as Mr. or Ms. in emails to students without prior knowledge of the students' gender self-identifications."[23]

Although it can certainly be argued that such a rule goes beyond what is necessary, there is a current and ongoing debate about how to regard, address, and include transgender students, some of whom have demanded the use of a different gender and pronoun designation (i.e., ze instead of he or she). Ginsberg, though, does not acknowledge this; rather, he describes such students as merely "sensitive" and argues that the real reason behind such a rule was "to create an enormous amount of new business for the office of the Title IX coordinator."[24] While it is true that some administrators (as with faculty and even some staff) may be empire-builders or may seek to increase their power and influence, in this circumstance, Title IX staff have to be vigilant about claims made and potential lawsuits based on supposed or actual discrimination or harassment. Further, they may also be working to make the campus more inclusive and equitable. Ginsberg's arguments may seem extreme, but they are representative of a certain segment in academia who, although they may not be as direct and vocal as Ginsberg, bristle and push back against increases in the administrative ranks while the tenure density of faculty decreases and, often, class sizes correspondingly increase.

Diversifying the student body and hiring more administrators and staff to support diversity and inclusion is only one of the ongoing diversity-related debates and issues at colleges and universities. Generally, less attention is placed upon diversifying the faculty and staff. Some faculty, like Ginsberg, respond vehemently to such attempts. Ginsberg claims that "the simple, if unfortunate, fact of the matter is that in many fields there are few women and virtually no minority faculty available to be hired. In a recent year, only ten African-Americans earned PhD degrees in mathematics and only thirteen in physics."[25] However, Ginsberg provides no documentation for his source(s), and even if he is generally accurate, his choice of fields that are among the least diverse display his bias. Would he still hold to this position for faculty positions in education, nursing, or the humanities, which are generally more diverse fields? Such a position as Ginsberg's is almost definitely bound to lead to a hostile and suspicious environment for newly hired historically underrepresented faculty (and staff).[26] It also serves to contribute further to an actual or perceived hostile environment for such faculty (and staff) who, it is generally safe to assume, already have a steep road ahead of them due to conscious and unconscious bias, not to mention discrimination and prejudice.

Despite the problems with his assertions, it is important to take Ginsberg seriously, as he is a strong proponent for faculty and, I believe, is vocalizing a sentiment that any administrator involved in diversity and inclusion efforts at a college or university will run up against at some point (if not directly, then indirectly). Further, Ginsberg's claims that college and university administrators may be trying to "intrude into and gain a greater measure of control over the faculty hiring process" has some truth to it.[27] Administrators, especially those in senior-level positions, often have to grapple with the extent to which they or their direct or indirect reports will be involved in the job search process and selection, especially when it comes to issues of diversity. To assume that faculty-driven committees (or any college or university job search committee, for that matter) always have the institution, school, or department's best interest in mind when hiring is to be naive. Faculty, staff, and other administrators may be more interested in hiring a colleague who is more like them or who may be a potential ally, or someone just competent enough (but not so competent as to raise the expectations for tenure and promotion). Moreover, if faculty, staff, or administrators on a job search committee are part of the department or unit where the hiring is occurring (which is generally the case), they may be biased.

While it is certainly true that human resources or equity-oriented administrators and staff may also be biased, their presence can bring a fresh, neutral perspective and one that may reflect the institution's priorities. Further, if at least one of the committee members has a strong and successful background in campus diversification efforts or is knowledgeable in the legal matters or in the realm of human resources, it is quite conceivable that their presence could improve the equity of the search process. At the same time, if this committee member is not skilled in these areas or if she or he is regarded with disdain by the rest of the search committee as an unwanted interloper, it can make the search process worse (and it could also shorten the career of the administrator who put this person or a required administrative presence on the search committee). This is part of the delicate calculus administrators need to make before making a decision as to whether to include administrative participation or even oversight on a job search committee. There is no easy answer. While Ginsberg is correct that departments and units tended to be much more autonomous in the hiring process in the past, he neglects to mention that there was also an increased amount of direct and indirect racism then and an abysmal lack of diversity at colleges and universities at this time as well.

Ideally, there would be no need whatsoever for anyone with a background in diversity, equity, or human resources to be involved in any part of a job search. However, colleges and universities, like any other organization, are vulnerable to actual as well as subtle but nonetheless significant forms of unconscious or implicit bias. One of the most important goals of those who work to improve diversity, inclusion, and equity on college and university campuses is the development of programs that aim to reduce unconscious or implicit bias. Indeed, it is very difficult for anyone to admit that she or he may be consciously or even unconsciously biased (and she or he is likely to be unaware of unconscious bias). It is especially challenging for faculty, who tend to pride themselves on their cognitive abilities and critical thinking skills, and who have the responsibility of evaluating their students equitably, to admit that they could be biased. In fact, this is one of the common objections students make when they receive unsatisfying grades (e.g., "My professor just doesn't like me"; "My professor just doesn't agree with me, and that's unfair."). Colleges and universities that offer workshops or sessions designed to identify implicit bias may hope that doing so will increase equity and inclusion, thereby increasing campus diversity. Whether the programs actually work to do this is open for debate, as it can be incredibly difficult, if not impossible, to gauge what effect(s) these specific workshops or sessions may or have had. One problem is follow-through. If, as is the case on some campuses, all one needs to do is comply with a workshop, those supposed revelations or lessons may not be carried forward when participating on a job search committee.

To address or minimize resistance, administrators have become sensitive to word choice when it comes to scheduling workshops that address implicit or unconscious bias. Instead of using the term "training," which many faculty and staff may feel is condescending and may uplift the facilitators into an overly powerful position as the "trainers," some colleges and universities, such as the University of California at Berkeley, have begun using the term "dialogue," while the Georgia Institute of Technology has used the term "diversity education" instead of "diversity training."[28] Further, these institutions have found it helpful for faculty to lead the sessions or at least be cofacilitators.[29] While there is certainly no magic solution to decrease unconscious or implicit bias (although I would argue that it can never be eliminated, or, at least, since one can never conclusively prove that it has been eliminated, it is better to presume that it still exists) even after the "successful completion" of an unconscious bias session, the more such workshops can be presented as something like "dialogues," which are led by peers (e.g., faculty), the greater the chance of some kind of success.

The aforementioned discussion mainly relates to hiring a more diverse workforce. Of at least equal importance is inclusion and retention of a diverse workforce, although neither tends to be focused as much on recruitment. In the case of faculty,[30] one can examine the proportion or percentage of minority faculty who are tenured and promoted. For administrators and staff, one can examine data on minority retention and promotion. While most colleges and universities have at least some kind of written policy about tenure (if they offer tenure) and promotion, the extent to which this policy or these policies are vague (or explicit) and followed is another matter entirely. In the *Chronicle of Higher Education*, Robin Wilson determined, though research and interviews, that "minority professors say they have to do more than meet the usual standards for high-quality teaching and scholarship. They have to work to fit in, they say, to seem more approachable and less threatening."[31]

Although these may be anecdotal claims based on little to no empirical evidence, if the data suggests that minority faculty have not been tenured and promoted at the same rate as their nonminority colleagues, it does make the claim more plausible and increases the desire, if not the need, for a wider investigation. Wilson's research also suggests that there is a strong sentiment among minority faculty members that the work some of them may do more than other faculty (e.g., interdisciplinary or progressive or even transgressive scholarship and teaching), which often makes them attractive during the interview process, may not seem as appealing to a deliberating committee when they are up for tenure and promotion. While administrators will never be able to eliminate concerns like these (or even eventual grievances), work can be done to help increase equity—for example, by examining the retention, tenure, and promotion rates for different demographics of faculty and staff; revising the written process and procedure for retention, tenure, and promotion; beginning or promoting campus dialogues as well as activities promoting diversity and inclusion; making changes to the job search process; and placing expectations upon unit heads to provide documentation that they have successfully increased diversity and inclusion in their respective areas.

On the surface, the future looks bright for the diversification of campuses. Writing for the *Chronicle of Higher Education*, Beth McMurtrie points out that there is a growing percentage and proportion of minority students completing high school and attending college. However, McMurtrie also identifies that minority students are more likely "to attend two-year colleges" and for-profit institutions.[32] They are also less apt to complete college. Even colleges and universities that have significantly reduced if not eliminated equity gaps, though, may not have become more inclusive. While administrators would be wise to consider what McMurtrie suggests that minority students generally want, such as "spaces and programming" for their respective groups, doing so can, ironically, lead to increased separation while diversifying the campus.[33] This can be seen, for instance, in how some campuses have begun separate orientations and graduations for students of color (e.g., Native American Welcome/Graduation, Black Students' Welcome/Graduation, Chicanx/Latinx Welcome/Graduation) in addition to the main event(s). It can be argued that historically underserved students benefit from developing and maintaining separate spaces just for them, but it can also be challenging to determine whether such spaces are ultimately beneficial in the larger cause of campus inclusion. This can also depend on the institution and surrounding area. Less diverse colleges and universities or surrounding communities might (unintentionally) foster a greater desire on the part of minority students to have separate welcoming and graduation events for their respective groups because they may not feel sufficiently integrated into the campus community.

Regardless, administrators generally want to assert that their college or university handles diversity and inclusion well. To state anything less may be viewed as an admission of failure on either their part or the part of the college or university. Indeed, a survey by *Inside Higher Ed* and Gallup indicates that "84 percent of college presidents said race relations on their campus were 'excellent' or 'good.' Yet, only 24 percent [of historically underrepresented students] said race relations on college campuses nationwide were good."[34] Could this have something to do with the fact that the vast majority of college presidents are aging White men,[35] most of whom are at majority-White institutions? It is important to recognize that acknowledging significant problems with racial relations on campus can be viewed as a professional failing as well as a personal failing (e.g., doing poorly with diversity and inclusion efforts could signal that it is not of great interest, let alone a priority, to the person or people in charge). Brave administrators will acknowledge that they or their college or university can do more. With all that seems to have been done to supposedly increase diversity and inclusion over the past years and decades, it is indisputable that we still continue to hear of shocking acts of racism, sexism, or other acts of hate or violence at college and university campuses nationwide. There is no way to know conclusively if these events seem to be occurring more because of increased (previously nonexistent) social media coverage, or if there has been a post-Trump backlash against perceived political correctness. Regardless, this has led some to determine that the only way they can ensure that their respective group or community will be sufficiently valued and respected is by attending a college or university that focuses specifically on their community and its values.

Ethnically/Racially Affiliated Institutions

Thus far, this chapter has focused on secular or nonspecifically affiliated public and private colleges and universities. Diversity may and often does mean something slightly or entirely different at such colleges and universities. In the case of ethnically affiliated colleges and universities, such as historically black colleges and universities (HBCUs) and tribal colleges and universities, to a large degree, diversity is a given, at least in the way diversity is traditionally defined in higher education (e.g., a certain percentage or a certain number of historically underserved students). However, "diversity" takes on greater meaning and implication at such institutions. Even colleges and universities that are not ethnically affiliated can take note of an analysis of "diversity" at HBCUs and tribal colleges and universities, as it can have larger implications on how "diversity" and other affiliated initiatives are viewed. Especially in the case of HBCUs, as there are many more[36] of them than tribal colleges and universities,[37] it is important to be aware of the term "historically" in context to the BCU (black colleges and universities).

While it may be generally understood that HBCUs do not exclusively enroll African American students, it may be surprising to many that some HBCUs do not even enroll a majority of African American students. For instance, Bluefield State College in West Virginia is an HBCU, but its demographics are, as of 2017, 85 percent White and 8 percent African American.[38] West Virginia State University, another HBCU, has similar demographics.[39] Although these two colleges and universities are the exception more than the rule, among other HBCUs, the percentage of overall African American students can range from more than 80 percent to less than 50 percent. How much these percentages should matter is a good question. If the term "HBCU" is taken literally, with an emphasis on "historical," then Bluefield State and West Virginia State are certainly HBCUs. However, if one important component of HBCUs is to serve the current, larger African American community or population, it is hard to see how either institution fits the criteria of a (current) HBCU. Moreover, there is an ongoing debate as to whether HBCUs should open themselves up more or less to non–African American students and whether "diversity," at least in a conventional sense, really applies. On the one hand, an institution that has 80–90 percent of any ethnic group will be, by definition, not diverse. On the other hand, if "diversity" means inclusion of historically underserved groups or social justice initiatives aimed at increasing the equity and representation of such groups, then HBCUs with a very high percentage (e.g., 80–90 percent) of African American students certainly fit the mold.

Overall, enrollment trends have not been favoring either HBCUs or tribal colleges and universities.[40] In recent years (since 1980), enrollment at both HBCUs and tribal colleges and universities has not kept up with the increase in student enrollment nationwide, and this does not take into account the greater number of non-Black students at HBCUs.[41] While it has been reported that "freshman enrollment is up at 40% of HBCU schools," other HBCUs continue to struggle, with three closing in the past three years.[42] As with private institutions, HBCUs have experienced a recent, growing bifurcation between more elite HBCUs (e.g., Howard, Spelman, and Morehouse) and less elite / lesser-known HBCUs (e.g., American Baptist College, Denmark Technical College, and Fort Valley State University). Public HBCUs have the ability to argue for additional state funding. They also have the ability to sue their states for additional funding. While some HBCUs have been successful in their protracted legal fights with their respective states (e.g., Mississippi, where HBCUs there "won a $500-million settlement"),[43] such "victories" can come with a price—namely, the promise that HBCUs will "increase their nonblack enrollments."[44] This has proven easier said than done for a number of reasons, including already-established and typically better-funded nearby colleges and universities that predominately cater to White students. Still, HBCUs have proven that they are especially valuable.[45]

At the same time, especially considering there are no historically Hispanic colleges and universities but rather Hispanic-serving institutions (HSIs), whose threshold for consideration is having a demographic of at least 25 percent Hispanic students, it begs the question of whether there ought to be analogous categories for African Americans and Native Americans. Since, according to a 2017 estimate by the US Census, 18.1 percent of Americans are Hispanic while 13.4 percent are African American and 1.3 percent are Native American or Alaskan Native,[46] if the same proportion was used for Black or African American-serving institutions,[47] for instance, as is currently used to determine the threshold for HSIs, any college or university with more than 18.5 percent African Americans would be Black or African American serving. This means or could mean that colleges and universities such as the University of Memphis (36 percent African American) and the CUNY College of Technology (30 percent African American) might be able to receive additional state and federal grants (as well as possible additional private grants).

While designations and funding are certainly important for HBCUs, tribal colleges and universities, and, for that matter, any institution that is seeking to reduce or eliminate any existing equity gap, even institutions that are demographically diverse or who are noted for distinctive programs aimed at reducing equity gaps can be challenged to become more inclusive. One reason that inclusion is so challenging, if not elusive, is because it is such a vague and subjective term. What, exactly, does it mean to have an inclusive campus? Is inclusion measured (or can it be measured) in retention and graduation rates? Can it be measured in how diverse academic programs, student clubs, classes, or other campus activities may be? Can it be measured by surveying students? If a particularly egregious act of racism or sexism occurs on campus, does that definitively mean that the campus is not really inclusive, or can it be seen as an isolated aberration? Does this or should it depend on the response(s) to the act? Although there may not be conclusive answers to these questions, one thing that can be agreed upon is that inclusion is a continual process, something that every campus should never feel that they can completely achieve, because (1) there is no definite way or objective manner through which to measure inclusion, and (2) even if a college or university appears to have a strong culture and track record of diversity and inclusion, all it takes is one significant incident, especially if the incident goes viral, to undo much of an institution's reputation for inclusivity. While this may seem unfair, and it can be so, it can also be valuable in forcing colleges and universities to never rest on their laurels and to be ever vigilant to minimize, if not eliminate, racism, sexism, and other acts of hate and violence.

Religiously Affiliated Institutions

Ethically affiliated institutions are not the only specialized group of colleges and universities. Another category of more specialized colleges and universities are religiously affiliated institutions. Religiously affiliated institutions, being private, are not subject to the federal dictate of separating church and state, as are public institutions. While there may not be clear and exact criteria for what makes a college or university religiously affiliated, there are some that are indisputable and proudly so (e.g., Brigham Young University, Baylor University, Yeshiva University, Azusa Pacific University), while there are others (e.g., Muhlenberg College, American Jewish University, California Lutheran University) that are debatably so (and, sometimes, do not even label themselves as being one). According to the National Center for Education Statistics (NCES), as of 2015, 19.4 percent of all institutions were religiously affiliated, and 9.5 percent of all college and university students nationwide were enrolled at a religiously affiliated institution.[48]

Overall, according to the NCES, while the number of religiously affiliated institutions has decreased over the past several decades, the number of students attending one has fluctuated, with increases from 1980 to 2010 and a decrease from 2010 to 2015. Although there was about the same percentage of religiously affiliated institutions in 2015 (19.3 percent) as there was in 2010 (19.4 percent), 12.3 percent of the total student body nationwide attended one in 2010, as opposed to 9.5 percent in 2015.[49] Looking further back, in 2000, 22.9 percent of colleges and universities in the United States were religiously affiliated, with 10 percent attending such institutions. Going back even further, to 1980, 24 percent of all students attended a religiously affiliated institution, whereas 8.3 percent of all students attended one. While it is hard to account for the fluctuation in students attending a religiously affiliated institution, the number of such institutions may have decreased because some either closed or became quasi-affiliated, such as California Lutheran University. Therefore, the number of students attending a religiously affiliated institution or quasi-religiously affiliated institution may have actually increased in recent decades, even though this does not necessarily mean that the students themselves have become more religiously observant.

Diversity issues can become considerably more complicated and thorny when considering religiously affiliated institutions, which, by nature, will inevitably cater to and seek a smaller number and a targeted pool of potential students. This can be both helpful and harmful for enrollment management since there are fewer students from which to recruit, but that smaller pool tends to be more interested in the institution (as most will share or their family will share the religious orientation or commitment). Still, this is little consolation for financially and enrollment-challenged religiously affiliated institutions, some of which have had to engage in a good deal of literal and figurative soul-searching to consider whether they should alter their institutional mission and focus to bring in larger class sizes. On the other end of the spectrum, some at religiously affiliated institutions do not want to become more inclusive, as they feel that it will impinge on their religious affiliation or identity.[50]

Even though it has been reported that "the proportion of minority undergraduates has steadily risen at evangelical schools— from 18 to 28 percent since 2004 (among all private colleges, minority students make up 33 percent of enrollments)"—there is concern that such colleges and universities may not be doing enough to help make their historically underserved students feel included and involved.[51] While these statistics may not align with what appears to be a decrease in the religious affiliation of college students over the past several decades,[52] there are several different explanations for why this may have occurred. First, those who have become even less religiously affiliated were probably not going to attend a religiously affiliated institution anyway. Additionally, the number or percentage of students who strongly affiliate with a certain religion may not have changed very much over the past several decades. In addition, a number of colleges and universities that may be technically religiously affiliated could have become more secular (or more open to secular students) in recent years.

Regardless, attending or serving at a religiously affiliated institution can have consequences. More specifically, religiously affiliated colleges and universities that seek federal funding for their institution and for their students (e.g., federal financial aid, including grants and work-study funding) can find themselves subject to federal mandates that prohibit discrimination. However, it is not always or often easy to distinguish discrimination when it occurs at religiously affiliated institutions. For instance, it is possible that a proudly Muslim or Jewish student may have difficulty being accepted to a Christian-affiliated institution because she or he is not considered a good "fit" by the admissions committee or she or he did not demonstrate sufficient institutional interest or commitment in her or his application materials. If these students are accepted and choose to attend, they may also feel not included by certain segments of the institution or even discriminated against, although either may be challenging to conclusively support or prove. While the aforementioned are forms of discrimination, it is hard to hold religiously affiliated institutions accountable for such actions, as admissions determinations are held behind closed doors. Further, religiously affiliated institutions tend to assert their own freedom of religion rights when determining their student body.

One means of overseeing religiously affiliated institutions is through either accrediting agencies or through the federal or state Department of Education. These entities, though, have not done much to shape or curtail decisions made by religiously affiliated institutions. Some argue that these institutions use or can use religion as a kind of halo, shielding them from claims of discrimination, prejudice, and inequity. To be sure, similar claims have been made against religiously affiliated organizations or individuals who may claim, for instance, that they have the right to not serve certain people (e.g., homosexual couples) because doing so goes against their religious beliefs.[53] Should such institutions be held more accountable by accreditors or by the federal or state government? Of course, there is no objective answer to this question.

Already, religiously affiliated institutions are regularly being granted exceptions to federal and state higher education regulations and laws, especially those that pertain to gender and sexual orientation, leading some to conclude that these institutions have received a free pass to discriminate against others.[54] In fact, it has been reported that the Department of Education "has not denied a single request (though it has stalled some for up to 10 years). It has also been willing to acknowledge religious exemptions for the first time in processing complaints."[55] While one possible option is withholding state or federal funds from religiously affiliated colleges and universities (or any colleges or universities, for that matter) that credibly appear to discriminate or treat their students or prospective students inequitably, thus far, this has not occurred. As Sarah Eekhoff Zylstra reports, when a California State senator "proposed withholding state funds from schools that ask for religious exemptions from sexual orientation and gender identity discrimination policies, Evangelical, Jewish, and Muslim leaders reacted strongly." Specifically, the potentially affected schools and their students vocally complained that "the bill particularly disadvantages minority lower-income students who can't afford to go to a private school without state grants."[56] The end result was merely a requirement for "schools to tell current and prospective students, faculty members, and employees if—and why—they have an exemption."[57]

The irony of this is that students often least served by religiously affiliated schools (e.g., historically underserved groups) have been the ones claiming discrimination because, they have argued, they would be the ones to suffer the most if their college or university loses its ability to provide its students with federal funding. While this may be true, the end result, it can be and has been argued, was the further discrimination of other historically underserved groups (e.g., the LBGTQ community). Moreover, by shifting blame on the state or federal government instead of on the schools themselves for their policies, their apparent lack of need-blind admissions, and their lack of interest in making college more affordable for students who come from limited means, these colleges and universities have cleverly been able to have their proverbial cake and eat it, too, by maintaining their (arguably discriminatory) practices, by claiming religious exception, and by having those most vulnerable be their strongest advocates.

While religiously affiliated institutions generally do not have mandates that one must be of a certain religion to attend, some have methods to filter their applicant pool (and ways to distinguish that applicant pool) so that their eventually matriculated students are either all or virtually all of a certain faith, or that they have great respect for that faith. For instance, at Brigham

Young University, which is strongly affiliated with the Church of Jesus Christ of Latter-Day Saints, students must adhere to an honor code that states that they "demonstrate in daily living on- and off-campus those moral virtues encompassed in the gospel of Jesus Christ." These "moral virtues" include living a "chaste and virtuous life," using "clean language," following a dress code, not imbibing any alcohol or caffeine, and not engaging in "homosexual behavior."[58] While one can be of a different faith and attend BYU, one would essentially have to follow the mandates of the Latter-Day Saints church if one wishes to attend (or remain in good standing there). In addition, students and faculty at BYU must receive an "ecclesiastical endorsement" each year. At Baptist-affiliated Baylor University in Texas, students are required to attend chapel sessions for a certain period of time, depending on whether they are transfer students or not.[59]

Other religiously affiliated institutions are less stringent in their religiously related requirements and embrace (or at least profess to embrace) those of all faiths and backgrounds. For some institutions, doing so may have been driven by necessity because of their need to attract a larger number of students in order to survive financially, whereas, for other institutions, being inclusive fits more with their identity and mission. In the vast majority of cases, unless one was or is a college or university administrator, faculty member, or staff member at a religiously affiliated institution, one will presumably never know how difficult a decision it may have been (and may continue to be) to become more secular, as these kinds of discussions and debates are generally held behind closed doors and involve the board of directors and trustees as well as college and university representatives. Indeed, attempts to secularize an institution may often be met with resistance if not outrage and flat-out rejection. Most religiously affiliated institutions that become secularized do so out of a desire to attract more students, better students, or financial resources. They may also do so because the institution wants to be better regarded as a (more) premier college or university. Along the way, some institutions that are unwilling to make such changes either may close completely, transform into a non-degree-seeking institution (e.g., a Center for Jewish Studies or a Center for Islamic Culture), or just muddle along, barely surviving.

Good examples of especially inclusive and diverse religiously affiliated institutions include Lutheran colleges such as Muhlenberg College in Pennsylvania and California Lutheran University. Despite having a Lutheran identity, Muhlenberg is nearly one-third (28 percent) Jewish and has a Hillel as well as a kosher section in one of its dining halls. California Lutheran University became an HSI in 2016, and it strongly promotes diversity and the welcoming of all faiths on its website.[60] Are these institutions really religiously affiliated institutions? Technically they are, and administrators there, no matter how inclusive (or noninclusive) the college or university may be or appear to be, will have to grapple with difficult issues that are usually not issues at public, secular institutions. There could be subtle ways one may feel excluded if one is not part of the core constituency of the institution (e.g., Muslims at a Catholic-affiliated college or university). It is true that a college or university can profess a surface-level commitment to tenants of diversity and equity while internally promoting core cultural or religious values, thereby effectively perpetuating its homogeneity. Although the opinions of students, staff, and the community are important, and these opinions can sway the direction of private, religiously affiliated institutions, these same institutions are often bound to one main constituency, their boards, who typically contribute to the institution precisely because of its religious or cultural affiliation.

Is there a point at which religion can demonstratively interfere with the free pursuit of knowledge and critical thinking or the academic integrity of the institution? While there is certainly some subjectivity to this question, I would argue that there are already-existing religiously affiliated institutions whose key principles and demands run contrary to the very mission of any self-respecting college or university. As one case in point, regional accredited Bryan College's (Tennessee) "statement of belief, which professors have to sign as part of their employment contracts, included a 41-word section summing up the institution's conservative views on creation and evolution, including the statement: 'The origin of man was by fiat of God.'"[61] Further, faculty at Bryan College must also "agree to an additional clarification declaring that Adam and Eve 'are historical persons created by God in a special formative act, and not from previously existing life-forms.'"[62] If this isn't the restriction of critical thinking and academic freedom, what is? Bryan College administrators may well argue that these provisions are "what they see as a marked erosion of Christian values and beliefs across the country."[63] Even if one accepts this, though, the purpose of a college or university should not be to perpetuate a specific religion or to indoctrinate but to educate students. Yet, Bryan College, along with other religious colleges and universities that require faculty (and staff) to sign pledges and commitments (e.g., Biola University, Azusa Pacific University) are able to maintain their accreditation with no consequences. Many of these same institutions have received religious exceptions from federal legislation, such as Title IX.[64]

While it might seem like the regional accreditation process is an appropriate venue to hold religiously affiliated institutions more accountable, since doing so would not directly impact students (e.g., regional accreditors can place institutions on warnings or on probation, which will not affect their ability to qualify for federal financial aid), in practice, this is not often done. The vast majority of administrators at religiously or culturally affiliated institutions go through the same institutional accreditation processes as other institutions do. However, some institutions that wish to operate according to their own principles and policies without any external intrusion have chosen to bypass accreditation. In his article "Mother Church or Uncle Sam," former president of Wyoming Catholic College Kevin D. Roberts explains why he and his institution opted out of the accreditation process. Roberts argues that "everyone agrees that the culture has shifted against Christians—quickly"—and cites a dismissive quote about religiously affiliated institutions by a professor at the University of Pennsylvania, who suggests that religiously affiliated institutions should be denied accreditation because they are "intellectually compromised institutions," in that they "erect religious tests for truth." Roberts also uses the example of Gordon College, which has a policy prohibiting homosexual practices. Even though Gordon was able to maintain its accreditation, according to Roberts, this example illustrates the "vulnerability of any Christian school that adheres to biblical teaching on sex and marriage," leading him to conclude that "Catholic colleges will be faced increasingly with a choice between these masters: Mother Church and Uncle Sam." While Roberts and his institution end up choosing "Mother Church," they also opted not to pursue regional accreditation. This, though, is often the exception, more than the rule, which is, as stated earlier in this chapter, that the Department of Education and regional accrediting bodies do not generally hold religiously affiliated institutions' proverbial feet to the fire.

Administrators at religiously (or culturally) affiliated institutions, or those considering joining one, should know that their behavior, opportunities, and environment can be shaped heavily by religious or cultural forces beyond their control. Such institutions may claim to be open and welcoming to all. In some cases, this can be accurate, but in other cases, it may not be accurate at all, despite the best intentions of many at the college or university, especially if one is not a member of the particular religion or culture. While some preliminary research (including getting a sense of what regulations one may be bound to, how other nonaffiliated faculty, staff, and administrators currently employed at the institution think or feel) can be done in advance of accepting such a position, it is important to recognize that religiously or culturally affiliated institutions may not stay static;

they can and often change in a number of ways, including becoming more or less religiously affiliated.

In the end, if an administrator is not particularly comfortable with the religious or cultural affiliation (even if the institution promotes itself as not having a specific religious or cultural affiliation, or a very loose one), she or he should think twice before accepting a position at such a college or university, unless there is no better option. For the right kind of college or university administrator, religiously and culturally affiliated institutions may indeed be a wonderful mix of the personal and the professional, but for others, they can be absolutely miserable and oppressive. As much as possible, administrators should know what they want out of a college or university and whether their values and priorities align with it before accepting a position there. In the end, there is little worse for an administrator to be in a leadership position at an institution in which she or he does not believe, just as there is little better for an administrator to be in a leadership position at an institution in which she or he does wholeheartedly believe.

Conclusion

The Future of the College
and University Administrator

The future's so bright, I gotta wear shades.
—Timbuk 3

I t is the year 2050. From out of your window in the central
administrative building at —— University, you see several students playing Frisbee on the large eco-friendly lawn of the campus quad. Other students lounge in adjustable lawn chairs wear-
ing their SmartShades or napping. Unless they are speaking, it
is often hard to tell if they are awake or sleeping. Sudden jerky
body motions may indicate deep REM sleep or deep Smart-
Shades engagement. You look at the left wall of your office where
your interactive iWall provides you with access to the internet
and Virtunet. Should you want to take a look at what's going on
in any building on campus, you can press any area of the interactive campus map and it will take you there in real time, and,
if you put on your SmartShades, can you see it in 3-D virtual
space. "Big administration is watching you," you chuckle to

yourself, but then you stop laughing, because you remember that the same thing may apply to you right now.

You have no time to scan the buildings now, though, as you have to make your way through a number of grievances about campus procedures, interfaculty disputes, and some possible student disciplinary actions due to honor code violations. You would love to leave these to your virtual assistant, Eliza, but artificial intelligence still has a ways to go when it comes to interpreting language and making judgments. Via your SmartShades, you arrange virtual meetings with the campus judiciary officer and legal counsel, both of whom are on call, although physically located hundreds of miles away. You are glad to have this virtual network of administrators, even though their presence and the presence of other virtual administrators who serve on call for multiple campuses has made you wonder how long your stand-alone position at —— University will last. It wouldn't be the end of the world, though, if it did end. You have enough saved up for a condo somewhere on the beach, because, after all, as a virtual administrator, you could live anywhere, and there is, at least, a steady demand for virtual, contingent administrative workers at colleges and universities.

You rest assured that, at least, in your lifetime, there will still be a need for administrators and managers in higher education, just as there will be for faculty and staff. You wonder what will happen in your children's lifetime, though. Just as Instructobots or Autos (short for automatons), as they are colloquially termed, are now regularly teaching certain lower-division courses (e.g., mathematics), Autos have also spread to academic and student affairs areas of advising, registration, and orientation. The higher up you go, though, in colleges and universities, the more likelihood you have of not being replaced. Indeed, just as the elite schools (e.g., Harvard, Yale, Stanford) have gotten even more elite and well-funded[1] in the past decades, there has been a flurry of consolidations and closings of a significant number of enrollment and fiscally challenged colleges and universities.[2] You feel safe at a mid-tier research and teaching-oriented university, and you feel safe in your belief that as long as there are faculty, staff, and students, there will always be at least some kind of need for administrators and managers to lead, evaluate, structure, and decide. You go back to the student grievances you have in front of you and get to work.

While no one, of course, knows the precise future of colleges and universities, there should be little need to fear (or embrace) the possibility that administrators and administrative positions could mostly disappear (although, in some areas, they could decrease, stay stable, increase, or even become more of a contingent workforce). In his monograph *The End of College* (2015), Kevin Carey suggests that in the not-so-distant future, we will see the growth of a monolithic University of Everywhere, where knowledge and education are ubiquitous and accessible to all. However, I do not share his view. Rather, I believe that there will continue to be distinct colleges and universities, which will be comparatively ranked and valued. Some will also continue to be better resourced than others. If students continue to advocate for additional, protective administrative layers to ensure, as much as possible, equal access, social justice, and individual rights or individual protection, there is a strong chance that the administrative ranks will continue to grow (or bloat, according to others) to accommodate the additional positions needed (although some may be part-time or temporary positions). In order to accommodate the growing ranks of college and university administrators, more graduate students may opt to pursue professionally advanced degrees in areas such as management, educational leadership, or higher education studies (or analogous programs) instead of more traditional, advanced study in the liberal arts and sciences.

At the same time, what may occur, especially if administrative roles tend to fragment further (e.g., specific positions specializing in classroom management and equity, additional student life and leadership positions, additional legal counsel and staff in Title IX and accessibility offices), is those same roles could decentralize, with administrators and staff working rather like online faculty (contractors) doing one "gig" at a time, either virtually or in person. However, another possibility is that concurrently, faculty, students, and community members could band together to successfully slow down, if not halt, the growing ranks of college and university administrators or the increased salaries of those in senior positions. Although, even if this occurred, it might not result in increased campus resources, increased tenure-track density, or decreased tuition and fees, as those resources, tuition, and fees could be diverted elsewhere, and artificial intelligence could replace some faculty.

While something like the development of an app (application) in which college and university administrators put out calls for temporary academic administrators, like Uber, Lyft, or TaskRabbit, may seem and may actually be extremely far-fetched (although not implausible or impossible), there could be further digitization of certain administrative areas such as advising, registration, payroll, and enrollment management. Indeed, there are already online or virtual advisors, and it is not difficult to imagine robotic advisors. Additionally, with what appears to be a nationwide push for higher education accountability and "proof" of return on investment, an increasing number of institutions may provide easy-to-access digital data (if not an app) that includes information about (if not direct guidance for) postcollegiate career placements, salary ranges, graduate school placement, and so forth. Could certain colleges and universities even go as far as making something like a guarantee[3] to students that they would receive a specific salary or the institution would at least partially refund their tuition upon successful completion of a degree (or perhaps to those who achieved a certain GPA or higher) or a program (and possibly after a certain period of time) and their own verifiable employment pursuits? Even if this does not occur, there might be more extensive partnerships with external organizations or corporations with higher education and a much greater emphasis placed upon and even increased nationwide ranking based upon career placement and average postcollegiate salaries.[4]

Regardless of what may or may not occur, what has stayed stable throughout the previous decades of higher education is that college and university administrators, like any leaders of important organizations and groups, should be inspiring communicators and innovators[5] who have a compelling vision as well as the ability to foster a culture of trust, respect, and inclusion. I do not see this vanishing. At the same time, if the recent #BlackLivesMatter and #MeToo movements are any indication, college and university administrators, especially at the senior level, need to be prepared that they could be held personally responsible for actions at their college and university that are not handled properly, or that are perceived not to have been handled properly. If an administrator is visually or orally recorded with a flat-footed, insensitive, or unsatisfactory response to an act of racism or sexism, that very ill-fated moment could mean the (beginning of) the end of that person's career, no matter what that person may have previously accomplished. In such cases, if there is a fall, it can be especially hard, not only on the individual who falls but on the entire institution. When considering this possibility, it may be tempting for many to retreat to the sidelines or to look for administrative positions (e.g., not at the senior staff or presidential level) in which one is not (part of) the face of the institution.

Still, even if this occurs, there will inevitably be a sufficient number of people who want to inhabit college and university administrative positions, perhaps driven by their egos, a desire for additional power or money, or, in the best-case scenario, a dogged determinism to lead an institution to better things. The danger is how the field of senior college and university administrators (like that of domestic politics) could be narrowed to mostly those who have the narcissism or arrogance to believe they are either immune or clever enough to navigate the sometimes treacherous administrative landscape with the force of their personality or belief in themselves. If this occurs, it will be detrimental. While faculty and staff are essential and integral to any college and university, without quality administrative leadership, a college or university is rather like a collection of independent contractors bound to little more than their own individual priorities and desires.

So, let's return to the original hypothetical situation presented at the beginning of this book, in which you, as a college or university administrator, are hard at work on potentially fraught issues on a Friday evening with no clear or immediate end in sight. Will you be energized by this work and feel that it is meaningful and significant, even though, at times, it may spill into what can never be completely circumscribed boundaries between your personal and professional life? Or will you bitterly curse (underneath your breath or possibly out loud if you are by yourself, in a soundproof room, or with trusted, equally salty colleagues) all of the additional time and energy you have to put into your position as well as your college or university, which eats into your personal life? While it is understandable to experience either of these extremes (and everything in between) at some point in an administrative career, if one finds oneself more in the second category than the first, college and university administrative life may not be a good fit for you. To be sure, it can be a hard and challenging life, fraught with politics as well as potential and real danger(s), but it can also be extremely rewarding.

My hope is that this book has provided a clear, thorough, and even insightful account and analysis of the world of college and university administrators. If you are thinking of a career transition, I hope that it has helped you realize whether college or university administration is right, or, if you are currently working as an administrator, that it will help you navigate and perform in your own position better. If you are not in the field of higher education, I hope that this book has increased your understanding (if not appreciation) of the important and distinct complexities of college and university administration. As much as the statement "Those that can, do. Those that can't do, teach. Those that can't teach become administrators" may elicit laughter and may have some elements of truth to it, it takes great skill, finesse, commitment, compassion, and dedication to be (or become) a strong college or university administrator. The best ones, in the end, boldly innovate, ethically lead, and enthusiastically inspire those who serve under or with them, directly or indirectly. Without the leadership of strong administrators, a college or university is something like a boat out at sea with no navigator or leader guiding it, vulnerable to natural forces largely beyond its control. If an administrator has a clear destination in mind or sight and is able to lead and inspire her or his shipmates to want to get there as well, the entire crew can embark on the journey together and, more importantly, transform the destination after everyone arrives there together.

Notes

Introduction. Don't Panic!

1. Buller, *The Essential Academic Dean or Provost*, xv.
2. Buller, *The Essential Academic Dean or Provost*, xv.
3. This is exactly what Buller does in *The Essential Dean or Provost*. He describes "essential principles" as "short and easily remembered" (xvi).
4. I am purposely distinguishing between staff and administrators, although I acknowledge that the two terms are ambiguous and there is overlap between them. Generally, administrators tend to be positioned higher, with managerial responsibilities as well as significant decision-making authority, whereas staff tend to be lower-level with little to no managerial authority and little to no decision-making authority. Some positions (e.g., dean, vice president, and provost) are clearly administrative and others are clearly staff (e.g., administrative assistant, receptionist, and admissions counselor). Others, though, are somewhere in the middle (e.g., academic policy specialist, facilities coordinator, executive assistant to the provost), pending the size and complexity of the institution.
5. While I do not have any data on how many college or university administrators attended training sessions prior or soon after beginning as an administrator in their current position, anecdotally, I have known of only a small minority (especially those who go into administration directly from the faculty) who have had the ability to do so, let alone have done so. Rather, the common path involves little to no training at all.
6. However, a mentor can only provide so much time and guidance, and she or he can never really supplant direct and indirect knowledge, experience, and engagement.
7. Buller, *The Essential Academic Dean or Provost*, 3.

1. These grievances included a lack of communication on my part and a claim of seniority on her part, along with a false claim that I had given this instructor her curricular materials (e.g., syllabi, reading list, and assignments). In hindsight, I believe that the first complaint (a lack of communication) was a failing on my part, and I probably should have considered seniority (in general) more.

2. In making this assertion, I acknowledge that there are other paths leading to a career as a college or university administrator, but these paths tend to be less common.

3. For instance, an EdD or a PhD in higher education leadership or variations of that title (e.g., educational leadership, organizational leadership), or the equivalent in work experience.

4. For a detailed and impassioned critique of supposed administrative bloat at colleges and universities, I recommend Benjamin Ginsberg's *The Fall of the Faculty* (2011).

5. Anyone who has taught at the college level can understand how faculty may become disenchanted or disengaged with teaching over time. Dealing with challenging, entitled, or underprepared students who may have behavioral issues or poor work habits, along with what may seem like relentless grading, can become tiresome. Further, faculty may become disengaged with research and scholarship, especially after they have done as much as they need to do in order to be tenured and fully promoted. Faculty may then wonder about the relative utility of what they may teach, research, or write. As Ryan Craig identifies in *College Disrupted*: "Depending on the discipline, anywhere from 45 percent (sciences) to 98 percent (arts and humanities) of published research is never cited in any other publication. A 2009 report from the American Enterprise Institute pointed out that over the prior five years, the number of published language and literature articles had risen from 13,000 to 72,000" (47).

6. Gunsalus, *The College Administrator's Survival Guide*, 12.

7. In fairness, it is normal for one to have additional expenses (e.g., childcare and home ownership) as one ages.

8. If staff share these feelings with faculty, it may be more in the "normal" way that many employees fear or disdain the power a supervisor over them or the power those above them have.

9. Garland, *Saving Alma Mater*, 89.

10. Garland, *Saving Alma Mater*, 89.
11. Chace, *100 Semesters*, 177.
12. This generally does not apply to staff, except in the general expectation that when they move into administrative roles, they will work at least occasionally (often frequently) during nonbusiness hours.
13. Gunsalus, *The College Administrator's Survival Guide*, 25.
14. As Gunsalus suggests, "It is a major transition to move from a professorship where one largely controls one's own intellectual agenda to a position in which one can be nibbled to death by administrivia: the tyranny of the in-box, telephone, drop-in visitors, email, and the latest form or survey required by some bureaucrat in University Hall" (*The College Administrator's Survival Guide*, 12).
15. Chace, *100 Semesters*, 193.
16. While less common, it is possible to be an autocratic administrator who is not a bully. For instance, a manager can set clear, meticulous, and what some might believe to be anal-retentive standards for his or her office or staff (e.g., desks should be organized in a certain way, papers need to filed in a certain order by a certain time), and not necessarily be bullying his or her staff (although that same staff may not feel the same way).
17. As an example, just weeks into a new position, my supervisor (an autocratic administrator) penned a pretermination letter for a staff member with my name on it. This letter alluded to events and activities that occurred before I had even been in the position, so I was understandably hesitant to sign the letter. At the time the letter was given to me, I responded in an overly emotionally manner and strongly resisted, when, in hindsight, I could have posed questions and come up with possible alternative approaches. My initial response upset the autocratic administrator, who literally said to me, "I'm getting angry now." While I subsequently decided to apologize and propose an alternative route with which both my supervisor and I could agree, he did express some disappointment in my perceived ability to make difficult decisions but graciously told me that "everyone deserves one pass when they first start." I thanked him for that, even though I felt demeaned and insulted by the entire experience.
18. When in tough times, such administrators might be easier to push aside or push down, as it might be assumed (for good reason) that, compared to most, they won't put up much of a fight.

19. Diplomats are not the same as listeners. While good listening skills may be a prerequisite for diplomats, other skills are just as important, if not more important, such as: communication, engagement, and political savviness.
20. This can be compounded if multiple "slackers" are dismissed within a short period of time.
21. I am focusing on staff and administrators here, not faculty, as, at most colleges and universities, there is a separate promotion and tenure process for faculty, and if that process is working at all, it should weed out the incompetent. Of course, it can be much easier to terminate or not renew part-time faculty or lecturers who do not hold a renewable or permanent position.
22. Flatterers are not consistently good allies, though, as their support for others will generally be private. When it comes to public displays, flatterers may compliment an administrator (and others), but they will usually not do so if it means conflicting with or contradicting someone else (or a group of people) who possess power.
23. This was a belief that a faculty member who reported to me once expressed.
24. Another faculty member who reported to me also expressed this. She insisted on changing the locks of her office, which we did once for her but refused to do a second time, when she made the same (now definitely unfounded) claim.
25. I purposely stated verbal praise as opposed to written praise. Written praise is more significant, as once it has been put in writing, it cannot be taken away. If, for instance, one provides repeated written praise for a staff member and that staff member's performance significantly deteriorates, it may be harder to take action if there is a record of written praise.

Chapter 2. Finances, Fund-Raising, and Budgeting

1. If this were the case, colleges and universities that have the biggest endowments (e.g., Harvard) would not have the need for a development or advancement office (or equivalent). This, though, is not the case.
2. Docking, *Crisis in Higher Education*, 4.
3. A good example is Sweet Briar College in Virginia, which was closed in 2015, despite having an estimated $90 million endowment at the time. While some or most of that endowment may have been in

restricted funds, and the campus was running a deficit, it was not insolvent at the time of closure (and subsequently reopened).

4. Docking, *Crisis in Higher Education*, 17.
5. Bowen, *Lessons Learned*, 61.
6. Jack Rosenthal, "A Terrible Thing to Waste," *New York Times Magazine*, 31 July 2009. https://www.nytimes.com/2009/08/02/magazine/02FOB-onlanguage-t.html.
7. Docking, *Crisis in Higher Education*, 40.
8. Docking, *Crisis in Higher Education*, 41.
9. Bowen, *Lessons Learned*, 119.
10. Bowen, *Lessons Learned*, 119.
11. As Basken reports, "The state legislature last month [May 2017] told the Montana University System to expect $4.5 million in budget cuts" ("Think You Know What Type of College Would Accept Charles Koch Foundation Money? Think Again," 19).
12. Basken, "Think You Know What Type of College Would Accept Charles Koch Foundation Money? Think Again," 20.
13. Martha McCluskey identifies how "advocacy groups and journalists have found evidence that Charles Koch's extensive philanthropy to colleges and universities over the last decade has been tied to ideological control over academic content and faculty hiring in several institutions" ("Following the Money in Public Higher Education Foundations: Academic Austerity in the Midst of Academic Wealth").
14. Indeed, there is recent evidence that grassroots efforts to either hold those who grant gifts accountable or to block potentially politically motivated gifts may have increased and been successful. The Charles Koch Foundation, for instance, has donated to a smaller number of new colleges or universities in the past few years than previous years, despite their efforts otherwise.
15. "Academic Research Increases Funding in Nation's R&D Landscape," 12.
16. As McCluskey explains, "Campus foundations are technically separate legal entities from their affiliated public higher education institutions, incorporated as nonprofit tax-exempt charities dedicated to supporting specific state institutions. By acting through a foundation, a campus can receive, spend, and invest funds directly, often bypassing university governance procedures and the restrictions that would normally apply to state appropriations and to state

procurement" ("Following the Money in Public Higher Education Foundations: Academic Austerity in the Midst of Academic Wealth").

17. A good example is George Mason University, which, although public, has "received more than $45 million in Koch donations since 2005 but has claimed privacy regarding the details." The university's president is on record stating: "Listen, when a donor provides a gift to us or to any foundation, many of them, they in fact don't like to have publicity of the details of their gift and we recognize that, and we respect that. That is not just a practice of our university foundation but pretty much of any 501(c)(3) in the country" (McCluskey 28).

18. McCluskey, "Following the Money in Public Higher Education Foundations."

19. This could even go beyond the general 25 percent some staff and administrators are able to receive (pending approval) on top of their full-time salary.

20. This can be the case at both private and public colleges and universities. In fact, the most telling and tangible example of the relatively exalted status of fund-raisers I have seen was at a public institution. At this institution, in the most popular and convenient parking structure, the first floor was reserved for administrators and staff from advancement (and only them).

21. Craig, *College Disrupted*, 40.

22. Craig, *College Disrupted*, 40.

23. While it is rare, an administrator may even receive an inquiry about a salary increase as soon as the first week or even the first couple days in a new position, as I have.

24. The exception to this may be if one is a human resources administrator, in which case one may have a larger obligation to uphold some kind of campus-wide procedures or general equity when it comes to salaries and benefits.

25. Often, it is better not to specify who is holding up the process, if one is not sure if the person or persons one is speaking to can be trusted, or if it may get back to the person or persons holding up the process that one disclosed their names to others.

Chapter 3. Free Speech, Censorship, and Harassment

1. Further, more than any other administrators, those working in the area of student affairs or human resources may be heavily involved

in potentially fraught issues related to student rights, free speech, political correctness, hate speech, harassment, censorship, and academic freedom.

2. This is a situation expertly detailed in fiction by Philip Roth in his novel *The Human Stain* (2000). In *The Human Stain*, a professor uses the word "spooks" to describe perpetually absent students who turn out to be African American, although he did not know the race of these students at the time. (Ironically, we later discover, the professor is partially African American himself, although he has been passing for White most of his life.)

3. Ross, "College Is Too Late to Teach Free Speech."

4. For example, by multiple accounts, this occurred or was perceived to occur with Jared Kushner and Ivanka Trump in the Trump White House, leading to divisions, polarizations, jealousy, media leaks, and animosity, as well as the ouster of a number of Trump's cabinet members or staff.

5. Stone, "Free Expression in Peril."

6. Pending the situation and the faculty member as well as the potential for the meeting to turn contentious, it may be advisable to have someone else present at the meeting.

7. At the same time, some administrators are just more popular than others for multiple reasons (e.g., charisma, perceived integrity, enthusiasm, energy).

8. Granted, there is a case to be made that even with such faculty, widespread acclaim can be symptomatic of a larger, unaddressed problem, such as rampant grade inflation.

9. This is usually the case if the individuals are rational. Mentally unstable people can react in illogical or unpredictable ways, and even stable people can sometimes act impulsively, irrationally, or vindictively if they get especially upset or are under extreme duress.

10. This being stated, there may be some areas in college and university administration—namely, financial aid and residential life—in which, at times, it may be productive to have parents involved. If an administrator goes this route, though, it can be risky, as once the door is fully opened to parents, she or he can get overwhelmed with the amount of contact from them.

11. This exact situation happened to me in my first year as a department chair of humanities, when I inherited two challenging and generally

nonperforming faculty who wanted to meet with me at the same time for anything curriculum related. In hindsight, I made the mistake of accommodating their request, which, after I later gave them both less than stellar performance reviews, provided them with the opportunity to claim that I said things that I did not.

12. This is not an exact science. There will be times in which an administrator will meet with someone she or he may be unsure about and he or she may close the door. She or he will then have to make an immediate decision as to whether or not to open the door. Pending an administrator's position and the situation, faculty, staff, and students may have the right to speak confidentially. One can ask in advance, or at the very beginning of the meeting, what it is about, but part of one's decision on how to proceed should be based on perceptions of the trustworthiness and stability of the person with whom one is meeting.

Chapter 4. Vision, Strategic Planning, Branding, and Image

1. While a stealthy administrator might be able to navigate her or his way to what she or he wants without crafting or articulating a vision statement, she or he will probably still need to craft a strategic plan with specific priorities, which is often like a more specific vision statement anyway.
2. "Soka University of America."
3. "Campus Ethnic Diversity"; "Soka University of America."
4. Seymour, "Higher Education Has Lost Control of Its Own Narrative."
5. If an administrator does this, though, the question is how many faculty or staff to bring in and when. Unless one really trusts in the ability of the faculty and staff to guide the process in the way or ways one wants, it is generally better to wait until there's a least some initial buy-in to the general ideas and focus.
6. "Mission Statement." Yale University. Accessed 15 August 2018. https://www.yale.edu/about-yale/mission-statement.
7. "Vision, Mission and Core Values." University of Mississippi. Accessed 15 August 2018. https://olemiss.edu/aboutum/mission.html.
8. "New American University: Toward 2025 and Beyond." Arizona State University. Accessed 15 August 2018. https://president.asu.edu/sites /default/files/asu_charter_jan_2019_web.pdf.

9. "About Cal Lutheran." *California Lutheran University*. Accessed 15 August 2018. https://www.callutheran.edu/about/quick-facts.html.
10. "Mission Statement." El Camino College. Accessed 15 August 2018. http://www3.elcamino.edu/about/mission.asp.
11. In the *New England Journal of Higher Education*, Roger Sametz explains: "Not too many years ago, a school's brand just was. Few people used the 'b' word. A college or university went about its business, became known for particular strengths and weaknesses, accrued what we would now call brand attributes over time (party school, really hard to get in to, innovative curriculum), and, through word of mouth and its alumni, earned its reputation in the higher ed landscape. Communications and marketing didn't play a huge role in the process" ("Brand-Building for Innovators," 1).
12. Docking, *Crisis in Higher Education*, 25. Further, Docking states that "students envision warm and inviting Homecoming parades and quiet walks between classes with new friends and classmates. They see chapel services on Sunday mornings and graduation ceremonies on the college green. All of these images are positive, and all are inviting to many prospective college students. We don't need to change our brand; our brand is just fine" (25). Yet, this description (with the possible exception of chapel services) could apply just as easily to public institutions as private institutions. It takes more than a generic depiction of a college to make a student want to attend a specific one.
13. Schmidt, "UC-Davis Was Ridiculed for Trying to Sway Search Results. Many Other Colleges Do the Same," A16.
14. Fichtenbaum also argues that "administrators increasingly view branding as an important way to attract students in an environment where individual institutions of higher education are seen as competing with one another." However, Fichtenbaum rejects this argument to conclude that branding illustrates that "we have been transforming higher education from a public good into a commodity." He concludes that "spending millions on branding is against the public interest. Colleges and universities instead need adequate funding to hire faculty who can participate in true shared governance and in peer review of publicly funded research" ("Branding and the Corporate University," 48). While Fichtenbaum makes a valid

point in that branding efforts can be extremely costly and offer little to no objective evidence of effectiveness and of themselves, it is not fair to conclude that they have no important effect(s). Successful branding efforts can assist with enrollment, fund-raising, national reputation, and public-private partnerships, among other things, even if it may be challenging to objectively demonstrate that specific results have occurred due exclusively to the brand.

15. Fichtenbaum, "Branding and the Corporate University," 48.

16. Quiggin, "Brands of Nonsense."

17. In the *Chronicle of Higher Education*, Scott Talan argues: "Professors are brands" themselves, in terms of either how they promote themselves or how they are regarded by others. For Talan, resistance or protest to branding is useless because "even if you object to the notion of being a brand, you still are one. Your colleagues, fellow staff members, and students have views of you that they share with others both online and in real life. Are you the tough professor who rarely gives A's? The fun one whom everyone seems to like? The absent-minded professor with mismatched socks?" ("Is Professorial Branding for You? Yes, It Is.").

18. Hewlett's research also suggests that when it comes to effective communication, "content is the least important aspect" (*Executive Presence*, 48). Rather, her studies determined that "what makes a speaker persuasive are elements such as passion (27 percent), voice quality (23 percent), and presence (15 percent). Content matters a measly 15 percent" (48–49).

19. In *Executive Presence*, Hewlett conducted lengthy and widespread polling and statistical analysis of administrative leaders and executives. While her analysis relates more directly to the business world, it is still applicable to the executive or senior management ranks in higher education. More specifically, Hewlett's extensive surveys that "involved nearly 4,000 college-educated professionals—including 268 senior executives"—were designed to discover "what coworkers and bosses look for when they evaluate an employee's EP [executive presence]" (5).

20. Even if an administrator does not have children, she or he can still connect with faculty and staff about their children. While it is true that one may not have one's own stories to relate (although one may have analogous stories about nieces, nephews, or family members),

one can still inquire about the children and families of others. If an administrator does have children (especially young children), although it can be argued that she or he may be able to connect better with faculty and staff who are also parents, she or he may also have to juggle childcare responsibilities, which could affect visibility in the workplace. In the end, though, there is little to nothing one can do about this unless it appears to become an issue for one's colleagues, direct reports, and supervisor.

21. Hewlett's research identifies gender biases, specifically that weight may be more of a factor for women (skinnier is generally better) and height more of a factor for men (taller is generally better) (*Executive Presence*, 94). As there is nothing one can do about height, and there may be little one can (or would want to) do about weight, this may end up just resulting in an unequal playing field, whereby women perceived to be heavier and men perceived to be shorter may be at an inherent disadvantage as compared to those who are not. While Hewlett's research does not generally investigate ethnic, racial, or religious differences, it is not hard to imagine that, as with virtually all professions, some vestiges of White privilege persist if not flourish at the senior level in college and university administration.

22. In this hypothetical example, Dean Smith is female. I have chosen to make Dean Smith female on purpose. Unfortunately, given lingering gender stereotypes and sexism, women in administration can face greater scrutiny than men face if they are not married or do not have a family.

23. Granted, all three can be image related or evaluated at only a skin-deep level. For instance, scholarship can be evaluated in terms of quantity over quality (e.g., the number of books or publications). It can also be evaluated based on publisher (e.g., reputed university presses or journals) as opposed to on its content. Similarly, teaching can be evaluated based on student evaluation statistics or appealing courses and syllabi. Service can be evaluated based on the charge of the committee and the number of committees a person may be "sitting" on, rather than the extent or quality of the work contributed. Likeability or "collegiality" can also be a factor. However, even though these are sometimes explicit or implicit factors, none is truly effective indicators of the quality of a faculty member's teaching, scholarship, and service.

24. More specifically, Hewlett's research suggests that "appearance," specifically in regard to "grooming" and "polish," is a significant factor in developing leadership, respect, and command in the executive world (*Executive Presence*, 8). In other words, dress, look, and act the part of a senior administrator (which is similar to a senior executive in the business world), and one is more likely to be considered and respected as such.

Chapter 5. Management, Leadership, and Ethics

1. Buller, *The Essential Academic Dean or Provost*, 4.
2. Buller, *The Essential Academic Dean or Provost*, 4.
3. Although, in our contemporary climate, in which students have been asserting their individual or collective rights and in which accusations of "harassment" or "verbal abuse" have increased, faculty, especially untenured faculty, may feel less secure in responding to a student in this fashion.
4. Susan Cain, in her *Quiet: The Power of Introverts in a World That Can't Stop Talking*, provides compelling arguments about the value of introversion and strong examples of effective leaders who are or were introverts.
5. Gunsalus, *The College Administrator's Survival Guide*, 1. This tends to be applicable to faculty who become administrators. In the case of career administrators, faculty generally tend to devalue their intelligence and competency overall.
6. Buller, *The Essential Academic Dean or Provost*, 15.
7. Buller, *The Essential Academic Dean or Provost*, 15.
8. Buller, *The Essential Academic Dean or Provost*, 599.
9. Buller, *The Essential Academic Dean or Provost*, 599.
10. Buller, *The Essential Academic Dean or Provost*, 12, 600.
11. Garland, *Saving Alma Mater*, 92.
12. Garland, *Saving Alma Mater*, 107.
13. Farnsworth, *Leadership as Service*, xi.
14. Farnsworth, *Leadership as Service*, 93.
15. Hewlett, *Executive Presence*, 40.
16. Anecdotally, I have noticed that staff and administrators who complain of being overwhelmed or slammed with too much work do not generally have, nor do they provide details of, an overwhelming list of tasks and priorities. In fact, pushing them on this can often

(but not always) be enough to get them to back down, at least on this one issue.

17. Especially behind closed doors, one may not be told this as diplomatically as "consider what you can do." Rather, it may be as direct and blatant as "We need to accept him" or "I need you to do this for me," as I have been told by a senior-level administrative supervisor.

18. Brandt, "Don't Let Faceless Complaints Replace Reasoned Discourse."

19. Keenan, "Practice What You Teach," 17.

20. In his essay "Ethical Behavior Starts at the Top," UC Irvine business professor Christopher Bauman argues that scholarly research suggests that "when leaders are getting away with unethical behavior, employees are more likely to act unethically without punishment."

21. Menzel, "Leadership in Public Administration," 315.

22. Menzel, "Leadership in Public Administration," 316.

23. Hewlett, *Executive Presence*, 26.

24. Hewlett, *Executive Presence*, 26.

Chapter 6. Diversity, Inclusion, and Religious Affiliation

1. A good case in point is *Fisher v. University of Texas*, in which a White student sued the University of Texas over perceived racial bias in the admissions process that led to her (Fisher's) nonacceptance. While the University of Texas's decision was upheld by the Supreme Court in 2016, not only was this a narrow ruling (4–3), but the court did not uphold the use of quotas, only that race could be considered as a factor (among other factors) in admissions decisions (*Fisher v. University of Texas*).

2. "New Hampshire," US Census Bureau, accessed 27 July 2018, https://www.census.gov/quickfacts/nh, and "Hanover CDP, New Hampshire," US Census Bureau, accessed 27 July 2018, https://www.census.gov/quickfacts/hanovercdpnewhampshire.

3. "Dartmouth Diversity and Demographics," College Factual, accessed 26 July 2018, https://www.collegefactual.com/colleges/dartmouth-college/student-life/diversity/. While Dartmouth has a lower reported percentage of White students, at 49 percent, this figure is comparatively skewed downward because it includes 9 percent International/Nonresident Students and 8 percent Other. As

49 percent of the remaining 83 percent is 59 percent, it stands to reason that Dartmouth's demographics for White students are closely aligned with that of the nation.

4. As is the case with many elite institutions, Asian Americans are comparatively overrepresented (15 percent at Dartmouth compared to 6 percent nationwide, or 19 percent if one does not take into account International/Nonresident and Ethnicity Unknown). African Americans and Hispanic students, however, are underrepresented, at 7 percent for the former and 8 percent for the latter. Even if one does not take into account International/Nonresident and Ethnicity Unknown, African Americans would only comprise 9 percent of the student body and Hispanics 10 percent. These figures are less than the national averages of 13 percent for African American and 18 percent for Hispanic.

5. "Madison City, Wisconsin," US Census Bureau, accessed 26 July 2018, https://www.census.gov/quickfacts/fact/table/madisoncitywisconsin/LND110210.

6. "Wisconsin," US Census Bureau, accessed 26 July 2018, https://www.census.gov/quickfacts/wi.

7. "Wisconsin Diversity and Demographics," College Factual, accessed 26 July 2018, https://www.collegefactual.com/colleges/university-of-wisconsin-madison/student-life/diversity/.

8. "Ole Miss Demographics: How Diverse Is It?" College Factual, accessed 26 July 2018, https://www.collegefactual.com/colleges/university-of-mississippi-main-campus/student-life/diversity/.

9. "Diversity and Inclusion," University of Mississippi, accessed 26 July 2018, http://diversity.olemiss.edu/.

10. "California," US Census Bureau, accessed 26 July 2018, https://www.census.gov/quickfacts/fact/table/ca/PST045217.

11. Poon, "Haunted by Negative Action," and Schmidt, "Asian-Americans Give U. of California an Unexpected Fight over Admissions Policy."

12. Schmidt, "Asian-Americans Give U. of California an Unexpected Fight over Admissions Policy."

13. The issue of racism and discrimination against Asian Americans in the US college or university admissions process has spread to elite, private institutions, including Harvard University, which has been sued for allegedly discriminating against Asian Americans in its admission process. Specifically, it has been argued that Asian

Americans are held to a higher standard than other ethnic or racial groups ("The Harvard Plan That Failed Asian Americans").

14. While there is slight variance among sources, as of 2018, women comprise anywhere between 56 and 58 percent of all college students in the United States, although, according to the *Washington Post* in 2014, men were admitted at a higher rate at a majority of the most competitive colleges and universities in the nation (Anderson, "A Look at Historically Black Colleges and Universities as Howard Turns 150").

15. Marcus, "Why Men Are the New College Minority," and Guo, "Women are Dominating Men at College. Blame Sexism."

16. For instance, see Joan C. Williams, "The 5 Biases Pushing Women out of STEM," *Harvard Business Review*, 24 March 2015, https://hbr .org/2015/03/the-5-biases-pushing-women-out-of-stem), and Luke Holman, Devi Stuart-Fox, and Cindy Hauser, "The Gender Gap in Science: How Long until Women are Equally Represented?" *PLoS Biology* 16, no. 3 (2018): 1–20.

17. Zimmerman, *Campus Politics*, 5; emphasis original.

18. Gluckman, "Higher Education Takes On the Tech Industry's Diversity Problem."

19. As Carol Patton identifies, "Over the last several years, more schools have been hiring chief diversity officers (CDOs). Based on results from a survey conducted by the National Association of Diversity Officers in Higher Education, 77 percent of the 196 CDOs who responded stated they're part of their school's executive or administrative staff" ("Diversity Initiatives Must Change with the Times," 20).

20. Bendici, "College Campus Diversity Chiefs on the Job."

21. Bendici, "College Campus Diversity Chiefs on the Job."

22. Ginsberg, "The Unholy Alliance of College Administrators and Left-Liberal Activists," 18.

23. Ginsberg, "The Unholy Alliance of College Administrators and Left-Liberal Activists," 17.

24. Ginsberg, "The Unholy Alliance of College Administrators and Left-Liberal Activists," 17.

25. Ginsberg, "The Unholy Alliance of College Administrators and Left-Liberal Activists," 19.

26. Ginsberg even contradicts himself by subsequently stating that "a crash program to hire minority scientists when none are being

produced seems misguided, to say the least" ("The Unholy Alliance of College Administrators and Left-Liberal Activists," 19). How did he get from ten or thirteen to zero?

27. Ginsberg, "The Unholy Alliance of College Administrators and Left-Liberal Activists," 17.

28. Pluviose, "Don't Call It 'Training,'" 10. David Pluviose further explains that UC Berkeley avoids the word "training," because faculty there (who are among the most talented and accomplished in the world), understandably, "don't resonate as much with the idea of being 'trained.'" Instead, they call it "dialogue" (Pluviose, "Don't Call It 'Training,'" 10).

29. Pluviose, "Don't Call It 'Training.'"

30. Diversifying faculty is often made a higher priority than diversifying staff for multiple reasons. First, staff at colleges and universities tend to be more diverse. Second, accrediting bodies tend to be more interested in the institution having a diverse and inclusive faculty than it having a diverse and inclusive staff.

31. Wilson, "A New Front of Activism."

32. McMurtrie, "How Do You Create a Diversity Agenda?"

33. McMurtrie, "How Do You Create a Diversity Agenda?"

34. Lederman, "Leading in Turbulent Times."

35. According to a 2017 American Council on Education study, the average college or university president in the United States is "a white male in his early sixties." While there have been small fluctuations over the past several years in gender and age, as of 2017, more than 80 percent of college or university presidents are White, and more than two-thirds are male. "American College President Study 2017," American Council on Education, accessed 28 July 2018, http://www.acenet.edu/news-room/Pages/American-College-President-Study.aspx.

36. According to the NCES, "In 2016, there were 102 HBCUs located in 19 states, the District of Columbia, and the U.S. Virgin Islands. Of the 102 HBCUs, 51 were public institutions and 51 were private nonprofit institutions" ("Fast Facts," National Center for Education Statistics, accessed 28 July 2018, https://nces.ed.gov/fastfacts/display.asp?id =667). The NCES also identifies that "the number of HBCU students increased 47 percent, from 223,000 to 327,000 students, between 1976 and 2010, then decreased 11 percent, to 292,000 students, between 2010 and 2016. In comparison, the number of students in all degree-

granting institutions increased 91 percent, from 11 million to 21 million students, between 1976 and 2010, then decreased 6 percent, to 20 million students, between 2010 and 2016" ("Fast Facts").

37. As of 2018, there are thirty-five recognized and accredited tribal colleges and universities in the United States, with a collective enrollment of more than seventeen thousand, a figure that, since 2000, has increased about on pace with the nationwide increase in college and university attendance ("Tribal College Map." American Indian Tribal Fund. Accessed 28 July 2018. https://collegefund.org /about-us/tribal-college-map/, and "Factsheets: Tribal Colleges and Universities," Postsecondary National Policy Institute, 2 January 2017, http://pnpi.org/tribal-colleges-and-universities-2/).

38. "Student Profile Analysis: Fall Term 2017 Census," Bluefield State College, accessed 29 July 2018, https://www.bluefieldstate.edu/sites /default/files/fall2017_census.pdf.

39. "2015–2016 University Factbook," West Virginia State University, accessed 29 July 2018, http://www.wvstateu.edu/wvsu/media /Research/WVSU-Fact-Book-2015-to-2016.pdf.

40. While enrollment at HBCUs has generally lagged behind the overall increase in college and university attendance from the mid-1970s to 2016, they experienced an approximate 10 percent decrease in enrollment from 2010 to 2016, followed by a more recent (in the past two years) increase in enrollment. According to the NCES, "Among Black students, the percentage enrolled at HBCUs fell from 18 percent in 1976 to 9 percent in 2010, then showed no measurable change between 2010 and 2016" ("Fast Facts").

41. Writing for the Pew Research Center, Monica Anderson identifies: "The percentage of HBCU students who were either white, Hispanic, Asian or Pacific Islander, or Native-American was 17% in 2015, up from 13% in 1980. Hispanic students, in particular, have seen their overall shares grow on HBCU campuses, increasing from 1.6% in 1980 to 4.6% in 2015" ("A Look at Historically Black Colleges and Universities as Howard Turns 150"). Overall, as the NCES states, "In 2016, non-Black students made up 23 percent of enrollment at HBCUs, compared with 15 percent in 1976" ("Fast Facts").

42. Rhodan, "Rebirth on Campus."

43. In Maryland, a similar legal case is in the works that would offer HBCUs in the state "a $100-million cash settlement," but the HBCUs

"want the state to help them develop distinctive academic programs that the white colleges will not duplicate—programs that will give them a recruiting advantage" (Harris, "Black-College Renaissance").

44. Harris, "Black-College Renaissance."

45. Harris identifies that HBCUs "make up just 3 percent of the nonprofit colleges across the country, but they graduate 17 percent of black students, and account for 24 percent of black science, technology, engineering, and math graduates" ("Black-College Renaissance"). Similarly, in "HBCUs and the Nation's Higher Ed Goals," Alvin Thornton states: "Although our nation's HBCUs are only 4 percent of its colleges and universities, they award approximately 22 percent of all bachelor degrees earned by African-Americans. In the critical areas of science and engineering, they award approximately 24 percent of all bachelor's degrees awarded to African-Americans and nearly 35 percent of all bachelor's degrees in physics, mathematics, biology and chemistry."

46. "United States," US Census Bureau, accessed 29 July 2018, https://www.census.gov/quickfacts/fact/table/US/PST045217.

47. I am just using the category of African Americans as an example as opposed to Native American/Alaskan Native, as the latter is a comparatively small group. If we used the same ratio for HSIs to determine indigenous-serving institutions, it would mean any institution with anything more than 1.8 percent Native American/Alaskan Natives. Because of the comparatively smaller numbers, this threshold is not particularly high, and it may be easier to reach this percentage without the institution doing more to serve its indigenous population.

48. "Table 303.90. Fall Enrollment and Number of Degree-Granting Postsecondary Institutions, by Control and Religious Affiliation of Institution: Selected Years, 1980 through 2015," National Center for Education Statistics, accessed 29 July 2018, https://nces.ed.gov/programs/digest/d16/tables/dt16_303.90.asp.

49. "Table 303.90."

50. *Religion Watch* details that "because most of the evangelical colleges affiliated with the Council for Christian Colleges and Universities originate from white and European theological and church traditions, the move to include other worship styles has proved challeng-

ing. At Wheaton College, an effort to include a black worship service was ridiculed by some students in one much publicized controversy" ("Is There a Diversity Problem at Evangelical Colleges?").

51. "Is There a Diversity Problem at Evangelical Colleges?"

52. In "College Freshman Are Less Religious Than Ever," Allen Downey states that "the number of college students with no religious affiliation has tripled in the last 30 years, from 10 percent in 1986 to 31 percent in 2016." Further, in "Why Religion Still Matters," Mary Beth McCauley suggests "over a third of Millennials self-identify as agnostics or atheists." However, this could be a phenomenon more specific to youth, as the number and percentage of older religiously affiliated Americans appears to be staying relatively steady.

53. A good, recent example is the 2018 Supreme Court case *Masterpiece Cakeshop v. Colorado Civil Rights Commission*, in which the Masterpiece Cakeshop claimed that they had the right to deny service to a gay couple who wanted them to make a wedding cake. The Supreme Court decided in favor of Masterpiece Cakeshop (7-2 decision).

54. As Sarah Eekhoff Zylstra identifies, "Since Congress finalized Title IX in 1975, 66 of its 246 exemptions have been given to CCCU members and affiliates. With eight more schools still on the pending list, more than half of the CCCU's 143 American schools have claimed an exemption" ("The Title IX Lives of Christian Colleges").

55. Zylstra, "The Title IX Lives of Christian Colleges."

56. Zylstra, "The Title IX Lives of Christian Colleges." Moreover, the Southern Baptist Convention's Ethics and Religious Liberty Commission focused on the same point, releasing a statement signed by 145 religious leaders that accused the legislation of being "its own form of discrimination" (Zylstra, "The Title IX Lives of Christian Colleges").

57. Zylstra, "The Title IX Lives of Christian Colleges."

58. "Honor Code," Brigham Young University-Hawaii, accessed 20 September 2018, https://honorcode.byuh.edu/.

59. "Spiritual Life," Baylor University, accessed 29 July 2018, https://www.baylor.edu/spirituallife/index.php?id=870498.

60. "About Cal Lutheran," California Lutheran University, accessed 15 August 2018, https://www.callutheran.edu/about/quick-facts.html. Its mission states nothing about its Lutheran basis: "The mission of the University is to educate leaders for a global society who are strong in

character and judgment, confident in their identity and vocation, and committed to service and justice" ("Identity, Mission and Core Values").

61. Blinder, "Bryan College is Torn: Can Darwin and Eden Coexist?"
62. Blinder, "Bryan College is Torn: Can Darwin and Eden Coexist?"
63. Blinder, "Bryan College is Torn: Can Darwin and Eden Coexist?"
64. As Zylstra explains, "A disproportionate number of those (49%) have come in just the past three years, after the DOE sent out 'Dear Colleague' letters to schools: first to inform them that they could not discriminate against transgender or gay students (2014), then to tell them that they had to treat students according to their gender identity (2016)."

Conclusion. The Future of the College and University Administrator

1. As Robert B. Archibald and David H. Feldman identify in their monograph *The Road Ahead for America's Colleges and Universities*: "The top 100 national universities and the most elite 100 liberal arts colleges all have seen substantial increases in their applicant pools, in their selectivity, and in the quality of the average enrolled student. Likewise, the quality of the faculty, facilities, and programming at a university ranked fifty-fifth today is probably better than it was forty years ago" (22).

2. What is more likely to occur is a growing bifurcation between the elite colleges and universities, where business will proceed mostly as before, and more open-access public and private institutions (including religiously affiliated institutions), which may compete with one another for more for students.

3. Of course, such an offer can and probably would be accompanied by a great deal of fine print that specified, among other things, the criteria to receive one's money back, which might include proof of sustained postcollegiate work, applications posted, and so forth.

4. A good example of a higher education–corporate synergy may be Arizona State University. Specifically, ASU president Michael Crow argues in his book (with William Dabars) *Designing the New American University* that ASU has become a model of the "New American University" by being generally accessible to the public while engaging in cutting-edge research, fostered largely through its

corporate partners, with whom it has worked on mutually beneficial projects that have benefitted the local community and state economy.

5. In particular, I agree with Cathy N. Davidson, who, in her monograph *The New Education: How to Revolutionize the University to Prepare Students for a World in Flux*, argues that the "core requirement" of a "new" (twenty-first century) education is to "prepare our students to thrive in a world of flux, to be ready no matter what comes next. It must empower them to be leaders of innovation and to be able not only to adapt to a changing world but also to change the world" (255). Similarly, in his monograph *Robot-Proof: Higher Education in the Age of Artificial Intelligence*, Joseph E. Aoun (currently the president of Northeastern University) argues "that college should shape students into professionals but also creators. Creation will be at the base of economic activity and also much of what human beings do in the future" (xvi).

Bibliography

"2015–2016 University Factbook." West Virginia State University. Accessed 29 July 2018. http://www.wvstateu.edu/wvsu/media /Research/WVSU-Fact-Book-2015-to-2016.pdf.

"About Cal Lutheran." California Lutheran University. Accessed 15 August 2018. https://www.callutheran.edu/about/quick-facts.html.

"Academic Research Increases Funding in Nation's R&D Landscape." *R&D Magazine*, 2018 Supplement: 12–13.

"American College President Study 2017." American Council on Education. Accessed 28 July 2018. http://www.acenet.edu/news-room/Pages /American-College-President-Study.aspx.

Anderson, Monica. "A Look at Historically Black Colleges and Universities as Howard Turns 150." Pew Research Center. 28 February 2017. http://www.pewresearch.org/fact-tank/2017/02/28/a-look-at -historically-black-colleges-and-universities-as-howard-turns-150/.

Anderson, Nick. "The Gender Factor in College Admissions: Do Men or Women Have an Edge?" *Washington Post*. 26 March 2014. https://www .washingtonpost.com/local/education/the-gender-factor-in-college -admissions/2014/03/26/4996e988-b4e6-11e3-8020-b2d790b3c9e1_story .html.

Aoun, Joseph E. *Robot-Proof: Higher Education in the Age of Artificial Intelligence*. Boston: MIT Press, 2017.

Archibald, Robert B., and David H. Feldman. *The Road Ahead for America's Colleges and Universities*. Oxford: Oxford University Press, 2017.

Basken, Paul. "Think You Know What Type of College Would Accept Charles Koch Foundation Money? Think Again." *Chronicle of Higher Education* 64, no. 17 (2017): 23.

Bauman, Christopher. "Ethical Behavior Starts at the Top." BizEd. 1 March 2017. https://bized.aacsb.edu/articles/2017/03/ethical-behavior -starts-at-the-top.

Bendici, Ray. "College Campus Diversity Chiefs on the Job." University Business. 25 September 2017. https://universitybusiness.com/college -campus-diversity-chiefs-on-the-job/.

Blinder, Alan. "Bryan College is Torn: Can Darwin and Eden Coexist?" *New York Times*. 20 May 2014. https://www.nytimes.com/2014/05/21 /education/christian-college-faces-uproar-after-bolstering-its-view-on -evolution.html.

Bowen, William G. *Lessons Learned: Reflections of a University President*. Princeton, NJ: Princeton University Press, 2011.

Brandt, Maria. "Don't Let Faceless Complaints Replace Reasoned Discourse." *Chronicle of Higher Education*. 10 September 2017. https:// www.chronicle.com/article/Don-t-Let-Faceless/241130.

Buller, Jeffrey L. *The Essential Academic Dean or Provost: A Comprehensive Desk Reference*. San Francisco: Jossey-Bass, 2015.

Cain, Susan. *Quiet: The Power of Introverts in a World That Can't Stop Talking*. New York: Crown Publishing Group, 2012.

"California." US Census Bureau. Accessed 26 July 2018. https://www .census.gov/quickfacts/fact/table/ca/PST045217.

"Campus Ethnic Diversity: National Liberal Arts Colleges." *US News and World Report*. Accessed 15 August 2018. https://www.usnews.com/best -colleges/rankings/national-liberal-arts-colleges/campus-ethnic -diversity.

Carey, Kevin. *The End of College: Creating the Future of Learning and the University of Everywhere*. New York: Riverhead Books, 2016.

Chace, William M. *100 Semesters: My Adventures as Student, Professor, and University President, and What I Learned along the Way*. Princeton, NJ: Princeton University Press, 2006.

Craig, Ryan. *College Disrupted: The Great Unbundling of Higher Education*. New York: Palgrave Macmillan, 2015.

Crow, Michael M., and William B. Dabars. *Designing the New American University*. Baltimore: Johns Hopkins University Press, 2015.

"Dartmouth Diversity and Demographics." College Factual. Accessed 26 July 2018. https://www.collegefactual.com/colleges/dartmouth-college /student-life/diversity/.

Davidson, Cathy N. *The New Education: How to Revolutionize the University to Prepare Students for a World in Flux*. New York: Basic Books, 2017.

"Diversity and Inclusion." University of Mississippi. Accessed 26 July 2018. http://diversity.olemiss.edu/.

"Diversity Initiatives at the University of Mississippi—Action Plan Update." University of Mississippi. 13 June 2016. http://chancellor .olemiss.edu/diversity-initiatives-at-the-university-of-mississippi -action-plan-update/.

Docking, Jeffrey R. *Crisis in Higher Education: A Plan to Save Small Liberal Arts Colleges in America*. East Lansing: Michigan State University Press, 2015.

Downey, Allen. "College Freshman Are Less Religious Than Ever." *Scientific American*. 25 May 2017. https://blogs.scientificamerican.com /observations/college-freshmen-are-less-religious-than-ever/.

"Factsheets: Tribal Colleges and Universities." Postsecondary National Policy Institute. 2 January 2017. http://pnpi.org/tribal-colleges-and -universities-2/.

Farnsworth, Kent A. *Leadership as Service: A New Model for Higher Education in a New Century*. Westport, CT: Prager, 2007.

"Fast Facts." National Center for Education Statistics. Accessed 28 July 2018. https://nces.ed.gov/fastfacts/display.asp?id=667.

Fichtenbaum, Rudy H. "Branding and the Corporate University." *Academe* 102, no. 6 (2016): 48.

Fisher v. University of Texas. Oyez. Accessed 18 August 2018. https://www .oyez.org/cases/2012/11-345.

Garland, James C. *Saving Alma Mater: A Rescue Plan for America's Public Universities*. Chicago: University of Chicago Press, 2009.

Ginsberg, Benjamin. *The Fall of the Faculty: The Rise of the All-Administrative University and Why It Matters*. Oxford: Oxford University Press, 2013.

———. "The Unholy Alliance of College Administrators and Left-Liberal Activists: How the Quest for Diversity Has Empowered Bureaucrats." *Modern Age* 59, no. 3 (2017): 17-27.

Gluckman, Nell. "Higher Education Takes On the Tech Industry's Diversity Problem." *Chronicle of Higher Education*. 5 November 2017. https://www.chronicle.com/article/Higher-Education-Takes-On-the /241663.

Gunsalus, C. K. *The College Administrator's Survival Guide*. Cambridge, MA: Harvard University Press, 2006.

Guo, Jeff. "Women are Dominating Men at College. Blame Sexism." *Washington Post*. 11 December 2014. https://www.washingtonpost.com /news/storyline/wp/2014/12/11/women-are-dominating-men-at -college-blame-sexism/?utm_term=.bd7528706ad8.

"Hanover CDP, New Hampshire." US Census Bureau. Accessed 27 July 2018. https://www.census.gov/quickfacts /hanovercdpnewhampshire.

Harris, Adam. "Black-College Renaissance: Students Are Once Again Flocking to HBCUs." *Chronicle of Higher Education*. 4 March 2018. https://www.chronicle.com/article/Why-Many-Black-Colleges-Are /242671.

"The Harvard Plan That Failed Asian Americans." *Harvard Law Review* 131, no. 2 (2017): 604–625. https://harvardlawreview.org/2017/12/the -harvard-plan-that-failed-asian-americans/.

Hewlett, Sylvia. *Executive Presence: The Missing Link between Merit and Success*. New York: HarperCollins, 2014.

Holman, Luke, Devi Stuart Fox, Cindy E. Hauser, and Cassidy Sugimoto. "The Gender Gap in Science: How Long until Women Are Equally Represented?" *PLoS Biology* 16, no. 4 (2018): 1–20.

"Honor Code." Brigham Young University–Hawaii. Accessed 20 September 2018. https://honorcode.byuh.edu/.

"Identity, Mission and Core Values." California Lutheran University. Accessed 20 September 2018. https://www.callutheran.edu/president /strategic-planning/identity-mission-values.html.

"Is There a Diversity Problem at Evangelical Colleges?" *Religion Watch* 31, no. 5. Accessed 24 July 2018. http://www.religionwatch.com/is-there -a-diversity-problem-at-evangelical-colleges/.

Keenan, James. "Practice What You Teach." *U.S. Catholic* 80, no. 2 (2015): 17–20.

Keller, George. *Transforming a College: The Story of a Little-Known College's Strategic Climb to National Distinction*. Baltimore: Johns Hopkins University Press, 2004.

Lederman, Doug. "Leading in Turbulent Times: A Survey of Presidents." *Inside Higher Ed*. 9 March 2018. https://www.insidehighered.com /news/survey/survey-college-presidents-finds-worry-about-public -attitudes-confidence-finances.

"Madison City, Wisconsin." US Census Bureau. Accessed 26 July 2018. https://www.census.gov/quickfacts/fact/table/madisoncitywisconsin/LND110210.

Marcus, Jon. "Why Men Are the New College Minority." *The Atlantic*. 8 August 2017. https://www.theatlantic.com/education/archive/2017/08/why-men-are-the-new-college-minority/536103/.

Masterson, Kathryn. "What Every Dean Needs to Know About Fund Raising." *Chronicle of Higher Education*. 4 June 2017. https://www.chronicle.com/article/What-Every-Dean-Needs-to-Know/240251.

McCauley, Mary Beth. "Why Religion Still Matters." *Christian Science Monitor*. 11 October 2015. https://www.csmonitor.com/USA/Society/2015/1011/Why-religion-still-matters.

McCluskey, Martha T. "Following the Money in Public Higher Education Foundations: Academic Austerity in the Midst of Academic Wealth." *Academe* 103, no. 1 (2017). https://www.aaup.org/article/following-money-public-higher-education-foundations#.XPZv5C2ZNuU.

McMurtrie, Beth. "How Do You Create a Diversity Agenda?" *Chronicle of Higher Education*. 15 May 2016. https://www.chronicle.com/article/How-Do-You-Create-a-Diversity/236427.

Menzel, Donald C. "Leadership in Public Administration: Creative and/or Ethical?" *Public Integrity* 17, no. 4 (2015): 315–318.

"Mission Statement." El Camino College. Accessed 15 August 2018. http://www3.elcamino.edu/about/mission.asp.

"Mission Statement." Yale University. Accessed 15 August 2018. https://www.yale.edu/about-yale/mission-statement.

"Mississippi." US Census Bureau. Accessed 26 July 2018. https://www.census.gov/quickfacts/ms.

"New American University: Toward 2025 and Beyond." Arizona State University. Accessed 15 August 2018. https://president.asu.edu/sites/default/files/asu_charter_jan_2019_web.pdf.

"New Hampshire." US Census Bureau. Accessed 27 July 2018. https://www.census.gov/quickfacts/nh.

"Ole Miss Demographics: How Diverse Is It?" College Factual. Accessed 26 July 2018. https://www.collegefactual.com/colleges/university-of-mississippi-main-campus/student-life/diversity/.

Patton, Carol. "Diversity Initiatives Must Change with the Times: More Higher Ed Institutions Hire Chief Diversity Officers to Oversee Range of Initiatives." *University Business* 20, no. 5 (2017): 20.

Pluviose, David. "Don't Call It 'Training': Higher Ed Diversity Officers Outline Key Guideposts in Developing Diversity and Inclusion Programming." *Diverse Issues in Higher Education* 34, no. 2 (2017): 10–11.

Poon, Oiyan A. "Haunted by Negative Action: Asian Americans, Admissions, and Race in the 'Color-Blind Era.'" *Asian American Policy Review* 18 (2009): 81–90.

"Quick Facts about Soka University of America (SUA)." Soka University. Accessed 15 August 2018. http://www.soka.edu/giving/annual-peace -gala/quick-facts-about-sua.aspx.

Quiggin, John. "Brands of Nonsense." *Chronicle of Higher Education*. 6 October 2014. https://www.chronicle.com/article/Brands-of -Nonsense/149091.

Rhodan, Maya. "Rebirth on Campus." *Time*. 4 June 2018. https://www .scribd.com/article/380179609/Rebirth-On-Campus.

Roberts, Kevin D. "Mother Church or Uncle Sam." *First Things*. October 2015. https://www.firstthings.com/article/2015/10/mother-church-or -uncle-sam.

Rosenthal, Jack. "A Terrible Thing to Waste." *New York Times Magazine*. 31 July 2009. https://www.nytimes.com/2009/08/02/magazine/02FOB -onlanguage-t.html.

Ross, Catherine J. "College Is Too Late to Teach Free Speech." *Chronicle of Higher Education*. 12 February 2017. https://www.chronicle.com/article /College-Is-Too-Late-to-Teach/239147.

Roth, Philip. *The Human Stain*. Boston: Houghton Mifflin, 2000.

Sametz, Roger. "Brand-Building for Innovators." *New England Journal of Higher Education*. 27 July 2015. https://nebhe.org/journal/brand -building-for-innovators/.

Schmidt, Peter. "Asian-Americans Give U. of California an Unexpected Fight over Admissions Policy." *Chronicle of Higher Education* 55, no. 31 (2009): A21-A22.

———. "UC-Davis Was Ridiculed for Trying to Sway Search Results. Many Other Colleges Do the Same." *Chronicle of Higher Education* 62, no. 33 (2016): A16.

Seymour, Daniel. "Higher Education Has Lost Control of Its Own Narrative." *Chronicle of Higher Education*. 6 November 2016. https:// www.chronicle.com/article/Higher-Education-Has-Lost/238321.

"Soka University of America." *US News and World Report.* Accessed 15 August 2018. https://www.usnews.com/best-colleges/soka-university -of-america-38144.

"Spiritual Life." Baylor University. Accessed 29 July 2018. https://www .baylor.edu/spirituallife/index.php?id=870498.

Stone, Geoffrey R. "Free Expression in Peril." *Chronicle of Higher Education.* 26 August 2016. https://www.chronicle.com/article/Free -Expression-in-Peril/237568.

"Student Profile Analysis: Fall Term 2017 Census." Bluefield State College. Accessed 29 July 2018. https://www.bluefieldstate.edu/sites/default /files/fall2017_census.pdf.

"Table 206. Fall Enrollment and Number of Degree-Granting Institutions, by Control and Affiliation of Institution: Selected Years, 1980 through 2010." National Center for Education Statistics. Accessed 29 July 2018. https://nces.ed.gov/programs/digest/d11/tables/dt11 _206.asp.

"Table 303.90. Fall Enrollment and Number of Degree-Granting Postsecondary Institutions, by Control and Religious Affiliation of Institution: Selected Years, 1980 through 2015." National Center for Education Statistics. Accessed 29 July 2018. https://nces.ed.gov/programs /digest/d16/tables/dt16_303.90.asp.

Talan, Scott. "Is Professorial Branding for You? Yes, It Is." *Chronicle of Higher Education.* 15 October 2017. https://www.chronicle.com/article /Is-Professorial-Branding-for/241438.

Thornton, Alvin. "HBCUs and the Nation's Higher Ed Goals." *Diverse Issues in Higher Education.* 19 April 2017. http://diverseeducation.com /article/95530/.

"Tribal College Map." American Indian Tribal Fund. Accessed 28 July 2018. https://collegefund.org/about-us/tribal-college-map/.

"United States." US Census Bureau. Accessed 29 July 2018. https://www .census.gov/quickfacts/fact/table/US/PST045217.

"Vision, Mission and Core Values." University of Mississippi. Accessed 15 August 2018. https://olemiss.edu/aboutum/mission.html.

Wang, Ming-Te, and Jessica L. Degol. "Gender Gap in Science, Technology, Engineering, and Mathematics (STEM): Current Knowledge, Implications for Practice, Policy, and Future Directions." *Educational Psychology Review* 29, no. 1 (2017): 119–140.

Williams, Joan C. "The 5 Biases Pushing Women Out of STEM." *Harvard Business Review*. 24 March 2015. https://hbr.org/2015/03/the-5-biases -pushing-women-out-of-stem.

Wilson, Robin. "A New Front of Activism: Cases of Minority Scholars Denied Tenure Call into Question Long-Term Plans to Diversify." *Chronicle of Higher Education*. 6 November 2016. https://www.chronicle .com/article/A-New-Front-of-Activism/238319.

"Wisconsin." US Census Bureau. Accessed 26 July 2018. https://www .census.gov/quickfacts/wi.

"Wisconsin Diversity and Demographics." College Factual. Accessed 26 July 2018. https://www.collegefactual.com/colleges/university-of -wisconsin-madison/student-life/diversity/.

"Yeshiva Demographics: How Diverse Is It?" College Factual. Accessed 26 July 2018. https://www.collegefactual.com/colleges/yeshiva -university/student-life/diversity/.

Zimmerman, Jonathan. *Campus Politics: What Everyone Needs to Know.* Oxford: Oxford University Press, 2015.

Zylstra, Sarah Eekhoff. "The Title IX Lives of Christian Colleges." *Christianity Today*. 23 November 2016. https://www.christianitytoday .com/ct/2016/december/title-ix-lives-of-christian-colleges-cccu -exemptions.html.

Index

faculty affairs, 11, 118
Family Education Rights and
Privacy Act (FERPA), 110-11
favoritism, 27-28, 86, 163
financial aid, 110, 191-92, 214, 219,
235n10
Fort Valley State University, 210
foundations, 70, 73
fraud, 34
fund-raising, 52, 62-71, 84. *See also*
advancement office
furloughs, 57

Gandhi, Mahatma, 149
gender gap, 197-98, 239n21,
244n35. *See also* sexism
George Mason University, 234n17
Georgia Institute of Technology,
205
Gonzaga University, 92
Gordon College, 220
gossip, 43
grading, 115-17
graduation rates, 3, 81-82, 123, 200,
211
grants, 25, 214
grievances
administrative, 113
and administrator involvement,
101-3
and campus speakers, 98
and decision-making, 153
faculty, 11-12, 207
faculty and staff, 15
and harassment, 117-18
and merit, 79
responding to, 42, 98, 108
and salaries, 76
student, 223-24
and trigger warnings, 95
See also complaints
guided discovery, 152
guidelines, 5

Hanover, NH, 190-91
harassment, 42, 90-91, 102, 117-19,
197, 235n1, 240n3. *See also*
sexual harassment
Harvard University, 146, 223
hate speech, 89-93, 97, 99, 101-2,
235n1. *See also* racism
"helicopter parents," 109
Hillsborough Community
College, 6
hiring
administrators, 32
faculty, 8
and interviewing, 17, 206
and search committees, 17,
173-74, 203-4, 206
staff and administrators, 175
university-wide, 173-77
See also recruitment
historically underserved groups, 3,
117
Holocaust, 101
hostility, 31, 43, 57-58, 203. *See also*
aggression
Howard University, 210
human resources
and administrators, 107
consultation, 42
and difficult faculty and staff, 45
effectiveness, 21, 34,
and evaluations, 177
and faculty, 11, 94
and grievances, 102, 106
and harassment, 117-18
and hiring, 84, 204
and meetings, 114
and personnel changes, 39, 47
protective, 41 44
and salaries, 75-77, 175-76,
234n24

idealism, 16-17, 180, 182
industry, 7, 19, 21, 62, 72

organizations, 199
positions, 90
power, 194
protections, 29
realities, 17
roles, 149
savviness, 48, 232n19
texts, 183
See also democracy
post-millennials, 91, 109
power
    abuse of, 105
    and administrators, 143, 156, 163, 169
    couple, 96
    desire for, 21-22, 26, 202, 226
    discrepancy, 96
    disequilibrium, 93, 106, 118, 151
    and diversity, 194
    and faculty, 25, 140, 153
    and flattery, 43, 232n22
    increasing, 38
    and management, 167
    and morality, 24
    in numbers, 158
    organizational, 150, 181
    and popularity, 46
    of positions, 18, 33, 54, 60, 127, 160, 176
    at private institutions, 165
    veto, 174
    and vulnerability, 8, 30, 114, 117, 164, 230n8
pragmatism, 182-83
prejudice, 203, 215. *See also* bias
Presentation College, 138
presidents, college and university
    as autocrats, 34
    and conflicts, 29
    and diversity, 188-89, 208, 244n35
    engagement, 160, 163-64
    and ethics, 182

and free speech, 2, 101
and fund-raising, 68, 84
and grievances, 106
and mission, 136
and power, 33, 150
reflections, 4
and salaries, 86
and tenure, 12
and terminations, 13
and visions, 122-23
Princeton University, 59, 138, 146, 223
procedures, 99-100, 223
professional degrees, 19-20
program review, 5, 42, 79-80, 157
promotion, 12-13, 19-21, 25, 36-37, 40, 102, 154, 178, 183, 204, 206-7, 232n21
provost, 4, 7, 16-18, 28-29, 33, 83, 85-86, 107, 151, 182, 229n4
public safety, 13, 90, 118
public speaking, 38

racism
    and admissions, 242n13
    and demographics, 191, 193, 195
    and free speech, 1, 89-94, 97, 99
    and grievances, 105
    and hiring, 204
    institutional, 192, 194
    on-campus, 208, 211-12
    reportable, 34
    responding to, 199, 226
    See also hate speech
reclassification, 79. *See also* restructuring
recruitment, 81, 110, 134. *See also* hiring
research and development, 70, 137, 230n5
residential life, 117, 235n10
respect, 31, 152-53, 156, 164, 226
restructuring, 60, 79, 172

vice presidents, 7, 18, 22, 160-61, 229n4
violence, 90, 94, 99, 185, 208, 212
Virginia Tech, 200
vision, 37, 87, 114, 120-23, 125-28, 130-31, 135, 168, 188, 226, 236n1

Wesleyan University, 26, 200
West Virginia State University, 209

Wisconsin, 192
work habits, 23-24, 35, 38-40, 46, 71, 77, 161-62, 166, 169, 178-79, 187, 240n16
Wyoming Catholic College, 219-20

Yale University, 6, 131-33, 146, 223
Yeshiva University, 191, 212
Yiannopoulos, Milo, 97-98